A Hispanic View

A Hispanic View

✦

American Politics and the Politics of Immigration

Raoul Lowery Contreras

Writers Club Press
New York Lincoln Shanghai

A Hispanic View
American Politics and the Politics of Immigration

Writers Club Press
an imprint of iUniverse, Inc.

For information address:
iUniverse, Inc.
2021 Pine Lake Road, Suite 100
Lincoln, NE 68512
www.iuniverse.com

ISBN: 0-595-25691-0

Printed in the United States of America

The country was stunned when the Census Bureau announced in 2001 that the American Hispanic population had leapfrogged past the traditional American minority "Black" population. That surprise announcement revolutionized American politics by turning it upside down and changing it forever.

American politics reflects the people that make up the country's population, particularly where they live and work. Thus, if one group is growing in numbers while other traditional groups remain static or drop in proportionality to the whole, American politics slowly but inexorably change. The Hispanic and Asian-Pacific Islander populations are growing proportionately larger and faster than the rest of the country. Concurrently, the White/Anglo and Black populations are not growing much and are, in fact, losing proportionality in the total American population.

Clearly, as the reader can see in the enclosed articles, we do not have a pure racial situation as Hispanics can be of any race, thus the Hispanic situation in America is not hamstrung by the racial conflict between Americans of the White and Black races that has dominated the Country for hundreds of years.

Millions of words have been published in recent years about Hispanics, how they got here, who they are and what part they play in the American political scene. Herein are some of those words, published as they were on the Internet's **www.calnews.com** between 1998–2002 on a weekly basis.

I salute those millions of immigrants who have come and continue to come to the United States of America, to work, to contribute, to become part of what President Ronald Reagan declared as the "Shining city on the hill." My words are designed to make their efforts understandable and acceptable. My words are designed to isolate their critics in a manner that all can see who and what the critics are and have been.

Immigration critics have always been with us. They can be called the "usual suspects." Their arguments are always the same, no matter whether they objected to Germans ("filthy" Benjamin Franklin called them), Irish (Irish need not apply signs throughout the East), Jews (Christ killers), Italians (grease balls), Chinese/Japanese (The Yellow Peril) and now Mexicans (Greasers, Beaners, Invading criminals).

I welcome them all, and I welcome the emergence of anti-immigrant and all critics of people who want to become Americans. Some come legally and some come illegally to the United States, but legality is but a simple political question that can be solved in Congress.

What isn't easy is dealing with the anti-immigration critics, for they sound so logical (What part of illegal don't you understand?); why can't all Hispanic immigrants speak English instantly, my grandparents did (The Big Lie); Illegals are stealing jobs from Americans (another Big Lie).

As a rule, the anti-immigrants are disingenuous in presenting illegals as "criminals." Some, of course, are. If, however, there are ten million illegals in the United States, why aren't more in jail? Are they smarter than the cops around them? No, they aren't smarter than the police, despite being smarter than the Border Patrol and the Immigration and Naturalization Service (INS). The critics, in general, are the liars of our generation and are true descendents of immigration critics like, of all people, Benjamin Franklin.

When, however, critics crawl out from under their rocks, they must be exposed. That's what I do. I do it on behalf of those who cannot speak for themselves. This book is dedicated to the battle against ignorance and bigotry and those who live off ignorance and bigotry.

Contents

INTRODUCTION

While most Americans have heard the words Hispanics and/or Latinos, few know what and who they are. When I started writing in 1988 about Hispanic affairs and views on issues, there was such a vacuum of information about and by Hispanics, it didn't take long to develop a market for my work among many newspapers, directly, then through the New York Times Syndicate New America News Service.

Then came the Internet's explosive growth. ***WWW.CALNEWS.COM*** became my Internet outlet and we commenced our mutual arrangement in 1998. Over 100 of these Op-Ed pieces have been published in CalNews.com.

Suddenly, readers and observers throughout the world could read about Hispanics, their issues and views, written by a Hispanic with years of political and business experience.

Week after week, the 700-800-900 word essays come forth from my word processor on myriad issues, but mostly about politics and immigration.

Politics dictate every aspect of our lives from the issuance of birth certificates to marriage certificates to death certificates. Politics also dictate immigration policy. Immigration policy has reflected the politics of America from the very first day of the United States of America.

Immigration policy, in the form of "a uniform rule of naturalization" (Article 1, Section 8 of the Constitution), used to be administered by local authorities corrupted by local politics. It was not unusual for local judges to be bribed by local political machines to swear in newly arrived immigrants, some as they stepped off the boats, as new American citizens as long as they registered Democratic to help elect the great Irish machines of large Eastern cities.

Concurrently American born Blacks were not allowed to be or become citizens and vote with only a handful of exceptions in northern states.

Comically, the grandchildren and great grandchildren of those illegally sworn in as United States citizens, are the loudest whiners about today's illegal immigrants who don't get sworn as they sneak in so they can vote Democratic.

What's even more interesting is that President Bush is more popular with new Hispanic immigrants than he is with native-born Hispanic Americans. Thus, we posit that many of today's non-citizen Hispanics will become Republicans when they become citizens because they are enamored with President George W. Bush.

The politics of these first years of the 21st Century will determine the course of the country and affect every citizen of the country and every person throughout the world who desires to live in a free country, a free market economy.

First, terms must be defined. What is a Hispanic? Are they all left-wing Democrats, or not? Are they all uneducated welfare parasites feeding at the public trough? Are they self-segregationists? Do they resist assimilation or Americanization when they arrive from South of the Border? Are they inclined towards socialism or a free market? Is there freedom of thought within the Hispanic community, or are they but a monolithic body politic marching as one over political cliffs like African Americans did in 2000?

Secondly, philosophical and ideological territory must be claimed, issue-by-issue.

The Op-Ed pieces included in this collection were written in response to contemporary issues and events. As this writer's crystal ball is not always accurate, we can look back on some of these pieces and note that the piece was wrong in its prediction, or, sometimes, even factually, as facts sometimes emerge long after events.

Where appropriate, notes will be added after an op-ed piece to clarify what actually happened, or whether or not the op-ed piece was even correct in its assumptions and conclusions.

The noun used in this collection to describe those in the United States who have roots, cultural, ethnic, linguistic or geographic south of the Rio Grande, in the Caribbean, and, perhaps, Mother Spain herself, is Hispanic, not Latino.

Most middle-class people with Spanish surnames, myself included, reject the word Latino. Many immigrants from Spanish-speaking countries also reject the term. Latino is preferred by less than middle-class people, just as an even smaller minority within Mexican Americans call themselves "Chicanos," a term rejected by over 90% of millions of Mexican Americans, or former Mexican nationals interviewed by the Census Bureau.

These pieces raise hackles among many, especially the pieces on immigration. That pleases me, for the debate rages every day in every city and state on immigration. The debate, however, is usually one-sided and factually false, for the American media is ages behind the demographic explosion caused by million-people a year immigration. Example: One critic wrote me that 62% of all prisoners in America are illegal aliens. Wrong. The state of California reports that as of May 31, 2002, 12.5% of its inmates were illegal aliens. Who is right, the critic or the State of California?

Is immigration good; is it good in large numbers; is the United States better off, or worse off because of immigration?

The readers can determine, here, for themselves who Hispanics are and what effect they have on American politics, as well as how politics affects immigration and how immigration affects politics.

PART I

A HISPANIC VIEW OF AMERICAN POLITICS

1

HISPANICS?

HISPANIC OR LATINO?

Raoul Lowery Contreras
December 1, 1999

For years I have campaigned against the Los Angeles Times-imposed word, "Latino," in describing the country's fastest growing ethnic "Group," those with Spanish-surnames, those who speak Spanish, et al. The LA Times set it's feet in concrete on the use of the word "Latino" and nothing has cracked that concrete since. Worst of all, other newspapers have followed the Times' lead and news coverage, accuracy and the community have suffered.

Now, I am not alone. In Agustin Gurza's November 30th LA Times column, he describes an in-house Times controversy about the use of theTimes imposed word "Latino." He quotes pioneering Times columnist Frank Del Olmo from a 1981 column in which Del Olmo wrote that he had convinced the Times to not use the word "Hispanic" because it is "that ugly and imprecise word." He added that "Latino" was less bureaucratic and that "nobody" actually called themselves "Hispanic."

Gurza's Del Olmo reference is fairly accurate, but lacks details. Frank Del Olmo had several reasons to object to the word "Hispanic." And, as he was the management favored Mexican-origin reporter at the Times, if not the only one at the time, he had great influence with Times management. The public had no input, only Del Olmo did.

Del Olmo had three specific reasons to oppose the word "Hispanic." One was that the Coors Brewery company of Colorado was using the word "Hispanic" to sell beer in the "Decade of the Hispanic." Coors was then being boycotted by radical Mexican-origin people—Chicanos—and unions for perceived slights against them by the ultra-conservative Coors family. Del Olmo bought into the boycott because he was more than left-of-center, if not a "Chicano," himself According to him, he grew up in a blue-collar union family that was the antithesis of a "free market" Republican household.

The second reason was that the word "Hispanic" was coined by the Administration of Richard Nixon in the early Seventies and became the "official" word used to describe people like Del Olmo and me. Contrary to conventional wisdom, the word "Hispanic" was not invented for use by the Census in 1980, but rather, was developed at the Department of Housing and Urban Development (HUD). Del Olmo's passions were such in 1981, that any Richard Nixon legacy was to be rejected.

And, lastly, as Gurza writes, "By their choice of language, journalists not only describe people, they define them for others." The third reason Del Olmo objected to the word "Hispanic" and championed the word "Latino" was that "Chicano" had been roundly rejected by all Mexican Americans but the most radical, blue collar, less educated, under-class people of Mexican-origin. Del Olmo pushed "Latino" as a substitute for the rejected "Chicano." Unfortunately, he was in a position to push this substitution into the language of the "Newspaper of Record" in the West. Other papers and broadcast stations took up the word because it was the "style" of the LA Times. Frank Del Olmo single handedly branded millions of people.

Del Olmo was wrong in 1981. The Los Angeles Times has confused the entire reportage of the fastest growing group on the country by insisting on following Del Olmo's blue-collar bromide. Other than the

Times, very few people in the real world use the word "Latino." I recall a very confused New York Newsday reporter asking me the difference between Hispanic and Latino. Her confusion is interesting because the same company owned both New York's Newsday and the LA Times.

I tried to make the words clear to her by stating that Hispanic usually meant educated middle-class people who work hard, yearn to live in good neighborhoods, want their children well-educated and depend less on government than the working or non-working poor. Latino, being a substitute for Chicano in California, means less than well-educated, less than well employed, if employed at all, more dependent on government and a tendency to blame others for their lot.

Hispanic is used everywhere (except the LA Times) and is now ingrained in the language by usage and dictionary definition. The people have voted with their usage and Latino is not the word of choice. It doesn't sound right when used with American—Latino American has no ring to it. As far as formal recognition, "Anglo," for example, is defined in dictionaries as "non-Hispanic white," not non-Latino white. Besides, Latino can mean Italian, or Romanian, or any group with Latin as the basis of their language.

As for "Americans" who object to the use of either term, when Irish Americans quit using Irish Americans to identify their selves, we will quit also.

In twenty years, when the population of California has mostly Spanish-surnames, few people will remember the wrestling match between Hispanics (Contreras) and Latinos (Del Olmo) and that most Hispanics wore coats and ties and most Latinos didn't. They will also know that Hispanics won the match.

(NOTE: Not long after columnist Gurza stepped forward to challenge Frank Del Olmo, he was fired by the Times. A guy named Steve Lopez was brought from the East to add a Spanish surname to the Times' roster of Del Olmo and Martinez. Lopez is a longtime Time Magazine guy who is no more Angeleno Hispanic than William Jefferson Clinton is a sophisticated Upper East Side New Yorker. Del Olmo is the "House Latino" at the Los Angeles Times, just as he was before the Chicago Tribune bought it from the Chandler family. His presence does little to balance the newspaper's coverage of the community.)

HISPANICS VOTE DEMOCRATIC; HISPANICS VOTE REPUBLICAN

Raoul Lowery Contreras
January 4, 1999

As Democrat Gray Davis is sworn in as the first Democratic Governor of California in 16 years and only the fourth in this century, an independently elected Lt. Governor joins him. Democrat Cruz Bustamante, former Speaker of the Assembly is the first Hispanic to win statewide office since the 1870s. He will not be the last.

Hispanics now are 13% of the California electorate. Hispanics are the fastest growing segment of California and, in fact, the nation. Thus, for a political party to win elections in California or other important parts of the country, it must attract Hispanics reaching out for a better life.

This past November election demonstrated two mighty examples of this reach. In California, newly enfranchised Hispanics, new citizens, registered by a ratio of 4 to one Democratic and delivered almost 77 per cent of their vote to the party of Gray Davis and Cruz Bustamante, the Democrats. According to exit polls, Republican gubernatorial candidate Dan Lungren received but 23 per cent of the Hispanic vote. He had expected 35 per cent, which, with a 10 per cent higher Republican turnout would have elected him. As it is, because Hispanics voted a Democratic ticket, California is now almost tied with Hawaii as the most Democratic state in the country.

California Hispanics punished the Republicans for an anti-Hispanic, anti-immigrant and anti-illegal Mexican immigrant campaign fueled by former San Diego Mayor, Governor Pete Wilson. He had funded and promoted the floundering Save Our State (SOS) initiative sponsored by some of the worst racists in California.

The Wilson-SOS campaign would have imbedded into state law massive violations of the civil and constitutional rights of almost 30 per cent of California's population, that of Mexican-origin. Wilson sponsored television ads in favor of SOS, forever joining the Governor at the hip to racism—as far as Hispanics, the ultimate target of SOS, were concerned. They carried those anti-Wilson feelings into the 1998-voting booth.

But, California was the only place such political punishment against Republicans by Hispanics was manifested. Nationwide, Hispanic political support for a Republican Congress increased by 44 per cent, rising from 1996's 25 per cent to 1998's 36 per cent. In Florida, Cubans voted en masse for Republican Jeb Bush for Governor and helped him gain Republican majorities in both houses of the state legislature. In Texas, Mexican American voters flocked to the polls to give Republican George Bush 49 per cent of their vote and gave him majorities in such historically Democratic counties as El Paso, a county that had never, never, voted Republican. In Arizona, they similarly voted in higher percentages for Republicans, including U.S. Senator John McCain, a candidate for President.

So, 1998 provided us with two examples of Hispanic voter flexibility and power. Heavy Democratic voting by Hispanics in California delivered the state into Democratic hands for the first time in almost a generation; and heavy Hispanic voting for Republicans in Texas and Florida, where the Brothers Bush now govern one in eight Americans, buried Democrats.

Looking at the electoral mathematics of the situation, either party that carries two of these three states, California, Texas and Florida will win the Presidency. President Clinton won in 1992 and 1996 by carrying California and Florida, but would have lost each time had he lost California.

The Republican formula for denying the Democrats the White House in 2000 is not very complicated. They must carry Texas and Florida and make a strenuous effort in California. Thus, they must take their success of 1998 among the Hispanics of Texas and Florida and use the same methods, and, perhaps, the same candidates in California.

They must also use the same methods, policies and philosophies among the numerous Hispanic voters of Illinois, New Jersey and New York, to keep these states always in political doubt.

Between now and November, 2000, both Democrats and Republicans must look to California to frame their 2000 goals, for California is the great prize.

Democrats can attempt to label the national Republicans with the Pete Wilson wedge politics mantra that worked so well in California. Pete Wilson did his utmost to destroy the Republican Party in the eyes of Hispanics, just so he could win re-election. Such an every-Republican-is-a-Pete Wilson plan was a smashing success in California.

Republicans can lift the Bush Brothers and their Republican parties and "compassionate conservatism" above the fray and run in Spanish like they did in 1998. Such a plan was a smashing success in 1998. I predict: That the Presidential race of 2000 will turn on how Hispanic voters vote in Florida, Texas and California; That both parties will set records in spending to attract Hispanic voters. That though California Hispanics might not forgive Pete Wilson, Republican, they will vote in higher numbers for a good Republican candidate for President. Hispanics in Texas and Florida have manifested a tendency to vote Republican in big numbers—will California Hispanics follow their lead?

Hispanics will be the key to the White House next year, just as they were this time for the statehouse in California. Actually, Hispanics must be the key, for we can trust no one else to safeguard our interests, we tried that with Pete Wilson, once upon a time.

(NOTE: George W. Bush followed the suggestions in this article that succeeded on all counts. In 2000, more Hispanics voted for Bush than any other Republican in modern history, far more than for the previous record holder Ronald Reagan. My suggestion that the entire election hinged on votes in Texas, California and Florida was accurate in that Hispanics carried the day in Florida and that state's critical electoral votes went to Bush, the winner. In California, Bush garnered 25% more Hispanics than the GOP candidate for governor did just two years before. Hispanics were the key to the White House, all 537 of them who voted for Bush rather than Gore in Florida.)

HISPANIC AMERICA IS NOT LEFT-WING

By Raoul Lowery Contreras
February 26, 2000

Recently (February 8th), the NATIONAL HISPANIC LEADERSHIP AGENDA (NHLA), a coalition of 32 large Hispanic organizations released a report that graded the Congress on a "Hispanic" scorecard. NHLA trashed individual Republicans while deifying Hispanic Democrats. The report is baloney.

"The survey's purpose, stressed NHLA leaders, is to help Latino voters know if their representatives in Congress are looking out for their community's interests," writes Charles Erickson of the Washington, D.C.

based "Hispanic Link." The NHLA's "purpose", however, is all baloney.

What we actually have here is a political smear job by leftwing Latinos who do not represent the country's 32-million Hispanics. They chose eleven issues that they say are Hispanic issues and graded individual congressmen on how they voted on them. That scenario is also baloney. See, it doesn't matter what issues they chose because they aren't objective, they, the choosers of the sample issues, are leftwing big government statists.

For example, how did congressmen vote on eliminating the income tax "marriage penalty"? Certainly Hispanics, who have a higher rate of marriage than other ethnicities, will benefit enormously by relief from the marriage penalty that forces couples, especially educated couples, to pay more in taxes than single people.

Example, how did all these congressman vote on health plans that included tax breaks for small business when Hispanics are forming small businesses at three times the rate of the rest of the country? Certainly the Hispanic entrepreneur needs tax consideration if he is to carry expensive health insurance for his employees.

Example, how did congressman vote on impeaching the President? Certainly, if law and order Hispanics truly believe in the Constitution and the law, then a vote for impeachment would have been in the Hispanic community's interest. Over 50-percent of Americans now consider impeachment of President Clinton to have been correct.

Example, how did congressmen vote on welfare reform? Certainly, a vote to do away with welfare as it existed in the first Clinton administration was a vote for the Hispanic community, wasn't it? Or is a welfare state chock full of free money dependent, subservient Hispanics in the best interests of the Hispanic community?

Example, American 4th graders are no better off today than they were 7-years ago if one believes national test scores. How did congressmen vote on various education initiatives of the Clinton Administration when they have not fixed bad education, the dagger at the throats of Hispanic children?

Example, how did congressmen the NHLA rates so highly vote on the revolutionary Satellite/Low Power Television bill last year that preserves the tiny foothold Hispanic television entrepreneurs have in the country?

The true test of how a congressman's vote helps or hurts the Hispanic community is whether or not such a vote makes Hispanics more or less dependent on a larger government. Did the congressman vote to keep government out of the way of the burgeoning Hispanic community? Or did they vote for costly obstacles to Hispanics seeking more opportunity and education?

In other words, using a leftwing, radical, socialist yardstick, did your congressman vote for a leftwing radical socialist government that hobbles and economically penalizes Hispanics? Did their vote help Hispanics that want to run their own lives, want to work hard and enjoy the fruits of their own labor; or, did they vote to keep the Hispanic community on the welfare rolls?

The NHLA doesn't represent the Hispanic community Like many so-called national Hispanic groups, the NHLA is but one more leftwing, socialistic group that deifies people who vote for more government and for more shackles on individual Hispanics and to over-tax Hispanics who make money.

Who, then, represents the "Hispanic community?" Certainly, leftwing groups don't; they represent leftwing people, not Hispanics in general. They don't represent me, nor do they represent the U.S. Hispanic Chamber of Commerce, the very guys who create hundreds of thousands of American jobs. No, they only represent a handful of welfare check supplicants, not payroll check writers.

Given all this, 30-minutes spent with Republican National Chairman Jim Nicholson proved to be very illuminating. There is no doubt that Chairman Nicholson is sincere in reaching out to Hispanics for the 2000 election.

"The concerns of most Hispanics mirror those of national Republicans," he says. Better education for Hispanics has not been accomplished under President Clinton, but must be before the entire Hispanic community collapses from lack of education. Hispanic unemployment, though lower in January than anytime since President Nixon's administration, is 62-percent higher than "whites." The highest taxes since World War II are draining the fruits of Hispanic labor and business and they must be cut. No progress has been made on securing Social Security that is projected to collapse in a few years. As only 4-percent of Hispanics currently collect Social Security, Hispanics—paying into it now—want it fixed before they start collecting benefits. The Democrats torpedo school choice even as Hispanics overwhelmingly support school choice and vouchers.

Leftwingers, nor their values, reign in the Hispanic community. The National Latino Political Survey conducted by the U. of Texas discovered that less than 35-percent of Hispanics considered themselves to be "very liberal," or "liberal." Most said they were "moderate", "conservative" or "very conservative." That, unlike the National Hispanic Leadership Agenda, is the real state of mind of national Hispanics. National Republican Chairman Jim Nicholson is right. Most Hispanics think like most Republicans.

(NOTE: With the ascendancy of Bush and his Hispanic supporters in Washington, organizations have surfaced that are far more middle-class and Republican in orientation than before Bush. The Latino Coalition, for example, has commissioned surveys that totally contradict findings of the leftwing groups indicating that their surveys may not be legitimate, to begin with.)

A HISPANIC REPUBLICAN ROMP, FINALLY

Raoul Lowery Contreras
June 6, 1998

Bingo! ¡Caramba!

Hispanic Republicans won big on primary election night throughout California as California Hispanics romped up and down the state. One, Rob Guzman, lost the Republican nomination in the 42nd Congressional District by only 272 votes. Eunice Guzman won the Republican nomination for the 32nd State Senate District. Ruben Barrales became the first Republican Hispanic to be nominated for State office, that of Controller, in over a 120-years.

It is in State Assembly contests that Hispanic Republicans truly romped. In Sacramento's 5th District, Sam Paredes ran a strong second for the GOP nomination. Sacramento Republicans gave Irma Belmontes-Boreman enough votes to run a strong second for the 9th District GOP nomination.

Five Hispanic Republicans were nominated in Democratic-leaning districts to run in November's Election. In Sonoma's 7th District, Republicans nominated Bob Sanchez; Monterey Republicans nominated Phil Chavez in the 27th District; Azuza Republicans nominated Henry Gonzalez to run in the 57th District; Whittier Republicans nominated Albert Nuñez for the 58th District; and, San Bernardino Republicans nominated Irma Escobar as their nominee for the 62nd District.

But the big news is that the lone Hispanic Republican in the State Assembly, Rod Pacheco of Riverside, who is running unopposed for reelection in November will likely be joined in Sacramento by Santa

Maria's Abel Maldonado (who defeated Rene Bravo, by the Way), the Republican nominee in the Republican 33rd Assembly District. Also joining Assemblyman Rod Pacheco will be Robert Pacheco (no relation), who was nominated by Republicans in the Republican 60th District; and, Charlene Zettel, who grew up as Charlene Gonzalez of East Los Angeles and Flintridge, and was nominated by Republicans in the Republican 75th District.

From one Republican Assemblyman to four in just two years. Wow! Assuming they all win, the current thrust of the California Republican Party is working despite recent schisms between the Republican party of California and Hispanics. State Chairman Mike Schroeder has deliberately led the Party apparatus on the road to round up every California Hispanic it can—to vote Republican. Is there any better way than to put forth Hispanic Republicans for office?

Closer examination of these vote results reveals something even more important than just Hispanic Republicans running for office, but rather, where they run. These four potential Hispanic Republican Assembly people are running in suburban districts—heavily Republican districts. To win nomination, these Republican Hispanics had to win in overwhelming Anglo constituencies. In other words, they had to be superb candidates. Superb candidates usually win.

Take, for example, Charlene Zettel of the 75th District, a suburban San Diego District that includes Poway, Santee, Ramona, Alpine, Lakeside and all the rural areas in-between. This is a district that voted for Propositions 187, 209 and the stop-bi-lingual-education proposition, 227, by huge majorities. She won the nomination with 45% of the vote, beating two very conservative Anglo men in a district that has never elected a Democrat—ever. This East Los Angeles young lady moved to the Pasadena area when ten and attended Catholic schools through graduation from Sacred Heart Academy. She graduated from the University of Southern California and started a career as a health professional. She moved to the San Diego area almost thirty years ago and did all the community things an active modern woman does, particularly in education.

She was attacked by conservatives as being too liberal, too inexperienced and too woman, but she won the nomination anyway—with big numbers. Her 45% dwarfed the 32% and 23% her opponents garnered. Luckily, Charlene Zettel was able to raise the necessary funds to run and she needed them. Apparently, this race was the most expensive Assembly race in the State. Well over a million dollars was spent.

San Diego's Republican Party Chairman, Bob Marvin is delighted Charlene won and expresses himself with a big "WOW" for his representative-to-be for many reasons including qualifications and guts, but also for the fact she is a Mexican American, a 100-per cent Mexican American.

State Party Chairman Mike Schroeder says of Charlene and all the other Hispanic Republican nominees, "I could be no more pleased to have such a bounty of highly qualified nominees."

He says it all started a year ago when he convinced the Party to go after Hispanics with an energetic campaign. Santa Maria's Abel Maldonado, for example, began his campaign at that time at a Hispanic Republican conference sponsored by the Party, among the very people who attended the conference. Schroeder and the Party Political Director, a young energetic Hispanic, Mike Madrid, have turned the conferences into a road show covering the entire state, weekend by weekend.

As to the Democrats and their Hispanic candidates, they are mostly inner-city candidates, lots of them. At the state level, they scored well with Cruz Bustamante's nomination for Lt. Governor and he will probably win. Term-limited-out State Assemblywoman Diane Martinez was nominated for Insurance Commissioner and will probably lose. A very telling result was in the Democratic race for State Treasurer, where a South Gate City Treasurer, Albert Robles, received more votes (868,251) than did multi-millionaire big money spending candidates for Governor, Al Checci (682,479); or, Jane Harman's 664,005.

Robles spent no money, made few, if any, public appearances, or sent out mailers.

Hispanic voters of all political stripes voted on Primary day and will hit the polls again in November. Because they are voting and running for office in record numbers, in both parties, California is a better place to live in today, I think, for all people, not just Hispanics.

(NOTE: The four Republican Assembly candidates, Pacheco, Pacheco, Zettle and Maldonado did win and immediately formed a Hispanic Republican caucus of four. Rubern Barrales lost for Controller, but went on to become President Bush's Assistant and Director of Inter-governmental Affairs. Bustamante won the Lt. Governorship and became the first statewide elected Hispanic since 1875. Dianne Martinez was wiped out by Republican Chuck Quackenbush for Insurance Commissioner and disappeared from the political scene. He later resigned in an earthquake insurance scandal. One of his top political assistants was convicted of ripping of $200,000 in insurance funds and is in prison. Quackenbush is living in Hawaii, uncharged because the Democratic Attorney General didn't want to have to criminally charge Quackenbush's Democratic predecessor, John Garamendi, for conduct unbecoming, to say the least.)

HISPANIC REPUBLICANS GROW AND GROW

By Raoul Lowery Contreras
September 22, 2000

Hispanic Republican, is that an oxymoron? No. Though California Hispanic Republicans dropped in numbers during the Governor Pete Wilson inspired anti immigrant hysteria of the middle 1990s, their numbers have begun to increase as a result of courting by presidential candidate Texas Governor George W. Bush.

We know these things because the Hispanic Republican Association in San Diego County, home to 700,000 Hispanics, had professional planner Richard Amador Babcock (Master's Degree in Public Administration) conduct a formal scientific study that provides us with a wealth of data to examine.

Between 1992 and 1998, the number of registered Hispanic Republicans dropped 18% from 32 percent of registered Hispanics in the County to 26 percent. Considering that Hispanic Republican registration had risen every election for more than two decades, the drop must be attributed to the anti immigrant hysteria of 1994. Why? Because a third of registered Hispanic Republicans are foreign born. Foreign born didn't appreciate Pete Wilson and his Mexican hating allies picking on them, so some dropped their Republican registration.

In 1998, 168,000 Hispanics were registered to vote in San Diego. 48,000 were registered Republican and 20,000 were registered as Decline to State (who are open to vote Republican). Registered Hispanic Republicans make up 29 percent of the San Diego Hispanic electorate (statewide, only 19%) and will have a larger share when registration closes in early October. 5,000 new San Diego Hispanic Republicans have registered and more are expected in coming days.

Hispanic Republicans are younger than Hispanic Democrats; Hispanic Republicans have a higher percentage of their registration in the 30-49 age group. Hispanic Republicans make more money, with a median household income of $53,423, Democrats $50,280. This income disparity reflects in residential patterns. There are 803 precincts in the County in which Hispanic Republicans outnumber Hispanic Democrats. These precincts tend to be in higher economic level areas, such as North and East County.

Women outnumber men as registered voters in both parties, though among Republicans the genders are more balanced (51% Women, 48% men) than among Democrats (55% to 44%).

In general, those Hispanics in the 18-24 age group are registered in far higher percentages than non Hispanic Whites (15.84% to 9.65%), while the converse is true among 65 years and older, where non Hispanic Whites are almost double Hispanics of the same age (20.10 to 11.7%).

Over all, only 58.21 percent of California Hispanics eligible to vote have registered, while 72.04 percent of non Hispanic Whites are registered voters.

But enough of these statistics and percentages—there is good news and bad news in the study we examine here. The bad news is that while there are over 10,000,000 Hispanics in California, only about six in ten eligible are registered to vote and their voting rate is lower than other Californians. Nonetheless, 1.5-million of them are expected to vote this November (NALEO Election Handbook). This, despite low registration and voting, will be significant.

We also learn the Hispanic Republicans are growing in numbers and that they live in almost every precinct in civilized society. They tend to live well materially, and tend to be better educated, younger and tend to vote in higher percentages than their Hispanic Democrat counterparts.

All in all, Hispanic Republicans are growing in numbers and are strategically placed to have a serious impact on the future of California and the nation.

Hispanic Republican is not an oxymoron; it is a fact, a real important political fact.

(NOTE: In May of 2001, surveys conducted by AFL/CIO unions and Democrat Sergio Bendixen concluded that former Vice President al Gore would have defeated President Bush in a rerun among Hispanics by a two to one margin. Then came September 11th. Bendixen conducted a new survey for a Democratic client in May of 2002 and concluded that President Bush and Al Gore were statistically tied in a rerun for the Presidency. This survey follows those in the Los Angeles Times that reported that President Bush had more support post-September 11 among Hispanics than he did with the general population. More surveys concluded that President Bush had more support among foreign-born Hispanics than among the native born.)

HISPANICS AMBUSHED, AGAIN

By Raoul Lowery Contreras
March 5, 2000

Well, the cultural dissemblers are out in force again, this time buttressed by a questionable poll by John Zogby who interviewed 735 "Hispanics" (out of a estimated population of more than 33-million). Included in the survey, according to Zogby were immigrants, non-citizens and registered voters.

What we don't know is exactly what proportions of those groups were surveyed, what part of the country they were surveyed in and exactly who was surveyed, nor a definition of "Hispanic." We don't know if the "Hispanics" interviewed were Puerto Ricans, all of whom are natural-born U.S. citizens, New York-Washington Heights Dominicans, almost all of which are immigrants, or Mexican—origin people, most of whom are natural-born U.S. citizens, or recent Mexican immigrants.

What we do know is that mischievous anti-immigrant people, groups and newspapers are waving the Zogby Poll about like it is "Scripture" and proof of all their anti-immigrant rants. For example, Dan Stein, executive director of the Federation for American Immigration Reform (FAIR), issued a press release based on the Zogby Poll.

Among many pearls of ersatz wisdom, we find: "Those who claim that Hispanic voters were allegedly 'driven away' from the Republican Party by former Governor Pete Wilson's support of measures to control illegal immigration can point to no data to support that contention." Wrong!

Stein continues, "The old canard blaming Pete Wilson for the failure of some immigrant blocs to vote Republican is getting old and tired. It wasn't true then and it is not true now." Wrong, again!

There's nothing in the poll that indicates any truth to Stein's conclusions. Moreover, we have concrete data from the last two California elections, plus Republican Party Surveys, plus registration percentages at New Citizen ceremonies that conclusively prove that California Mexican American voters ran away from the Republican Party. Those that have quit the Republican Party, have publicly stated that they did so because of Pete Wilson's mean-spirited support of the unconstitutional Proposition 187. It, among other things, would have expelled American citizen children from public school if the unmarried father of the child is illegally in the country, despite the mother's legal residency in the country.

First, less than 23% of California's Mexican Americans voted for Prop. 187, a far cry from the 55% that told pollsters they supported Prop. 187 before their sample ballots arrived in their mailboxes. There is no doubt that most people who voted for Prop. 187 never read it. For example, this talk show host challenged the audience to prepare for a week to debate me on Prop. 187. With a huge audience tuning in, not a single person who called into debate had ever read Proposition 187. With 20-million people in Southern California, one would have thought that at least one person had read Prop. 187—30-days before the election besides me.

So, proof number one that California Hispanics rejected Pete Wilson's anti-immigration efforts is the four of five votes they cast against Proposition 187. Proof number two is that Pete Wilson had secured 50% of the Los Angeles County Mexican American vote according to exit polls in Governor Wilson's first gubernatorial win in 1990, but less than half that in 1994. Proof number three is a survey conducted for California Republican legislators that concluded that Republicans could not count on more than 20% of Mexican American voters in the immediate future if they didn't turn away from Pete Wilson's anti-immigrant positions. This survey was publicly released and discussed, but apparently didn't reach Mr. Stein.

Proof number four was the disastrous 1998 election in which Roman Catholic California Attorney General, Dan Lungren, a lukewarm supporter of Prop. 187, campaigned strenuously to appeal to fellow Roman Catholics in the Mexican American community. He was rejected for his efforts, losing over 70% of the Mexican American vote, matching the total failure of Robert Dole when he ran for President in 1996. Compare these efforts and results to Ronald Reagan and Richard Nixon, each of whom received 35-45% of the Mexican American vote in their successful presidential runs

Lastly, let's look at the hundreds of thousands of immigrants who have become American citizens lately. Among former Mexicans in California, over 60% have registered Democratic, a huge increase over the traditional 50% who used to register Democratic before Pete Wilson. That's proof number five.

One realizes that John Zogby's cultural survey falls on its own weight by considering all Hispanics to be like each other, that all Hispanics are monolithic in thought and that all Hispanics are stupid. Dan Stein makes the same false assumptions.

I'll wager that most of these surveyed "Hispanics" never heard of Proposition 187, nor read it, nor even know who Governor Pete Wilson is. I'll wager that most "Hispanics" surveyed by Zogby live in the East, while most American Hispanics live in the West. I'll wager that Zogby's poll doesn't have 65% Mexican-origin respondents, though that is the percentage of Mexican-origin people among all American Hispanics. How do I know?

Proof number six: There are more Mexican-origin people within sight of Los Angeles City Hall than all the Puerto Ricans, Cuban Americans and New York Dominicans—COMBINED. I wonder if John Zogby knows that, apparently Dan Stein and FAIR don't.

(NOTE: The previous article totally discredits the Zogby Poll and Dan Stein of FAIR.)

2

THE PRESIDENTIAL CAMPAIGN OF 2000

FREEDOM AND HONOR IN THE WHITE HOUSE?

By Raoul Lowery Contreras
January 2, 2000

There is a little six-year-old boy in Miami that has more COJONES and desire to live than most people in most countries. His name is Elian Gonzales. He is the Cuban boy who was rescued at sea by American patrols. The boy had held on to an inflated inner-tube for days after his mother drowned while trying to bring the boy out of Communist Cuba to the United States.

A Clinton Administration deal with Cuba mandates that the boy be returned because he didn't make it to the Florida beach on his own. That deal is the worst foreign policy deal made in decades. Fulfilling the mandates of that dumb deal and the dumb underlying law the Clinton Administration sponsored to curry favor with Communist dictator Fidel Castro may violate every principle upon which this country was founded.

Sure, there is supposed to be a father in Cuba, if he is the real father. Sure, parental rights are paramount in most cases of relationships between parents and children, but not always. Is it not correct for society to intercede between parent and child when physical, emotional or sexual abuse exists?

The factual situation in the case of Elian Gonzales is that he is now on U.S. territory. He is in the guardianship of Florida-residing relatives under Immigration and Naturalization Service (INS) bond and supervision. His father demands the return of the boy, according to government controlled reports out of Cuba. The relatives are fighting that demand. President Clinton's administration says the INS will decide the case of Elian, the relatives stand by with lawyers to contest what the Clinton Administration will obviously and probably do—return the child to Fidel Castro's Cuba.

Should Elian Gonzales be returned to his father in Communist Cuba? Or, should the boy be allowed to stay with his relatives in Miami? Should the boy be sentenced to a possible lifetime of socialistic nonsense and denial of human and political rights? Or, should the boy be granted a lifetime of human and political freedom and material plenty for which his mother died trying to provide him?

Would sending the boy back to Cuba be the quintessential case of child abuse, in fact, the ultimate case of abuse? Can we send that boy back purposefully despite the ultimate sacrifice of the boy's mother for freedom? Can we dismiss her sacrifice so Bill Clinton and Fidel Castro can smoke cigars together, or whatever they do with cigars?

Is the desire of the boy's father higher on the human scale than a six-year-old boy's future? Where do we draw the line between parental rights and a child's right to life? We draw it here. The boy must be allowed to stay in the United States and Congress must pass the special legislation necessary to make the boy's freedom possible. There are many reasons why this should be.

American citizenship, by law, follows maternity and always has in this country, and did under English common law dating back to the early

1600s. Custody generally follows maternity when it is court assigned throughout the country. It was the mother's desire that the boy live in the United States, not in Cuba. Our child prevention infrastructure should coalesce around the mother's desire as manifested by her attempt to bring the boy out. Where are the ultra-liberal feminists when we need them?

Instead of a clear-cut decision by the Clinton Administration to support the mother's desire for her boy's freedom, we find equivocation and wimpiness. What we find a White House influenced by phony government sponsored demonstrations in Cuba, the land where anti-government political demonstrations and free elections are not allowed.

We find a White House that has no guts, no COJONES. We find a White House without the guts of a six-year-old boy who fought the elements, the sea and death for five days. The boy has absolutely no control over the situation. His fate and future are in the hands of William Jefferson Clinton and his ACHICHINCLE (ah-chee-chee-nkleh, gofer) Albert Gore, Vice-President and candidate for President, and the Presidents ersatz wife, U.S. Senate Candidate Hillary Rodham Clicnton.

Clinton, Rodham Clinton and Gore will agonize over whether returning the boy has more political pluses than allowing him to stay. When they arrive at that determination, Elian Gonzales will embark on the rest of his life. Will it be in a free United States of America with loving relatives guiding him to adulthood; or, will it be in Communist Cuba where people are not allowed to speak their mind, do what free people do and live the life of a six-year-old in America. I bet Clinton, Rodham Clinton/Gore will send the kid back.

The child, not William Jefferson Clinton, Fidel Castro, Al Gore and Rodham Clinton, is what's important here. If the White House decides to send the boy back, every freedom loving American must punish them for the crime of sending a boy back to Cuba, the crime of the ultimate child abuse. Every freedom loving Hispanic must stand with the boy and his mother's wish of freedom for him. They must punish anyone who abuses this child. We must remember a loving mother who gave her life for her boy's freedom when we cast our votes next November.

(NOTE: When this article was written, the national debate on Elian Gonzalez raged everywhere. When this article was published in the Philadelphia Inquirer and reprinted on myriad websites, the e-mails clogged my computer. Though President Clinton publicly stated he would stay out of the issue, he lied. One of his impeachment attorneys turned up as the attorney for Elian's Cuban father. Clinton's Attorney General personally involved herself in the issue and personally ordered machine gun armed INS agents to storm the Miami house of Elian's relatives in a pre-dawn raid to take Elian away, to turn him over to his Cuban father. One press photographer took a prize-winning picture of 6-year-old Elian screaming with a machine gun barrel in his face, held there by a ski-masked federal agent.

Two giant political repercussions were caused by the machine gun in Elian's face: First, outraged Florida Cubans voted in mass for George W. Bush in November, 2002, and elected him President. In 2002, the same outraged Cubans massed their votes and chased former Attorney General Janet Reno into political oblivion when an unknown Tampa lawyer beat her in the Democratic primary for the opportunity to run against Governor and Presidential brother Jeb Bush.)

CAN PRESIDENT G.W. BUSH SAY MUCHAS GRACIAS?

By Raoul Lowery Contreras
March 12, 2000

The Presidential candidates are, as expected, Governor of Texas, George W. Bush, and Vice-President Al Gore. How will "Hispanics" vote this fall? Will they vote for Vice-President Gore or for the Governor of Texas?

First of all, we must detail the quadrilateral nature of the "Hispanic" vote and it's geography. The reader must disbelieve any commentator who claims the Hispanic vote can be quantified as a monolithic vote. Period.

The "Northeast" Hispanic lives in a belt starting in Boston on the north, through New York, west to Philadelphia and into Chicago/Detroit. This Northeast Hispanic voting population is primarily Puerto Rican and Dominican, though Mexicans in Chicago/Detroit are increasing in numbers through recent immigration. These people are so Democratic they wouldn't vote Republican if someone paid them.

The "Southeast" Hispanic populace consists mostly of Cuban-origin people in Florida. The Cubans of Florida helped elect George Bush's brother, Jeb Bush, governor and have a healthy regard for the Bush name. These people generally vote Republican and there is no reason to think they will deviate from their normal path this November.

The "Southwest" Hispanic lives in Texas, New Mexico, Colorado, Nevada and Arizona. These people are overwhelmingly of Mexican-origin, either here for almost five hundred years, as in New Mexico, or by recent immigration from Mexico, as in Las Vegas.

Using political carbon-dating, we discover political variations among these Southwestern Mexican-origin people. Mexican people who have immigrated into the U.S. in recent years have registered Democratic upon gaining citizenship. Those who came before 1980, registered Democrat, but voted Republican in Presidential elections. They were happy with Presidents Eisenhower, Nixon, Reagan and Bush. More importantly, as educational and economic levels rose for the children of immigrants, they registered and voted Republican in greater numbers than their parents. Observers and political witnesses must note the almost 50% of the Mexican vote for Governor Bush in his reelection two years ago in Texas. Witness also the argument over these percentages from the left-wing. They claim that Bush only received 39-percent, not 50-percent. Big deal.

The "Western" Hispanic lives in California, with a few in Washington State's Yakima Valley. Subtracting out the huge cohort of recent, non-citizen immigrants, one is left with a predominately middle-class, fairly sophisticated Mexican-origin population that leads the world in forming new businesses and flooding the state's college campuses with new students. Again, political carbon-dating reveals length of time in the U.S. as a litmus test on voting habits. Recent immigrant/new citizens, riled as they are with Proposition 187 Republicans, registered Democratic. Long time resident citizen Mexican-origin people are 40-percent registered Republicans.

In 1996 and 1998, as many as 80-percent of California Mexican-origin people voted Democratic as a result of the anti-immigrant hysteria stoked by Republican Governor Pete Wilson and his support of the unconstitutional Proposition 187. However, while they were punching the ballots for Democrats, middle-class Mexican Americans voted to do away with Affirmative Action by voting for Proposition 209, the California Civil Rights Act. They were mad that California blacks overwhelmingly supported the anti-immigrant, anti-Mexican Proposition 187. In voting against Affirmative Action, they joined many Republicans on just one more issue.

In the recent primary, middle-class Mexican-origin people renominated four incumbent Hispanic Republicans to the State Legislature, and nominated 10 more Hispanic Republicans for legislative seats up in November and four candidates for Congress. If only 30-percent of California Mexican Americans vote Republican, and 90% of Republicans vote Republican, the Republican Presidential candidate can win the state's 54 electoral votes.

The Presidential campaign of 2000 is joined between Governor George W. Bush and Vice-President Al Gore and the election can turn on "Hispanic" votes, but not those of the Northeast. Governor Bush has little chance to win in Massachusetts and New York (Total: 44 electoral votes). He can win Pennsylvania, Michigan and Illinois without the "Hispanic" voter in those states. "Hispanic" votes aren't critical for a Republican in the Northeast because those people never vote Republican.

The Cubans of Florida, thus the state, are a lock for Governor Bush. Texas is a lock for Governor Bush, with help from the state's Mexican voters. New Mexico, Colorado, Arizona and Nevada are locks for Governor Bush. These states all have Republican governors, elected with the help of Mexican American votes.

California (54 electoral votes), thus, is the prize in play. Gore cannot win the Presidency without California. He can only count on 10 states and the District of Columbia with 96 electoral votes. Bush, on the other hand, can count on 25 states with 198 electoral votes, including the 57 electoral votes of Texas and Florida. I count 14 states in play with 187 electoral votes. 270 electoral votes elect the President.

Will Mexican-heavy Los Angeles and mostly Anglo Northern California produce enough Democratic votes to offset heavy Republican majorities in non-Los Angeles Southern California (San Diego, Orange, Riverside, Ventura, Santa Barbara and San Bernardino Counties)? Or, will enough middle-class Mexicans in Los Angeles vote their minds instead of their registration to provide Democrat Al Gore far fewer votes than he might otherwise expect? They've done it before. A majority of California middle-class Mexican Americans voted for Ronald Reagan for President, as they did for President Richard Nixon.

(NOTE: New Mexico went for Al Gore by fewer than 400 votes. The other states noted as locks were just that, though Florida went for Bush by only 537 votes after numerous counts and recounts. It should be noted that American Blacks have taken great umbrage at comments in this article. Nonetheless, most Mexican Americans reject the Jesse Jackson-Al Sharpton view of issues and events and gleefully vote against those people and their issues when given the opportunity, as in the Affirmative Action vote in California. The same Mexican Americans will reject Ward Connerly's proposal to do away with race boxes on university, employment and mortgage loan applications in March of 2004.

Reason: Mexican Americans are not as stupid as Ward Connerly assumes they are. His "color-blind society" arguments are designed to appeal to dumb people who think that all race problems have been left behind. Intelligent people see Connerly as a "stalking horse" for wealthy white racist associates that he hangs around with to take their contributions and use them for his personal benefit. News reports show that Connerly collects funds for his Racial Privacy Initiative (RPI) using a tax deductible fund and paid himself over a million dollars.)

BREAKFAST WITH GEORGE W. BUSH

By Raoul Lowery Contreras
May 8, 2000

The crowd was mostly Anglo, mostly forty-something-plus and very hungry. Like most major hotel banquet rooms, the service was slow, but for the first time in memory, the wait staff was not 100% Mexican. Hotels being particularly vulnerable to the Immigration and Naturalization Services' ability to clean out hotel staffs with just the threat of a raid, Anglos and Blacks were now serving breakfast. It was slow and the food was not hot. It didn't matter, the thousand people had come to see and hear the Governor of Texas wax poetic on Cinco de Mayo, the Fifth of May.

Governor George W. Bush came to my city specifically to reach out to the California Hispanic community. He had done the same the day before in Santa Ana, the large, mostly Mexican city between Los Angeles and San Diego. There he walked the streets, shook hands, ate tacos and kibbutzed with Mexican Americans who fell all over themselves to meet the man who might be the next President of the United States.

When he entered, an electric political current ran through the room. He walked among the tables personally meeting each person, shaking their hands and addressing them by their first names. What a wonder laser printed nametags are. Eventually he came to my table, shook my hand, called me Raoul and looked me in the eye. I asked him if he was one of those little kids in Midland, Texas I used to see on my yearly transit through that small 1950s town in Texas where he grew up. Midland, you know Midland, he asked.

Yes, Governor, though I lived in San Diego, my stepfather was a real Texan and used to take us every year to "vacation" in Texas. The Governor laughed. Yes, he said, even if Texans live in San Diego, a great vacation place, they have to return to Texas, like swallows to San Juan

Capistrano. He autographed my breakfast ticket, thanked me for being there, and moved on.

The Cinco de Mayo breakfast, sponsored by San Diego Republican Party and the United States and Mexico Foundation, proceeded with introductions, then, finally, the Governor of Texas and candidate for President, George W. Bush.

"Family values," he said, "do not stop at the Rio Grande River." Though we must "enforce" our border, he understands the duty of any father to "feed his family." "Thus," he continued, he "fully understood the need and duty for a Mexican father to come to the US to work, to support his family." We must, he posited, develop a "guest worker program" that can match people who want to work with those who need work performed.

A strong NAFTA (North American Free Trade Agreement), Bush told his audience, is just one way to help build a strong Mexico. A strong Mexico that produces many jobs and a friendly Mexico is absolutely necessary and is, perhaps, the most important foreign policy goal this country can have. Since NAFTA's implementation, Bush pointed out, two-way trade between the US and Mexico has grown from about $37-billion to $200-billion worth of trade. Jobs, (a million jobs a year in Mexico according to Mexico and millions in the USA) are being created in each country because of NAFTA, Bush stated. As President, Bush will demand more negotiating ability (Fast Track) from Congress so he can negotiate free trade throughout the Hemisphere. The crowd enthusiastically received these comments.

No wonder his comments were so well received. San Diego has an unemployment rate of 2.5% and thousands of jobs have been created because of more trade with Mexico. Everyone in the room knows how valuable NAFTA has been to our region and Governor Bush knows that also. No one in San Diego who wants a job, whether they are

White, Black or Brown or female, is unemployed. There are gazillions of jobs seeking workers in San Diego and Orange counties.

At the press conference after the breakfast, one pesky reporter kept asking Governor Bush why more Hispanics weren't present. She maintained that only 10% or so of the audience was Hispanic and didn't that bother him. He shrugged and asked, "Who's counting?"

Nonetheless, they were there and they are but the tip of the iceberg. Bush is mining the Hispanic community for every single vote. He will get more Hispanics than most people expect. He will make the California race a close one because Hispanics are responding. He does not need to carry a majority, just 30% or more. He can do that.

Why? Because, Hispanics look into Governor Bush's eyes and read his soul. He is for real. He does not tell us, like Al Gore, that he wants a grandchild to be born on Cinco de Mayo. Bush tells us that he wants to lead us to a better America, an America of and for all of us. We believe he means it. That's why Hispanics are beginning to move into George Bush's column. He is for real.

(NOTE: George W. Bush carried San Diego County. He lost to Gore in the state. Nonetheless, his Hispanic vote set a record nationally in actual votes cast for him by Hispanics. He went on to win Fast Track negotiating authority from the Congress in 2002, a feat former President Clinton could not do because he couldn't get his fellow Democrats to support him.)

AFTER 500 YEARS, DEMOCRACY COMES TO MEXICO

By Raoul Lowery Contreras
July 3, 2000

Sunday, July 2, Mexicans voted for President and they will never look back. After almost 500 years of existence, Mexicans stood on their democratic hind legs and swept authoritarianism, corruption, and the world's oldest one-party "democracy" aside, forever.

Former Governor of Mexico's Guanajuato State, Vicente Fox, will be inaugurated as the next President of Mexico on December 1st of this year. Assuming that all goes well, this will be the first peaceful transfer of power from one political party to another in the history of Mexico. Francisco Labastida, the ruling party's candidate graciously conceded defeat to the National Action Party's Fox. Why even spoiler leftist candidate Cuahuatemoc Cardenas conceded defeat to the man he called a "traitor" and "liar."

Ruling party faithful humbly accepted defeat election night. No mobs hit the street. Thousands of victorious Mexicans flooded the streets of Mexico City around the "Angel of Independence" Monument chanting "Fox! Fox! Fox!"

Mexican President Ernesto Zedillo hit the airwaves minutes after the Federal Election Commission issued the "Quick Count" proclaiming that Mexicans had spoken and that the vote must be respected. Ah, the quick count...

At Eleven P.M., precisely, the Independent Federal Election commission (IFE) spokesman Jose Woldenberg came on national television, with millions of Mexicans watching, to give the official "Quick Count" in which all parties had agreed beforehand. A number of ballots from thousands of voting places were plucked at random from transparent ballot boxes and counted. Percentages where then calculated and forwarded by phone, fax or computer modem to IFE's Mexico City headquarters, where they were tabulated between the close of voting and 11:00 P.M.

Chairman Woldenberg then announced what everyone already knew from exit polls—PAN candidate Vicente Fox had clearly won the Presidency of Mexico. He won with a final vote projected to be between 39% and 45%, with the PRI's Labastida coming in second with between 36% and 39.8% and Cardenas third with between 15.1% and 18%.

Fox won after a three-year campaign. Fox changed political campaigning in Mexico and forced the ruling PRI party to hold an "open" national primary. Fox took Mexican presidential politics into nationally televised debates and won both easily. Fox brought religion back into Mexican politics with an "in your face" confrontation with the traditionally anti-clerical (and heavily Masonic) PRI by waving a Virgin of Guadalupe banner at a PAN rally. He declared for all that he is a staunch Roman Catholic and that the Church should have a say in education.

Fox preached free markets and the people agreed. Fox preaches free enterprise and micro-enterprises and the people agreed. Fox decried the "PRI as Corruption and corruption as the PRI." The people agreed. Fox declared against abortion and displayed his four adopted children as alternatives to abortion. The people agreed. Fox declared that each person is important. The people agreed. Fox declared that each vote counted. The people agreed. Fox declared that the youth of Mexico is the future of Mexico. The people agreed. Fox declared that Mexico's women are important and the people agreed. Fox declared that the people must be heard. The people agreed.

The people trooped to the polls in record numbers and voted for Fox. Over a third of the young (18-29) voted for him, 44% of the 30-49 year olds voted for him. Only the aged didn't, for they have known nothing but the PRI since 1929. Women voted for Fox; men voted for Fox. Fox carried the urban vote, where two/thirds of Mexicans now live.

Fox won because he referred to Mexicanos (men) and Mexicanas (women) in each speech he gave, giving women the political respect they never had.

Mexicans can thank each other for democratically changing governments. They can thank former President Carlos Salinas for deciding more than a decade ago to respect the vote so Mexico could ally itself economically with the USA and Canada in NAFTA. Mexicans can thank NAFTA for its huge successes in creating millions of new jobs in Mexico and for making Mexico an exporting powerhouse. Mexico can thank President Ernesto Zedillo for unburdening the Mexican system of the traditional tapping of his successor and throwing the ruling party into chaos by opening the nominating process.

Fox's victory speech had two outstanding thoughts: "A Democratic government is a respected government." And, "May God bless this government and country."

Mexico enters the new century a democratic country when Vicente Fox becomes President. Mexico is blessed. Now if only the Vicente Fox government can come to pass. There was once a favored presidential candidate named Colosio. He was shot to death while campaigning six years ago—and he was the nominee of the ruling party.

(NOTE: President Fox took office six weeks before President George W. Bush. The two met quickly, with Bush making Mexico his first foreign visit. Both Presidents agreed to negotiate a plan to bring millions of Mexican workers illegally in the United States into a legal status of some sort. That would have happened if September 11th hadn't occurred. First, American attention was diverted to a war on terrorism.

Secondly, Fox hesitated in jumping into a pro-American enthusiastic fight on terror, despite Mexican nationals being killed on September 11th. Thirdly, the Clinton-recession that started in the last 10 months of his administration slowed down the economic interchange between the US and its second largest trading partner, Mexico, causing the Clinton recession to reach into Mexico.)

A BURNING BRIGHT BUSH

By Raoul Lowery Contreras
July 24, 2000

Like a comet racing across the sky, blazing with sheer star power, there's a 24-year-old man crisscrossing the United States bringing light into the darkest recesses of what used to be called the ghetto, called now, the barrio. From Detroit's Mexicantown to East Los (Los Angeles), he goes shaking hands, talking in Spanish, bringing light. His name is George Prescott Bush.

His uncle is running for President; his father is the Governor of Florida; his mother was born and raised in Mexico's famous shoe manufacturing city, Leon, in the state of Guanajuato, the home of Mexico's President-elect, Vicente Fox. He and I spoke over the phone today during a break in his Michigan campaign appearance schedule.

How do you like campaigning for your uncle, George W. Bush? "I love it," he told me. "It is completely different than my previous campaign experience, campaigning for my father (Jeb Bush, Governor of Florida). This, is the big league (s)."

Have you been stumped by any questions while campaigning? "Yes," the 24-year-old graduate from Rice University responded, "Someone asked me the details of the Anti-Ballistic Missile (ABM) Treaty with the Soviet Union." What did you say in response? "Let me get back to you on that."

Presidential candidate relatives, sons and daughters, are not new on the campaign trail, you, however, are considered to be something special, why? "I think it's because this campaign is definitely an opportunity for me; my role is unique, my role is special." Why? "Because, I'm proud to be a link between my uncle and Hispanics; between Hispanics and the issues of this campaign."

George P. Bush, Hispanics and issues...? "This campaign allows me to seize the opportunity to discuss real issues, issues that are important to Hispanics and to do so from a background that includes Spanish and English, and that includes a Mexican born and raised mother. In other words, I understand the issues Hispanics relate to better than people who don't have my background."

What kind of reception have you received in the field? "Young Hispanics have been very enthusiastic. People, I'm told, who are not interested in politics, people my age, are all over the place. It's amazing to me how enthusiastic they are. I do run into entrenched hardcore Democrats who refuse to listen, but..."

What kind of reaction do you find among Hispanic Republicans? "Great. They think this campaign is so important. They tell me this is the opportunity to bring them out of the shadows, to prove to the country that not every Latino is a Democrat and that not all are closed-minded to the Republican Party. It also is an opportunity to show the Republican Party that we are here and worthwhile."

George Prescott Bush will enter law school at the University of Texas in Austin in two months, leaving the full-time campaign trail. He does say, however, "I'll help on weekends, if my uncle wants."

Let's examine if his uncle, George W. Bush, can use his nephew after September. Governor Bush has flatly stated that he has targeted the national Hispanic vote with particular emphasis on California and Florida. Governor Bush reminds all that he almost carried the Texas

Hispanic vote with 49% and that doubled his first Hispanic vote in his 1994 victory.

How best to go after the Hispanic vote than to let the world see his nephew, the obviously mestizo, mixed blood, young man who glides between Spanish and English, perfectly? How best to tell Hispanics that he cares for them and their issues than to present his nephew, the son of a Mexican mother? How best to get back useful intelligence of what Hispanics are thinking than to present his articulate nephew on the campaign trail?

George Prescott Bush, 24, history graduate from Rice University, handsome, named the 4th most eligible bachelor in the country by People Magazine, is all over the place, pumping for his uncle George W. Bush for President. Detroit one day, Los Angeles the next at 8:00 A.M. opening a campaign headquarters, joining his grandmother, former First Lady Barbara Bush, at an evening fundraiser, then shaking hands Sunday at a California fair. Beats licking stamps and stuffing campaign envelopes, n'est-ce pas?

Will Hispanics benefit from George P. Bush's campaign for his uncle? Yes. He is very visible, he's smart, articulate and he is everywhere. It's not often a presidential candidate's relative is truly relative to the campaign. George P. Bush is. Governor George W. Bush is very, very lucky.

ILLUSION OF INCLUSION

By Raoul Lowery Contreras
August 12, 2000

Crack! Crack! Crack! This was the sharp sound of an overseer's whip on the back of black slaves being punished for transgressions of the white man's rules on the plantation. It is the same sound made by Al Gore and his puppets at the Democratic National Committee plantation as they whipped the stuffing out of Loretta Sanchez, Democratic Congresswoman from Orange County.

Actually, for the first time in public, Al Gore tripped over a Mexican American and he simply and purely reacted as a typical plantation overseer, he cracked the whip against this woman who broke his rules. Loretta is one of the most well known Mexican Americans in the country, a woman who is revered as an almost saint by many in the Democratic Party. Loretta, of course, was famous for beating old Republican B-1 Bob Dornan in Orange County, a county perhaps more conservative than Mississippi.

The Democrats were so delighted by her long shot win over Dornan that they appointed her a National Committee Vice Chairperson and were able to blackmail Congressional Republicans into keeping her in the House, despite overwhelming evidence that 5,000 ineligible voters cast ballots in her win over Dornan. They paraded her around like she was a saint, a female Hispanic saint, a symbol of the best of the Democratic Party. With her as an icon, Democrats calculated that they would corral Hispanic votes for as far as we can see into the future. Her position was cemented when she politically slapped an inept Bob Dornan the second time around by thousands of votes and sent him into permanent retirement.

So, with the enthusiasm and energy of a convert (Loretta used to be a Republican) she plunged into raising money for Hispanic Democrats with the crowning achievement of her brief political career being a super jackpot of Hollywood treasure right in River City, the City of Angels. On the eve of the Al Gore Convention, the flashy "babe" from Orange County organized her $5000-a-plate fund-raiser at the infamous monument to Hedonism, the Los Angeles Playboy Mansion of Playboy magazine founder, Hugh Hefner.

Suddenly, the Buddist Temple fundraiser, the proud former tobacco farmer and inheritor of Big Oil shares, Mr. Al Gore, Vice President of the United States throws a moral fit. He decides that the Playboy Mansion might send the wrong signal and might associate his morals with his impeached immoral boss, President Bill Clinton. Never mind that Al Gore has accepted campaign contributions from Hefner and his daughter ($1500) and the Democratic National Committee (DNC) has received and spent $30,000 from Playboy Enterprises.

Al Gore decided that the pesky Mexicana had to be humiliated for making him look "bad." So, he had Joe Andrews his ACHICHINCLE (ah-chee-cheen-kleh, gofer) chairman of the DNC, threaten Loretta with banning her from speaking at the National Convention, with stripping her Party title away and not endorsing her reelection if she didn't cancel or move the fundraiser from the Playboy Mansion.

She caved, of course. What else could she do? Al Gore can now smirk about how moral he is, even as he spends Playboy money. There's also Chinese money, and tobacco money (Philip Morris sponsored the Democratic Governor's Gala at the Convention this year), all to elect Al Gore President.

One question of the "inclusive" Democrat candidate Al Gore: Would you have slapped Loretta SANCHEZ around in public like you did if she were named Smythe, or Clinton?

(NOTE: Al Gore is racist to the core. He smacked Loretta around, supported racial profiling by the Clinton Forestry Department in Northern California aimed at Mexicans and was used as evidence by Black Secret Service agents in their lawsuit charging discrimination. Specifically, the agents alleged that Gore ordered Black Secret Service agents away from him at campaign appearances so they wouldn't appear in photos with him. Other than appointing a Black woman campaign manager, then ignoring her, can anyone dispute Gore's Old South racism, a racism he obviously inherited from his arch-segregationist Senator father)

KEY VOTES IN NOVEMBER

By Raoul Lowery Contreras
September 9, 2000

Democrat Al Gore has reinvented himself into an "us versus them" candidate. Surveys show that much of the American public (54%) is invested in the stock market, so, will it buy a Marxist-Leninist-Communist like class warfare campaign?

Left-wing Mexican Americans will relish the Gore campaign. They are, however, but a small portion of the over-all Mexican American vote, a vote that could decide November's election. According to the Latino Election Handbook of the National Association of Latino Elected and Appointed Officials (NALEO), an estimated 1.5 million Mexican Americans will vote in California; 220,000 in Arizona; 146,000 in Colorado; 100,000 in Illinois; 223,000 in New Mexico; and, 1.2 million in Texas. Texas is a Bush state, it is not in play, nor is Colorado (Bush) or Illinois (Gore).

No matter how much the left wing screams, there aren't many of them. Only 10% or so of Mexican Americans classify themselves as left wing. More importantly, 50% of Mexican Americans call themselves conservative and 33% call themselves liberal, according to the national Public Broadcasting Latino Poll 2000 that was conducted by Dallas' Rincon and Associates.

If, then, the campaign is based on conservative values, Democrats lose, for the 50% that call themselves conservatives would naturally vote Republican. On the other hand, if the campaign is based on little people fighting Big Oil, Big Business, Big HMOs and Everyone-is-against-us-because-we're-Mexican, then more than 60%, or so, of Mexican Americans will vote Democratic. That 60% includes the poor (30% of the total) and working poor (low wage workers, about 30% of the total).

Most political pundits haven't a clue about how these millions of potential Mexican American voters will vote or why, for they know little of the Mexican American. To prove the point, watch Al Gore torture Spanish words. George W. Bush trots out his young half-Mexican nephew George P. Bush on the campaign trail and silly left wingers and sycophantic journalists demand to know why it is important for the President of the United States to have a Mexican sister-in-law and nieces and nephews who are Mexican Americans.

While pundits punt and left wing Mexicans snivel (being a minority within a minority), political eyes turn to three particular states: Arizona, New Mexico and California.

Arizona is simple. Its 8-electoral votes went for Clinton-Gore in 1996. A Bush win in Arizona is now a given. New Mexico's political history includes the second Mexican American Republican governor in U.S. History and the first Mexican American publicly elected U.S. Senator, a Republican, no less. California, with its history of having the first Mexican American governor in the United States and the first elected Mexican American congressman and Chairman of a Congressional Standing Committee, is the American political brass ring.

New Mexico and Arizona need to be watched because the Clinton-Gore ticket carried both in 1996. Republican Bob Dole won 159 Electoral College votes in 1996 (270 are needed to win the Presidency), thus, states like Arizona and New Mexico that voted for Clinton-Gore are critical if one assumes that George W. Bush's electoral foundation is made up of the same states Dole carried in 1996.

California is important, not just because it has 54 electoral votes, but because George W. Bush can win the Presidency without carrying the state. Around 8-million Californians will vote this November, thus, the 1.5-million Mexican Americans who might vote are 800-pound political gorillas.

If 50% of those 1.5-million are conservative and thus vote for Bush, that's 750,000 votes that are mostly registered Democratic. Those votes would hand the state to Bush and destroy Al Gore's chances. If, however, only 40% of the 1.5-million vote for Bush, with the other 60% voting as expected, Bush might also take the state with those 600,000 votes added to a higher-than-normal Republican turnout of middle and upper class whites and Asians.

Class warfare by Al Gore can easily backfire in California and deliver the state to Governor Bush. Why? Because 600,000 Mexican American Bush votes will cancel the California Black vote, the only vote Al Gore can actually count on in the Golden State. White men are for Bush; so are white married women, while single white women and Blacks are for Gore. Canceling the Black vote with middle-class Mexican American votes offers a comic ethnic scenario for pundits. They are not capable of understanding the middle-class Mexican American phenomenon, for all they see is those who are poor.

In this, they are conditioned by what Gregory Rodriguez wrote in the Los Angeles Times. He maintains, and I agree, that the public perception of the Mexican American is conditioned by a small group of "academics" from the "St. Cesar Chavez School of The Poor and They're-Picking-on-Me-Because-I'm-Mexican" and lazy journalists. That perception is wrong. Election Day may offer concrete proof that Rodriguez and I are right.

So, which will it be, a campaign of conservative values or of class warfare a la Gore? Either way, Gore just might lose California and if he can't win California, he can't win the Presidency, period.

(NOTE: Gore, of course, carried California and lost the election because Bush carried Texas and Florida. Arizona went for Clinton-Gore in 1996 but rejected Gore in 2000 and returned to the Republican fold. New Mexico, with the largest percentage of Hispanic votes, went for Gore by a measly 366-votes. Bush increased his Hispanic vote in California and laid the foundation for California victory in 2004.)

THE HALLOWEEN COALITION RISES UP, AGAIN

By Raoul Lowery Contreras
October 29, 2000

The ugly anti-Mexican, anti-Hispanic "Halloween Coalition" has risen again to flail away in the Presidential election race between Al Gore—their boy—and George W. Bush, their enemy. Any Hispanic who considers listening to the "Halloween Coalition" and voting for its boy, Al Gore, is committing economic and social suicide.

The "Halloween Coalition" was born to fight the North American Free Trade Agreement (NAFTA) in 1993, a hugely successful trade arrangement with Mexico that has lifted Mexico into our world and has helped create millions of American jobs.

The "Halloween Coalition" consisted of Big Labor (the AFL/CIO/ Teamsters), Greens and the type of person who rioted in Seattle earlier this year. Gluing the "Coalition" together was Jesse Jackson and most American Blacks. It was a race card then and it is a race card today.

Jesse Jackson is nothing but a race card dealer. He was in 1993 and is today. In the NAFTA debate, Jesse Jackson and most American Blacks fought heavily against NAFTA and the heavy majority of Hispanics who supported it. They turned a trade agreement into a racial question (charging that Black jobs were being sent overseas and to Mexico).

Jackson and his henchmen poisoned the race well between Hispanics and Blacks so deeply that when the racist Proposition 187 emerged in California, Blacks overwhelmingly supported its passage. Despite the obvious unconstitutionality of the Proposition sponsored by white racists who would just as soon deport Blacks to Africa as Mexicans to Mexico, Blacks voted just like white California racists voted.

Has-been Jackson is back. He's on talk and news shows throughout the country, hustling for Al Gore among Blacks. Nonetheless, Blacks are lagging in their support of the Gore/Lieberman ticket for the simple reason that many Blacks, for better or worse, dislike anyone Jewish. Remember Jesse Jackson's "Hymietown" reference to New York City? Many "politically correct" Americans are aghast at that thought and criticize commentators who point it out, but it is true, nonetheless. Criticize all you want.

Jackson is laying heavy political artillery on George W. Bush. His shots are cheap and usually untrue. Ironically, his campaign is an "us versus them" class warfare campaign on behalf of a Southern White guy whose father proudly voted against the Civil Rights Act of 1964. That anti-civil rights, anti-Black vote doesn't matter to Jackson, Republican Bush must be defeated. Jackson personifies the Confederate General Nathan Bedford Forest credo of take no prisoners (General Forest ordered the murder of over 300 Black Union soldiers when his troops captured Ft. Pillow in Missouri—he also founded the Ku Klux Klan)—Forest is a hero of fellow Tennessean Al Gore, but Jackson ignores this fact as he does the reverence of the Confederate flag by both Gore and President Clinton.

Joining Jackson is the National Association for the Advancement of Colored People (NAACP), a non-profit 501(c)3 organization to which contributions are tax exempt. The NAACP (actually a NAACP front group—the National Voter Fund) is spending $2-million in large urban centers with a crybaby television campaign featuring a relative to James Byrd, the Black dragged to death behind a pick-up truck in Texas.

She relates that she went to Texas Governor George W. Bush and pleaded with him to support a new "hate crime" bill. Bush refused, but took the position that if it reached his desk from the Democratic legislature, he would sign it. Two of Byrd's killers have been sentenced to death, the third to life without parole. No new "hate crime" law would have added anything to these sentences.

Jackson and NAACP are also picking away at the death penalty's application during Governor Bush's tenure. Jesse Jackson even compared one Black convicted murderer to Jesus Christ. Jackson implied during a pre-execution vigil that Bush is a murderer and as most of those executed are Black and other minorities, Bush is also a racist.

Hell hath no fury like Jesse Jackson (and the NAACP) when he levels his verbal cannons. Nonetheless, Jesse Jackson ceased to be a real political force when his "Halloween Coalition" was slaughtered in the NAFTA debate. George W. Bush was and is an ardent supporter of a hugely successful NAFTA. Jackson loses again.

(NOTE: American Blacks voted 91 or so percent for Al Gore. Jesse Jackson succeeded in his efforts to paint George W. Bush as a racist. The political problem is that Blacks have now written themselves out of the American Presidential picture for all time. Even though they voted in record numbers in Florida, Bush still carried the state. Thus, as Bush or any other Republican only needs to carry two of three states (California, Texas or Florida) along with the normal Republican voting states, Blacks don't mean much in national politics anymore. They can vote for a Democrat in every state they live in and do so at a 100% clip and the Democrat will still lose if he loses California, or loses Texas and Florida. In California, in 2004, the entire Black vote can be cast for a Democrat and he will lose the election if 40% (800,000) or more of the state's Hispanics vote Republican. Blacks have made themselves nationally irrelevant in Presidential elections by slavishly casting their votes for Democrats, especially racist Democrats like Al Gore and Senator Byrd of West Virginia, the former Ku Klux Klansman.)

BUSH BEATS GORE IN PHOTO FINISH

By Raoul Lowery Contreras
November 27, 2000

At 7:30 p.m. (Eastern time) on Sunday, just as my San Diego Chargers won their first game of the season (1-11), my candidate for President, George W. Bush, was certified by the Florida Secretary of State as the winner of more votes for President in Florida than Vice President Al Gore.

Within minutes of certification, Democratic Vice Presidential candidate Al Lieberman whined his way through a statement claiming that not all votes cast were counted and that the Republicans threw up stumbling block after stumbling block in an effort to disenfranchise Gore/Lieberman voters.

Lieberman had started the whining and cry babying when he went on national television and charged, without any offer of proof, that Republican mob rule had intimidated the Miami/Dade Democratically controlled vote Canvassing Board into dumping a manual recount of over 600,000 votes. Again, without any proof whatsoever, Lieberman charged that a Republican mob had intimidated local officials into abandoning a manual recount of votes cast for President.

Lieberman and his Democratic acolytes practically cried about the incident they claimed intimidated the Miamians. But, they were crocodile tears, based on falsehoods, lies and pure mendacity.

The incident occurred on Wednesday in the government building where the Miami/Dade Canvassing Board was counting ballots. Recall that the same board had rejected a manual recount to begin with, then was pressured by the Gore people and Democratic Party to recount, despite legal justification. Now came Wednesday morning and the Board decided, for whatever reason, to move their location to a smaller room and to eliminate public observers and most reporters. These people, reporters included, swarmed to the new location and chanting "Open the Doors!" Many of these protesters wore coats and ties. Yes they had to be kept out by locked doors; yes, rumors abounded that a thousand Cuban American Bush supporters were on the way to protest. Yes! Yes! Yes!

Nonetheless, despite the garbage like allegations by Joe Lieberman, Congressman Jerry Nadler (D-NY) and Washington, D. C. Democratic Representative Elizabeth Holmes Norton, all offered without a scintilla of proof, there was no intimidation. How do we know? We know because the President/Chairman of the Miami/Dade Canvassing Board, David Leahy, says so. The Miami/Dade hand recount was abandoned because there simply wasn't enough time, according to him, to complete the count by the Florida State Supreme Court imposed deadline of 5:00 p.m. of Sunday, the 26th of November.

Of course, that very deadline may be illegal as the United States Supreme Court has taken a Bush appeal to set aside the Florida State Supreme Court decision of Tuesday, November 21, that allowed the statutory deadline set by the Florida Legislature to be ignored. They set a new deadline and there are many who consider that law-making, not judicial interpretation. Law-making by a court is illegal.

We have, then, a certified winner of the Florida Presidential vote. His name is George W. Bush, the Governor of Texas. But, hold on, the Al Gore legal beagles will flood the courts with more law suits in attempts to set the election results aside, to "contest" the election results.

Some of their arguments will be that though the Palm Beach hand recount washed over the time limit, those votes should be counted despite the drop-dead deadline set by the Florida Supreme Court. Another argument is that Miami/Dade should be ordered to recount the entire county despite the Canvassing Board's rejection of a manual recount twice. Another argument is that all absentee ballots should be thrown out in Seminole County because some of them were partially filled out by Republican volunteers—not dates and signatures, but such things as addresses and voter registration numbers, both public records, by the way. Naturally, Bush carried Seminole County by a wide margin.

So, the Democrats will cry-baby about "mob rule," physical intimidation by Republican "thugs," false absentee ballots and a conspiracy among Bush supporters in Florida government to make sure Al Gore doesn't win the election.

Despite all this, Bush has won the election on election night, he won after a recount, he won after the overseas absentees were counted and he won again after the votes were recounted, including all dimples, in Broward County, where Gore won two to one. Bush has now won four times, even when Democrats counted phantom dimpled ballots.

What a relief! Democrats can't steal elections anymore. Democratic Canvass Boards couldn't steal the election; Democratic judges couldn't steal the election even with a 7-0 margin in the Florida Supreme Court.

Joe Lieberman can quit crying, for he and his boss lost the election. Al Gore can go home and whine for four more years. Al Gore can watch his titular leadership of the oldest political party on earth slip to Hillary Clinton.

Yes, all this because Florida Cuban Americans voted in a landslide for George Bush, the next President of the United States, almost.

(NOTE: Joe Lieberman remains a cry-baby; Al Gore lost control of the Democratic Party to Bill Clinton, the recounts all confirmed Bush's victory and it was Bush who was sworn in as President on January 20th.)

AL GORE'S TRUE COLORS

By Raoul Lowery Contreras
December 5, 2000

There are almost three million people in San Diego County with over a million of them Democrats. Most live in the City of San Diego, a handful live in Escondido and a majority of the City of El Cajon (pop. 95,000) is Democratic.

There are four Al Gore-appointed Electors from San Diego County to the Electoral College who will cast their votes for Vice-President Gore on December 18th in Sacramento. Escondido attorney Thor Emblem is the only North County Democrat, while two El Cajon Democrats, Kristie Mann and Ron Obendirfer join him on the delegation. The fourth is Craig Roberts, the President of the San Diego Democratic Club, the area's largest Democratic organization and its only Gay, Bisexual and Transsexual political club.

Unlike the majority of Democrats in San Diego County, these four Electors are all non-Hispanic whites. The majority of Democrats in San Diego County are Hispanic, Black, Asian and some Whites, so why are all-Whites in the San Diego County Democratic Electoral College representation—100%, lily White?

Doesn't this fact truly demonstrate the White segregationist family background of Al Gore? It was his father, the Senator from Tennessee, who voted against the Civil Rights Law of 1964. It was also his father who took the Gore family to all-white restaurants and left the Black nanny of Junior's in the car to eat scraps brought out by Al Gore Junior.

Perhaps there are reasons why Al Gore Junior picked an all-White Electoral College delegation from San Diego that we are not aware of, nor can fathom, but somewhere there is something "Rotten in the State of Denmark." Pardon me, Mr. Bard, but that phrase is so appropriate here. Or, perhaps, it should be something is "rotten in "Carthage," the alleged "home town" of the soon-to-be former Vice-President.

There were many hints during the campaign that Al Gore Junior was truly his segregationist, racist father's son. Take, for example, the fact that though my Mother was a Hispanic-Woman Gore delegate to the Los Angeles Democratic National Convention, she received only a smattering of official Gore campaign e-mails and faxes. Five, count them, five, e-mails came from the Hispanic campaign coordinator of the Al Gore Junior campaign for her.

Compare that, if you will, with as many as two dozen e-mails from the national Bush campaign to this writer day after day. I wasn't a delegate, but the e-mails came and came. They really paid attention to a writer named Contreras.

So who was paying more attention to Hispanic voters, Al Gore Junior or George W. Bush? To listen to the Gore Hispanic supporters one would believe that they fantasized their candidate into almost sainthood and so voted. In retrospect, they and their fantasies are laughable. In the first concrete action in California, Al Gore Junior totally ignored the majority of San Diego Democrats and the 750,000 San Diego Hispanics in naming his Electors. What a guy!

Al Gore's doomsday clock is ticking away the final seconds of his abortive bid to overturn the voters of America in the country's first ever legally contested Presidential election and we find that the very place where he could have made a difference and selected Hispanics, he fumbled the ball.

Mind you, this is not a plea for "quotas" but rather a statement of fact. And people wonder why I'm a Republican.

A PRESIDENT OF AND FOR ALL OF US

By Raoul Lowery Contreras
December 17, 2000

George W. Bush, President-elect, will be sworn in at Noon, the 20th of January, thanks to James Madison and his fellow founders of the United States of America and men and women named Gonzalez, Contreras, Rubio, et al. While the Founding Fathers are long gone, Miami's Little Havana streets are still wet from the salt water dripping off the legs of refugees from Communist Castro's Cuba.

Thanks to Communist Castro, President-elect Bush will bring into government a whole new generation of people willing to implement a philosophy of trust the people before government. Education will benefit, not from more money being thrown at it, but at money aimed like a rifle shot at specific problems. Children will learn to read under George W. Bush. Adults will learn how to read in Florida and learn how to vote when they can read instructions.

Those of us who work and pay taxes will pay less in taxes under George W. Bush. Of that, I am sure. Small business people will be happier and more prosperous in the new Presidency. Large businesses will have less regulatory pressure on them. States will have money block granted to them without a morass of rules and regulations. Hi-tech miracle companies will breath easier than Microsoft has under the Clinton Presidency. People who lend money will charge less interest and company bottom lines will increase as productivity increases and export trade grows.

Yes, the politics of America will be softer on the one hand because George W. Bush is a likable man and tougher on the other hand because those he vanquished will never give up their fight. They will claim they "wuz robbed." They will attack the Supreme Court for ending the Gore legal crusade, a Quixotic one at that, with a one-vote margin. They will charge the Court with politics. They will disrespect and demean a Justice's wife (Thomas) because she is recruiting people for the new Bush Administration. Another (Scalia), will be attacked because his son works for a law firm in Washington that detailed their best appellate lawyers to the Bush legal forces. It will be, in this sense, a brutal four years in front of us. A President Bush will reviled and hated by elements of our society, as was President Richard Nixon.

Like Nixon, I expect, President Bush will accomplish far more than his critics will give him credit for, though less than his adherents will claim. Nonetheless, will little black children in the inner-city benefit from a Bush Administration? Yes. The wheels of progress will turn slower in the inner city, but any progress will be measured exponentially for those areas look and act like nuclear war sites. Will Hispanic children benefit from a Bush Administration? Oh, yes, emphatically yes.

President Bush will extend a hand to the black community, a black community that has declared war on George W. Bush and his Republican Party. Will the black community respond in the affirmative? We don't know, but, no matter. He will try, for it is a family tradition in the Bush family going back to his grandfather, United States Senator Prescott Bush of Connecticut.

It is in his outreach to the Hispanic community that we will see real progress and acceptance. Bush targeted Hispanics in a major way and it paid off. Not only did 4.5-million Hispanics vote for him, but, I suspect that many more would have if they had just a bit of personal experience with him. Well, now we'll all have personal experience with him in the next four years.

Attention will be focused on Hispanic education, business, neighborhoods and those employed (by lower taxes) and those unemployed (more job creation caused by more foreign trade and lower interest rates). People named Gonzalez, Rubio and Garcia will be a huge part of the Bush Administration, for in that we do have a track record to examine. Texas Hispanics are enjoying a bonanza of positions in Texas state government, full and part time. The numbers are staggering when one compares them to, say, Hispanic appointments of California Governor Gray Davis.

It will be interesting to see the number and quality of Hispanic appointments by President Bush vis a vis those of President Clinton. I'll wager that Bush appoints more than Clinton ever dreamed of appointing. Consider this, President Clinton had two opportunities to appoint justices to the Supreme Court and managed to avoid any Hispanics while appointing two wealthy white Jewish justices.

President Bush will appoint a Hispanic Justice to the United States Supreme Court and will do so from a pool of immensely qualified candidates first appointed to the federal bench by President's Reagan and Bush.

President Bush will, I think, raise the entire Hispanic community to a level best described as—WE MADE IT! Thanks George W. Bush, I know you will be a good President, a President of and for all of us. Gracias.

GONZALEZ, MARTINEZ, THE FIRST OF MANY

By Raoul Lowery Contreras
December 29, 2000

The other day I watched Los Angeles Congresswoman Maxine Waters bitterly state that she "would or wouldn't" congratulate General Colin Powell on his appointment as Secretary of State. It seems Maxine isn't happy that president-elect George W. Bush thinks so highly of this American Black male he has appointed Secretary of State.

Today I listened to Jesse Jackson more or less say the same thing.

What I did not see was Raul Yzaguirre or any other nationally known Hispanic complaining about President-elect making history by naming the son of a Texas construction worker, Alberto Gonzalez, one of the most powerful lawyers in the country, White House Counsel.

Nor did I hear Raul or any other national Hispanic complain about President-elect Bush naming the first Cuban immigrant to his Cabinet, Mel Martinez, Secretary of Housing and Urban Development.

In fact, the only complaints I've heard are from incompetent males of the Anglo persuasion and furious Blacks like Waters, Jesse Jackson and a plethora of Black Congress people who have turned anti-Bush-Republican whining into a very annoying art form.

President-elect Bush has dared to name Hispanics and Blacks to high positions in his administration, positions President William Clinton never managed in his eight years. And, more are coming.

Political issues like abortion and better education will be well served by the forthcoming Hispanic appointees. Partial birth abortion, particularly, will die in the USA. Abortion is just one Supreme Court justice away from becoming illegal or, at least, restricted. And before we hear the baloney that the majority of Americans are for "choice," let me disabuse the reader of that notion. It is not true among the Hispanic community, period. It might be among suburban white females, the type that adored Clinton, but the Hispanic community is against abortion by two to one, even when the deceptive word "choice" is used. That is a fact.

We look forward to an Attorney General that opposes abortion, as Senator John Ashcroft, the Bush nominee did and does. Sure he has some outmoded views on the Confederacy and the Civil War, but, much to my chagrin, some Mexican Americans served in the Confederate Army.

That Ashcroft view, however, doesn't disqualify the man from the job of Attorney General. In contrast, Democrat Al Gore supports the Confederate flag in Tennessee and supports his state's hero, Confederate General Nathan Bedford Forrest, the officer in charge of a monstrous massacre of Black Union troops at Ft. Pillow, Missouri Despite Al Gore's support of Forrest, the first Imperial Wizard of the Ku Klux Klan, I saw no Democrat raise that as an issue when Gore was running for President.

I'm reminded that a Republican Congressman told me before the election that Al Gore was dashing about like a mad man because he was frightened that a Republican Attorney General might take office and prosecute him right into prison for his law-breaking in 1996. John Ashcroft might be the man who does that, for the evidence is clear that Al Gore broke myriad federal laws while running for re-election in 1996. More importantly, Ashcroft will be in a position to recommend candidates for the Supreme Court when the next vacancy occurs.

Here we come back to Alberto Gonzalez, George W's pick to be White House Counsel. Bush had appointed Gonzalez to the Texas Supreme Court. Before that he appointed him first as Secretary of State for Texas, then as General Counsel to the Governor in his first term as Texas Governor. Isn't Counsel Gonzalez now a leading candidate for the United States Supreme Court?

But that isn't all the good news. George W. Bush can nominate Emilio Garza, Justice of the Circuit Court of Appeals based in New Orleans, to the Supreme Court. President Ronald Reagan appointed Garza a federal District judge; President Bush elevated him to the Appeals Court. He's a former United States Marine officer who attends church, Catholic mass, every morning before he goes to work. He's a good Judge. From California, Bush can pick Appeals Court Judge Ferdinand Fernandez, a crackerjack conservative judge immensely qualified to become a Supreme Court Justice.

What we have here is a surplus of riches, Hispanic riches, awaiting a President who, as we have seen, likes to appoint Hispanics to high positions in his administrations.

O Joy, O Rapture!

Maxine Waters, Jesse Jackson, People for the American Way and all the pro-abortion nutcases will have cows after January 20th. This time, for the first time, we won't have to suffer through appointments of window dressing lightweights like Henry Cisneros, Bill Richardson or Francisco Pena in lowly jobs that they failed in. We have men (and women, I hope) of real substance for the new President to select for the new government.

At the risk of sounding repetitious, O Joy, O Rapture!

LINDA CHAVEZ, GOOD PERSON?

Raoul Lowery Contreras
January 13, 2001

"To Raoul—from a fellow conservative and admirer, Linda Chavez, Nov. 29, 1991," so wrote Linda in my copy of her book, "Out of the Barrio," a book I helped her research. So, it goes without saying that I had more than a passing interest in her nomination by president-elect Bush to be the United States Secretary of Labor.

I was as surprised as anyone when the news broke Sunday during my radio show that Linda had given shelter to an illegal alien woman from Guatemala about the same time I was helping her with her book's manuscript. I was more surprised when she called her news conference Tuesday to withdraw her name from consideration for the Labor post. I thought she would tough it out, I thought she would martial arts them into political ambulances.

I thought she would spit in their eyes and stand tall like her distant cousin New Mexico's U.S. Senator Dennis Chavez (the second Mexican American to ever serve in the U.S. Senate); or, like Lt. Col. Manuel Chavez of Civil War fame in the New Mexico Volunteers-but she caved.

She caved, I think, because she found herself isolated and besieged by the media and by President-elect Bush's staff. Linda obviously caused her own problems by not blurting out the name and dates of her illegal alien and when she lived in Linda's Maryland house almost ten years ago. Had she done so in the original interviews with Bush people, they probably would have overlooked the problem because, as it turns out, the Chavez charity has caught the nation's imagination. She truly did a "Christian," charitable thing-she helped out a battered, down on her luck woman who couldn't speak English. So, she didn't check for a "Green Card," so what?

Must we, as citizens, do the work of "la Migra?" No. Marta Mercado managed to fool government immigration agents between Guatemala and the USA, so why should Linda have checked. She said today that she suspected all along that Marta was illegally in the US. In the final analysis, that's what did her in.

Did Linda "employ" Marta Mercado as a housekeeper, dog walker, or did she just take her in to help a woman in trouble? Semantics and legalisms aside, eyewitnesses declare that there was no obvious employer-employee relationship between Linda and her Guatemalan houseguest. Was there "harboring," as defined in Immigration Law? No. "Harboring" includes smuggling, payment, conspiracy, criminal intent, etc., etc. There were none of these criminal elements in Linda Chavez helping out a Guatemalan illegal alien.

Could she, then, have legal problems over this incident? Probably not. But would Teddy Kennedy, temporary Chairman of the U.S. Senate's Labor and Education Committee, have dragged her through the mud to embarrass George W. Bush? Probably, Senator Kennedy hasn't much respect for Republicans, much less a female Hispanic one with a mind of her own and political positions that are an anathema to Teddy and his labor buddies. Moreover, Teddy Kennedy has proven time and time again that he is as bigoted as they come when it comes to voting for Black minority Republican judicial candidates like Clarence Thomas. So what could we expect from him when it came time to vote for a Hispanic Republican woman?

Yes, she has staked out positions on issues that are, frankly, to my right. Nonetheless, I don't think there should be a government imposed minimum wage because that is a gross interference in the free market. I, too, think government regulations on business can be onerous. I, too, think the government taxes business too much, just as Linda does. We part on English-only, but agree that her former employers in the English-only movement are racist. She dumped them. They turned on her.

Good, a person is best characterized by the quality of his or her enemies. Linda Chavez has proven in the past few days that her enemies elevate her to a high level, for from Teddy Kennedy, labor bosses and racist English-only fanatics came the anti-Linda Chavez momentum. Helping them, of course, was the anti-Hispanic fanatical Chicanos from La Raza and the Southwestern Voter Registration Project, groups that undermine Hispanics at every turn with their barrio baloney.

She would have been a good Secretary of Labor. She would have driven labor bosses nuts. She would have driven the Chicanos nuts, as well. With Marta Mercado, two Puerto Rican boys she's putting through Catholic school in New York City and Vietnamese brothers she helped when they first came to the U.S. and countless others we don't know about, Linda Chavez has proven she's a good person. What else could we ask for?

(NOTE: I visited with Linda Chavez three days after President Bush's inauguration in her Washington, D.C. office. She told me the Bush people dropped her and that when she appeared on national television to withdraw her nomination, she did so without any Bush people around to support her withdrawal. She would have been a great Secretary of Labor.)

BILL CLINTON, PRESIDENT OF MEXICO

Raoul Lowery Contreras
February 25, 2001

Observers call his Presidency one of the best and most effective in history. He handpicked his successor-to-be not once but twice. His trade negotiations brought the country to the highest level of exports in history. As he left office, however, instead of a triumphant departure, complete with a brilliant legacy, the President's last minute corruption and manipulations of his office caused the political roof to cave in on him and he had to leave the country to live in exile.

That was the real life experience of Mexico's former President Salinas de Gortari in 1994. His American contemporary, William Jefferson Clinton, the 42nd President of the United States, seems to have taken pages out of the Salinas playbook. Will ex-President Clinton have to leave the United States of America to live in exile?

One Salinas experience that Clinton mimics is possible corruption of relatives, in this case, the brother of the former First lady, Hugh Rodham. He was paid $400,000 by crooks, drug dealers and well-connected political hustlers to arrange pardons and commutations for crooks, drug dealers and well-connected political hustlers. Mrs. Clinton and her husband claim they had no knowledge that her brother was "paid" to work on the pardons and commutations. "Shocked, I'm shocked."

Senator Hillary proclaimed at a news conference that she was "disappointed," in the manner of Claude Rains in the movie "Casablanca" who mockingly cried "Shocked, I'm shocked" when he saw gambling going on, as a croupier slipped his winnings into policeman Rains' pocket. She used the word "disappointed" 20-25 times in ten minutes.

Question: A lawyer works on pardons and commutations for people he doesn't know. Is it safe to assume that such a lawyer might be paid for his work?

Like Salinas, cronies of Bill Clinton have benefited beyond measure, not in money but in—Voila!—another egregious pardon, that of fugitive Marc Rich. Rich fled the country 17-years ago, one step in front of federal marshals, to land in Switzerland after securing citizenship in Spain, Israel and, maybe even Bolivia. Rich was charged with criminally evading almost $50-million in income taxes, plus charges of violating the Trading-With-The-Enemy Act and hundreds of violations of various Department of Energy regulations, as well as racketeering charges.

No one knows if ex-President Clinton knows Marc Rich, but one thing is certain, he knows Rich's former wife, Denise. She contributed lots of cash for Clinton's campaigns and pet projects, took the 5th Amendment when asked to testify in a congressional hearing and has dropped out of sight. Clinton has stated that he pardoned Rich (and his gofer, Pincus Green) because the charges against Rich weren't justified. The problem, of course, is that Clinton made the midnight pardon without concurrence or even input from the Justice Department. Also, one wonders exactly what was discussed between Denise and the President in any of the hundred visits she made to the Clinton White House.

Question: Can we believe the President that he was justified in pardoning Marc Rich when the prosecuting office of the Department of Justice (Southern District of New York) was unalterably opposed to pardoning a fugitive from justice, of this particular fugitive?

Was Denise Rich and her hundreds of thousands of dollars worth of contributions to Clinton's library the keys to the smelly pardon of her ex-husband? Or, was the presentation of the back-door pardon to Clinton by his former White House Counsel, Jack Quinn, more important? Quinn, a Democratic Party hack, was reportedly paid $200,000 to convince his former boss to grant the Rich pardon just two hours before Clinton left office.

Together, we find that $600,000 was paid to Quinn and Hillary Clinton's brother to secure four, count them, four pardons (including a commutation). That's 150 big ones per.

Hillary's brother arranged a commutation of a 15-year sentence for convicted drug dealing mastermind and financier Carlos Vignali, a wannabe rapper and Los Angeles drug dealer whose Argentine-born father has donated thousands upon thousands of political dollars to a raft of Los Angeles Hispanic Democratic politicians. They wrote many letters on Carlos' behalf that in the end weren't necessary. Hillary's brother managed the successful commutation campaign in the White House while a guest of his sister Hillary and the President

Question: Does anyone think that President Clinton was not aware of his brother-in-law's legal representation of crooks and drug dealers for big bucks?

The resemblance of former President William Jefferson Clinton to former Mexican President Salinas continues with Clinton's brother (another Clinton pardon). Roger Clinton, a convicted drug dealer, is currently being charged with another crime as in the case of Salinas whose brother, Raul, sits in a Mexican prison convicted of numerous crimes, including murder.

Sanctimonious Mexican-haters constantly point fingers at Mexico for being corrupt and particularly point at former president Salinas as the ultimate in corruption. Considering hundreds of years of corruption in Mexico, Salinas' and the Mexican political system's corruption, one is not surprised by Salinas' exile and how the Mexican people despise him. One doesn't have to be a Mexico-hater to not be surprised.

Question: The personal/political self-destruction of former President William Jefferson Clinton from Monica's blue dress to a million dollars in contributions from Denise Rich and a brother-in-law who sucked up 400-big-ones from crooks and drug dealers isn't really a surprise—is it?

(NOTE: President Bush pardoned 13 Puerto Rican terrorists serving many-year-long prison sentences during his wife's campaign for the U.S. Senate seat of retiring Patrick Moynihan in a blatant effort to secure New York Puerto Rican votes. Interestingly, none of these convicted bombers and terrorists ever asked for a pardon. These pardons certainly forecast Clinton's fire sale of pardons as he was vacating the White House the evening of January 19th and the morning of January 20th, minutes before he became former President Clinton.)

3

THE BUSH PRESIDENCY-
YEAR ONE

BUSH AND FOX MEET

Raoul Lowery Contreras
February 18, 2001

After years of nightmarish relations between Mexico and the United States, the meeting between President George W. Bush and Mexican President Vicente Fox can best be described as a sociopolitical diplomatic dream come true for the two countries.

Three years ago, the Ambassador from Mexico could not meet with California Governor Pete Wilson publicly because Wilson was loathed by Mexico for his sponsorship of the nefarious (and ultimately judicially buried) Proposition 187.

Twenty-two years ago, President Jimmy Carter cracked a "Montezuma's Revenge" joke in Mexico City that drove a stake into the collective Mexican heart.

Then, President Carter's Energy Secretary turned down Mexico's request to be treated equally with Canada in the price of natural gas.

Shortly after William J. Clinton became President, he instituted "Operation Gatekeeper," a multi-billion-dollar beefed up Border Patrol frenzy that became a death sentence for hundreds of Mexicans looking for American jobs. Besides the body count, "Gatekeeper" did little to stem the flow of Mexicans illegally crossing the border.

Minimally balancing the ledger of U.S. /Mexico relations during this era were two events: The negotiation of the North American Free Trade Agreement (NAFTA) by President George W. Bush and its passage under President Clinton. Secondly, the 1995 multi-billion dollar loan and loan guarantee from the United States and allied international organizations that the Mexicans paid off early. Both events drew howls of protest from many Americans.

Also, in a position highly valued by Mexicans, there was the 1994 opposition to Pete Wilson's Proposition 187 by George W. Bush, candidate for Governor of Texas in the same November election in which Californians voted on Wilson's Proposition 187.

Eventually, of course, Pete Wilson was forced to retire from public life after a disastrous bid for the Republican Presidential nomination. George W. Bush went on to win a quarter (a record) of the Mexican American vote in his successful 1994 campaign to unseat Texas Governor Ann Richards, then doubled that vote in his 1998 bid for reelection. He went on to garner more Hispanic votes than any other Republican in history while winning the Presidency last November. This was not an accident.

George W. Bush made it clear during all his campaigns that he likes Mexicans. At the same time, the once-in-six-years Mexican Presidential election occurred and the winner, Vicente Fox, won not only as an outsider, he won as a friend of the United States.

Mexico and United States relations have come far since the Mexican Ambassador secretly met with Governor Pete Wilson. There certainly was no secret to the meeting of Presidents Bush and Fox in San Cristobal, in Mexico just days ago.

The obvious good relations between these two men are symbolic of what the U.S./Mexico relationship should be. Mexico and Mexicans have had profound influence on the United States over the past two centuries that is highlighted by the existence of over 20 million people in the United States of Mexican origin.

Americans, of course, have also influenced Mexico. That influence has not always been benign. By investment and economic exploitation, Americans developed Mexican petroleum and mineral resources in a one-way manner that led to the great Mexican civil war of 1910-1920 and its aftermath that led to expropriation of American and other foreign companies by a xenophobic Mexico.

Against that historical backdrop and huge Mexican oil and natural gas reserves, Presidents Bush and Fox discussed the energy crisis in California and the ability of Mexico to maximize its energy reserves to meet demands on both sides of the border.

As if by magic, Sempra Energy of San Diego announced that it will build a new power generating plant in Mexico's Baja California for $350-million that will produce enough energy to power 450,000 California homes, well over a million people. The plant will be fully owned by the American company and its entire output will go north to California. The company can get Mexican building and environmental permits in six months versus years in California.

Can ten or twenty such modern, clean power producing plants be built along the border to alleviate rolling blackouts and energy emergencies in our Sun Belt? Of course they can. Are energy from Mexico, profits for American investors and jobs for Mexicans dreams or coming Bush/Fox realities?

As they were meeting, Mexicans were sneaking across the border in twos, threes and dozens to illegally fill jobs throughout the United States. From seafood processing in Maine to mushroom pickers in

Pennsylvania to melon pickers in California to tobacco leaf sorters in Kentucky to chicken processors in North Carolina and apple pickers in Washington, millions of Mexicans live and work in the United States. This is a problem to some, an economic boon to others.

Presidents Bush and Fox announced the formation of a very special panel. It is made up of U.S. Secretary of State Colin Powell, Attorney General John Ashcroft, Mexican Foreign Minister Jorge G. Castaneda and Interior Minister Santiago Creel. They will discuss and, hopefully, negotiate short and long-term solutions on the issue of Mexican labor in the United States. In other words, they mean to solve the illegal alien problem that vexes so many people.

Mexico needs investment from the United States and the United States needs energy and Mexican workers. It looks like Presidents Bush and Fox have embarked on a course that will produce much satisfaction for both countries. It's about time.

(NOTE: This piece speaks volumes for what was occurring before the attack on the United States on September 11th, 2001.)

100 DAYS OF ACTION, JESSE JACKSON

Raoul Lowery Contreras
April 30, 2001

It has been a hundred days since I stood in the rain with thousands of other Americans and observed George W. Bush sworn in as President of the United States.

In a television interview on Spanish language Univision, I was asked to grade the President on his first 100 days. I chose three specific presidential actions and policies to comment on because these issues are very important to the 35-million American Hispanics:

1. The relentless campaign by President Bush to lower taxes for those Americans who pay taxes has been successful beyond the wildest imaginations of Republicans, faced as they are with a 50-50 Senate. Sure the President won't get $1.6 billion in tax cuts. What he will get is at least four times what the Democrats campaigned on last year. He will sign a tax bill that cuts billions upon billions from the coming tax bills of every taxpayer, but more importantly, taxes on the exploding Hispanic middle-class will be slashed. GRADE FOR THE PRESIDENT ON TAXES-A+.

2. On education, the Senate is debating the President's proposal to help bring reading scores up for fourth graders by first testing them and surveying for those schools that are failing their children. The debate is not on the President's proposal, but on the details and amount of dollars to be spent. Yes, the President has dropped his voucher proposal that would have issued vouchers to parents of discredited public schools so they could find a better education, but he can't win on every issue. By bringing liberals like Senator Ted Kennedy on board for his education proposal, the President has earned another GRADE OF A+.

3. Other than the day Mexico declared war on Germany, Italy and Japan in June of 1942, relations between the United States and Mexico have probably never been better than today. The credit, of course, goes to Presidents Bush and Mexican President Vincente Fox. A high level committee of Mexican and American officials is negotiating possible solutions to the problem of some Mexicans illegally crossing the Border to work illegally in the United States, albeit fulfilling a huge demand for their labor. Contrast these excellent relations with Clinton's policies on the Border that have led to the deaths of hundreds of Mexicans. President Bush deserves a GRADE OF A FOR ELEVATING RELATIONS WITH MEXICO to the best I have ever seen.

There are, of course, many other issues that have arisen during the hundred days, but these three will have the longest impact on the country. Certainly permanent lowering of income taxes is a healthy issue that affects everyone and is particularly beneficial to the emerging Hispanic middle class.

On education, Hispanic and Black children suffer the most in the hands of the predominately Anglo teaching and administrative corps. That must be corrected and the only way we can know about the problem is to measure it first. That's what President Bush is trying to do. Certainly, the teacher's unions are fighting the proposal with all their resources, but they will lose this fight. It must be noted that not all teachers are deficient in their skills, nor desire, nor even professional competence; nonetheless, many of our children are being condemned to a life of poverty by poor education in the first four grades of public schools.

On relations with Mexico, President Bush has crafted an aura of goodness and light around relations with Mexico that have even affected those two lights of the South, Georgia born and raise, Texas Senator Phil Gramm and North Carolina curmudgeon Senator Jesse Helms. Helms took his Foreign Affairs Committee to Mexico City to meet with Mexican legislators and President Fox himself. Gramm is putting together a guest worker program that would legalize most Mexican workers in the United States. As to who's against this great effort to improve Mexican/American relations, the usual suspects. Congressmen Richard Gephardt (D-MO), David Bonior (D-MI) and Marcy Kaptor (D-OH). These are all union sell-outs.

World-class sell-out Jesse Jackson is, as this is written, campaigning in Georgia against the Bush tax cuts, and will always campaign against trade and better relations with Mexico. On tax cuts, Jackson wants all money to be spent on his "constituency" in direct aid, not better education. He wants checks for his people not the ability to read and write. Proof: Exactly how many times did he criticize his buddy, President Clinton, for letting education suffer so much in the Clinton years?

There, in Jesse Jackson's opposition to the Bush tax cut and for his failure to drag President Clinton into implementing better education policy is proof that President Bush has passed his 100-day test with flying colors. Despite Jesse Jackson whines, our children are headed to a better education. Those of us who pay taxes will keep some of our own money and not watch it spent on Jesse Jackson's idea that you and I should reward his people for failing in the greatest country in the world.

Soon, thanks to President Bush's first hundred days, we won't have to put up with the whines of Mexican haters who hang their hat on illegal immigration, for illegals may become legal with a vote of Congress and President Bush's signature.

(NOTE: The tax plan passed, as did the President's education plan. Congressman David Bonior went on to be retired by reapportionment and defeat in the Democratic primary for Michigan governor. Marcy Kaptor keeps up her hate-Mexico campaign on behalf of labor unions, but Richard Gephardt has announced that he will offer a guest worker program that might legalize Mexican workers in the U.S. who are in the country illegally. Jesse Jackson continues to make a political ass of his self, like he did when he counseled adulterer Bill Clinton just before it became public knowledge that he, himself, had committed adultery many times and fathered a child out of wedlock that he supported by a less-than-honest payroll check to the mother of the child.)

A SPANISH BULLY PULPIT

Raoul Lowery Contreras
March 8, 2001

If racists didn't exist, I would have to invent them. If bigots didn't exist, I would have to invent them. Inventing them would be hard, but finding them is easy.

From California to Virginia, there exists a cabal of Mexican haters who do anything they can, say anything they can, and propose anything they can to humiliate, insult and degrade anyone of Mexican heritage, whether American or Mexican born. They have this hate because they think they are superior to Mexicans, even if the Mexican is racially white, blonde and blue-eyed. It is enough that Mexicans are Mexican for these people to hate.

Armed only with my computer and radio and television airwaves, I combat them at every opportunity. I do enjoy myself, for these people rank close to the bottom of the human scale of intelligence and accomplishment. In a phrase, they are limited Americans.

Little I do, however, resembles more than the little Dutch boy plugging a dike leak with his finger. But I do rile them, for they simply cannot compete with me and reason. I now have a terrific ally in deflating these haters. President George W. Bush is his name and his bully pulpit is much larger than mine.

On Saturday, the 5th of May, Cinco de Mayo, if you please, President George W. Bush addressed the nation in Spanish on dozens of Spanish-language radio station from Miami to New York to Chicago to California.

The Mexican haters, led by Los Angeles denizens, are bursting visible neck veins and unleashing tons of hatred towards President Bush. Here, from their very own web site:

"BUCHANAN WAS RIGHT"

"We gave Bush the benefit of the doubt, and now he has removed all doubt. George Bush has shown his true colors and they are RED WHITE AND GREEN—THE COLORS OF THE MEXICAN FLAG.

We gave Bush the benefit of the doubt, and now he has removed all doubt. George Bush has shown his true colors and they are RED WHITE AND GREEN—THE COLORS OF THE MEXICAN FLAG.—He wants to extend 245i! and allow Mexican trucks to enter the United States without immediate inspection. We were worried when he said he wanted to make migration (illegal immigration) "safe and orderly." Now he has removed all doubt. Listen to Bush. George Bush is selling us down the river."

There, the best friend American Hispanics, President George W. Bush, is now being charged with "selling us down the river." What river? The coming America in which one in four Americans will be Hispanic and one in three will have Mexican blood? That coming fact freaks these people out. They are not alone, of course. Columnist Georgie Ann Geyer tends to agree with them. Newsweek writer Robert Samuelson tends to agree with them. President Bush doesn't agree with them.

The Ku Klux Klan (KKK) agrees with them. White Aryan Resistance founder and former Grand Dragon of the KKK, Tom Metzger, agrees with them. Notorious former KKK leader David Duke agrees with them. The Federation of Americans for Immigration Reform (FAIR) and its silly founder, John Tanton, agree with them. In California, the notorious former police clerk, Barbara Coe and her California Coalition for Immigration Reform agree with them.

They, of course, don't reach many people, despite the sheer racial hate they promulgate. Oh, they claim a great victory in the form of the infamous Proposition 187 and its victory at the polls in 1994, but that was a long time ago. 187 was thrown out by the courts as unconstitutional. Its key leader declared bankruptcy immediately after the election. In that action it came forth that he had lied to the very people who supported him and voted for his Proposition. He had not worked in years, not paid taxes in years and didn't even pay rent. Illegal aliens worked, paid taxes and paid rent and supported themselves. A very "close" associate supported him. To the people of California, he represented himself as writing the Proposition because he was fed up with paying taxes to support illegal aliens. That was a lie. So was Proposition 187.

The lie, however, coalesced this group of Mexican haters and they have been peppering the Internet with their hate and lies since. The American people have rejected them and that rejection is part and parcel of the President broadcasting a short message on radio on Cinco de Mayo, the 5th of May.

Cinco, of course, celebrates the victory of 4,000 Mexican soldiers over 8,000 French and renegade Mexican soldiers east of Mexico City in 1862. It was celebrated at the White House on Friday, the 4th and again in the President's radio address.

The President has tweaked the haters with a heavy, heavy blow. The President made a lot more people, people who spoke Spanish before they spoke English, feel like real Americans for the first time. Bravo!

GEORGE W. BUSH AND 11,278 VOTES

Raoul Lowery Contreras
August 1, 2001

There are those who criticize President George W. Bush's strategy of getting a larger market share of Hispanic support and votes. They do so by attempting to confuse the issues by suggesting that they don't see enough potential voters for Bush to appeal to—to make a difference. They are wrong.

Other critics suggest that the largest Hispanic group, those of Mexican origin, don't care to vote Republican or to be Republicans, especially, these critics try to point out, recent immigrants from Southern Mexico. They are wrong.

Then, there are those who criticize the President's moves to form a "Special Relationship" with Mexico because it isn't fair to other countries and peoples. They are wrong.

On these three fronts, President Bush is right on point and target.

Are there enough Mexican origin voters in the country to make a difference? Critics say no, that there are only two states where they really make a difference, Texas and California. They maintain those states will not vote any differently in the Presidential election of 2004 than they did in 2000. California voted for Gore and Texas voted for Bush. They are wrong.

Assuming that almost every state will vote the same in 2004 as it did in 2000, where can Mexican origin people make a difference, if they can? New Mexico has the highest percentage of Mexican origin people in the country and it is proof that Bush's outreach can make a difference. There, Gore carried the state's five (5) electoral votes by the grand total of 366 votes. Thus if Gore voters vote Democratic again in 2004, Bush needs to get just 367 more Mexican American votes in New Mexico to carry the state and broaden his win in 2004.

In Oregon, Gore carried the state by 6,765 to win its seven (7) electoral votes. If every voter votes the same in 2004 as it did in 2000, Bush would need to win 6,766 more Mexican American votes from a burgeoning Mexican origin population than he did in 2000 to carry the state.

In Iowa, where the Mexican origin population has grown from zero to several thousand, Gore carried the state by 4,144 votes to claim its seven (7) electoral votes. If everyone votes the same in 2004 as in 2000, Bush would just need 4,145 more Mexican votes in Iowa to carry the state.

Now, is there any sane person who doesn't think Bush can pick up this handful of votes to carry these three states in light of the latest polls among Hispanics that show Bush getting 59% approval from Hispanics? Take out Puerto Ricans and Mexican origin people give Bush better than 60% approval ratings.

This is not an accident. Recently, the non-profit, non-partisan Latino Coalition surveyed 1000 Latinos aged 18 and older throughout the country (margin of error 3.1 percent), It published these results: Higher than national approval ratings by Hispanics for President Bush were attributable to popularity of the President's tax cut; respect for the Presidency; and, appreciation of Bush's outreach towards Hispanics. In fact, 61.2 percent approved of the tax cuts.

Additionally, 75 percent approve of Bush's plan to expand the North American Free Trade Agreement (NAFTA) to the rest of the Americas. 73.3 percent support school vouchers. 62.6 percent opposes abortion. 50.6 percent of the surveyed support job growth over environmental protections and restrictions.

Given, then, this reality and the political and statistical reality that Bush need only gain 11,278 more Mexican American votes in three states to increase his electoral college victory by 40 votes (20 less for Gore and 20 more for Bush), Bush is looking at a very comfortable reelection in 2004.

Wrapping up a successful Hispanic outreach for Bush are the forthcoming changes in immigration policy that Secretary of State Powell and Attorney General Ashcroft are suggesting for Mexican nationals living and working in the United States—without work permits. It also appears that a larger guest worker program for agricultural workers, especially those from Mexico, is in the policy mix being discussed.

Critics complain that focusing on Mexicans is unfair, that all illegals should be treated "fairly." They complain about the "Special Relationship" Bush is developing with Mexico and that it is just pandering for votes.

Where were these people when President Roosevelt had Congress declare war on Germany in 1941 even though Germany had not attacked the United States? Did they object to Roosevelt's "Special Relationship" with England? Or, how about the "Special Relationship" we have with Israel?

Why shouldn't we have a special relationship with Mexico, our next door neighbor. Mexico buys more from us than Europe does, and more than Japan and China combined. Mexico' sons have fought side by side with Americans in WWII and Korea. Almost ten percent of our population has family roots in Mexico.

Given all this, why shouldn't millions of Mexican Americans show their appreciation to George W. Bush by giving him some more votes in 2004. Just 11,278 votes in New Mexico, Iowa and Oregon will do.

(NOTE: This article was written just days before September 11th. President Bush had already lined up strong Hispanic support when the hijacked airliners were smashed into the World Trade Center, the Pentagon and a field in Pennsylvania. The Los Angeles Times post-September 11th poll reported that President Bush's popularity and support among Hispanics surpassed that of the rest of the country 89% to 88%. A Latino Coalition survey in September of 2002, showed Hispanic support above 60% and 5 points higher among foreign-born Hispanics. Considering he received 35% of the Hispanic vote in 2000, it appears that his Hispanic support will deliver many more votes than in 2002.)

50% WILL DO

Raoul Lowery Contreras
July 2, 2001

Isn't it interesting how some people are commenting negatively on President George W. Bush's strenuous outreach to the burgeoning American Hispanic polity and population?

From out of the patented anti-Hispanic woodwork they come, crying and whimpering how the Republic and the Republicans are ruining the country's politics by appealing, of all things, to the largest minority group in the country. They publicly complain that appealing to Hispanics is foreign to America.

Let's look at American political history. For example, let's examine the political anthem of the American White Anglo Saxon Protestant of the 1800s—Irish Need Not Apply. That simple benign statement and what was behind it, led the Irish to form their own political activities, clubs and political campaigns. Irish politicians appealed to Irish immigrants and Irish Americans on ethnicity, culture and on common religious grounds—Roman Catholicism.

They were successful beyond their wildest imagination. They took over city and state governments throughout the country. Once in power they filled the ranks of police, fire and civil service staffs with their own people to the point that Irish men and women still control those agencies in most large cities (Riordan in Los Angeles, Daley in Chicago, Murphy in San Diego).

After the Irish, the Italians came and they decided they wanted part of the political action. It is no secret that the two very best mayors of world capitol New York City, are named Fiorello La Guardia and Rudy Giuliani. Moreover, both these stellar mayors were Republicans. Is this an accident? No. They were and are products of a deep-seated effort by Republicans to recruit Italian American Roman Catholics.

Considering that most Italian Americans, at least in New York, are Republicans, it seems Republicans have succeeded with them.

Democrats and Republicans court Polish American enclaves in Michigan, Illinois and Ohio, with Republicans winning the contests almost every time these days. Chicago Serbs, Brighton Beach Russians, New York Orthodox Jews and Roman Catholics are legitimate political targets for American politicians, just as are veterans, school teachers, union members, business people, etc., et al.

So what, I ask, is the big deal about President George W. Bush looking for Hispanic votes?

During the Presidential campaign, the Bush apparatus organized a bilingual publicity effort to reach out to the country's 500-plus "Hispanic weeklies and a handful of Spanish-language and bilingual dailies. Publicity releases were written in Spanish and English. Spanish-speaking spokespeople were recruited to be interviewed on Spanish-language television and radio. Governor Bush made a point of addressing Hispanic issues of education and more economic freedom through lower taxation. He addressed immigration problems and better relations with Mexico.

When he took office in January, he launched a huge effort to better relations with Mexico, stood by Republican efforts to ease guest worker rules, pursued educational reform that benefits all minority children, but particularly Hispanic children. He successfully pushed for lower taxes and lower tax rates that will affect millions of working Hispanics. It appears he personally responded to the millions of Puerto Ricans who wanted the American Navy and Marine Corps live fire exercises out of Puerto Rican territory. He has ordered a stop to such exercises.

He has appointed highly visible Hispanics to highly visible government posts from his legion of Hispanic supporters. That is only the beginning—the morning line has short odds that President Bush will nominate a Hispanic to the United States Supreme Court. That, unlike President Clinton, who, in two full Presidential terms, betrayed his Hispanic supporters by nominating two Jewish lawyers to the Court instead of nominating the first Hispanic Supreme Court Justice in American history.

Now, can anyone tell me what President Bush is doing that is different than what has been politically done in the past with Irish, Italian, Polish and other immigrants who have come to the land of Truth, Justice and the American Way? Certain people object to his display of intelligent politics. Columnist Georgie Ann Geyer objects to President Bush visiting Spain by calling it a betrayal of American Red, White and Blue history. She states that American Hispanics don't even like their Mother Country. She states that Cubans fought Spain (true), as did Puerto Rico (false). Her position, of course, betrays her knowledge of American political history and of American Hispanics.

If President Bush was failing in his Hispanic aimed effort there might be room for criticism, but he is succeeding. According to Democratic Consultant Sergio Bendixen, George Bush is succeeding at attracting Hispanics. Actually, he told a group of Democratic Congress people and staffers that George Bush stands a better than even chance of winning, 50% of the Hispanic vote in 2004, about 40% more than he won in last year's victory over Al Gore.

Such a Hispanic vote revolt against Democrats will reconfigure the American political scene forever. If Democratic Consultant Sergio Bendixen can see the obvious, it is not hard to see Hispanics voting heavily Republican by the second or third generation, just as Italian Americans have. 50% will do. Comprende? Capiche?

(NOTE: The only factor that has changed since this article was written is the attack of September 11th, 2001, which cemented President Bush's Hispanic popularity and support to the point that he might exceed Sergio Bendixen's prediction of what might happen.)

4

THE BUSH PRESIDENCY—YEAR TWO

2002 DAWNS AS A HISPANIC YEAR

Raoul Lowery Contreras
December 29, 2001

The year has gone by quickly and momentously. We entered the year with Texas Governor Bush entering the Presidency with half the country against him, with a slight majority in the House of Representatives and a one-vote margin in the Senate.

George W. Bush had friends, nonetheless, and they weren't all rich white Texas oilmen. Bush's best friends were the hundreds of thousands of Hispanics who voted for him because they believed he just might be the first "Hispanic" President.

Sure, most Hispanics voted for Bush's opponent, Vice President Al Gore, but they did so unenthusiastically. They knew that Gore's boss, President William Clinton managed to not find a single qualified Hispanic jurist or lawyer to place on the Supreme Court, despite two openings during his eight-year tenure in the White House.

They knew that Al Gore never spoke up for a qualified Hispanic nomination to the Court and they knew that he never would. They knew that Al Gore supported Bill Clinton in his stab in the back of Mexico on implementing the NAFTA trucking provisions to feed the Teamster Union's bid for more power. They knew that Al Gore had already ordered-according to court documents-that Black Secret Service agents not serve immediately around him. Mexican Americans knew that Al Gore wouldn't know a Mexican if he tripped on one. They knew that Blacks were furious that George Bush was spending millions on a targeted Hispanic campaign and had lined up prominent Hispanics throughout the country in an AMIGOS DE BUSH organization with hundreds of official "surrogates" representing Bush in every town and city throughout Hispanic America.

Knowing all this, Hispanics trooped to the polls and gave Bush the best vote totals since Ronald Reagan swept through the Hispanic community like a swath.

Washington, D. C. was full of AMIGOS DE BUSH on January 20th for the Inauguration of George W. Bush. The night before the swearing in, thousands of Hispanics partied at the Omni Sheraton Hotel, eating Mexican and Caribbean food, dancing to the Tito Puente sound, to the sound of Santana and applauding Mexican Mariachi music. Dressed to the "nines," these Hispanics thoroughly enjoyed themselves and spoke approvingly of the new day in Washington, a new day full of Hispanics.

Hispanic men wore their tuxedos or military uniforms with great pride. There were even fur coats, real fur coats, draped on the shoulders of beautiful Hispanic women. A drenching rain greeted the revelers when they left, casting doubts that the Inauguration would be a dry one. It wasn't.

That night, hundreds of the world's best known Hispanics, including former Presidents from Latin America, ambassadors. Newt Gingrich and gorgeous Hispanic women partied until 5:00 a.m. at the Organization of American States to be greeted by the world's slowest car valet service and snow.

Over the next few months, Hispanic support for the President grew from its 35-percent vote total in November of 2000 to 59% in the national polls by Labor Day in September of 2001. A week later, on September 11th, Hispanics rushed to support President Bush when the country was attacked and did so in record numbers.

The Los Angeles Times poll in November concluded that 88% of Americans over-all supported President Bush in the war on terrorism sparked by September 11th. Hispanics, however, supported the President with 89%. Deducting the notoriously partisan Democratic Puerto Rican portion of the national surveys, over 90% of Mexican Americans support President Bush.

Now that the Congress has passed President Bush's educational reform bill, the tax cuts and have or are preparing to support the President's Hispanic nominees to important posts, we enter the new year, an election year, with huge Hispanic support of President George W. Bush. Conversely, we enter the New Year with a President who truly cares for the Hispanic population of the country. It will be a great New Year.

PRESIDENT BUSH'S HISPANIC POPULARITY SOARS!

Raoul Lowery Contreras
August 26, 2002

Flash! President George W. Bush would defeat Democrat Al Gore 50% to 35% today among Hispanics, if one believes a survey taken for the Latino Coalition between August 2 and 14.

Moreover, among the 1000 adult Hispanics surveyed, 62% approved of the way President Bush is doing his job. Among newcomer immigrants not yet citizens and eligible to vote, President Bush's approval ratings is a stratospheric 74%.

"The President," says Latino Coalition's Robert de Posada, "and the congressional Republicans are scoring the highest with the newest arrivals in America—Latinos who do not speak English and also among Latinos who are not registered to vote."

That makes perfect sense. Here's why—when an immigrant comes to America he or she generally strives very hard to become an "American." They, after all, come here to live and work in America, not Ireland, or Denmark. They come to become Americans—at least the overwhelming majority of them do. That is palpably true and why immigrant citizens tend to reflect the President they are most used to, in this case, President Bush. Honest observers cannot legitimately challenge that fact because they have little data to contradict my assertion.

Immigration critics constantly point to a few immigrants, such as many of those from Muslim countries, who place other allegiances higher than to their new country, but those numbers are statistically insignificant and are only propaganda efforts by immigration critics frantically looking for negative proof against immigrants. Facts, as President Ronald Reagan used to say, are stubborn things—very stubborn, indeed.

The facts are that among these 1000 adult Hispanics and specifically among those who are not yet citizens, President Bush has higher approval rates than among the general population and than among citizen Hispanics. Certainly the Hispanic approval rate of President Bush and congressional Republicans is higher than among Black Americans, Puerto Ricans, Dominican Americans and those who have doctorate degrees. Certainly, President Bush has higher approval ratings among Hispanics than he does among conservative immigration critics like Pat Buchanan, Sam Francis, Peter Brimelow, Phylis Schafly, Steven Sailer, or liberal critics like columnist James Goldsborough, et al.

So, where should President Bush reach out for support? Should he reach out to Hispanics of all levels of residency and citizenship who number in the millions? Or, should he reach out to a few disgruntled anal retentive immigration critics whose only claims to fame are lack of language skills, uniformly white skins and Northern European backgrounds?

The critics say the President should ignore Hispanics and concentrate on getting more "white votes." This, they say without smirks because, they say, Hispanics are and continue to become Democrats. As more Hispanics immigrate, critics claim, they will build a larger Democratic majority than currently exists.

But, they have no proof to back up their claims. There isn't a single survey ever taken that shows that all Hispanics or Hispanic immigrants are or plan to all be Democrats. There isn't a single Presidential election they can point to since 1952 in which no less than 25% of Hispanics voted Republican. George W. Bush actually received more Hispanic votes than any Republican in history, and, he won.

Now comes survey after survey concluding that President Bush has astronomical approval ratings among Hispanics. The Los Angeles Times post-9/11 survey concluded that 89% of all Hispanics approved of the way President Bush did his job, a higher percentage than among the general population. Subtracting out the intractable Democrats of Puerto Rican backgrounds, the approval rating for President Bush among Mexican Americans was in the 90's.

In May, a Democratic organization conducted a survey and it showed President Bush and Democrat Al Gore literally neck and neck in a survey measuring how Hispanics would vote in May for President.

The August survey concludes that President Bush would defeat Al Gore today by a substantial margin among Hispanics registered to vote. It also concludes that, unlike last year, congressional Republicans have improved their position and approval among Hispanics immensely. Last year Democrats had a 34-percentage point advantage in a generic congressional choice; this year, Democrats only have a 13-percentage point advantage. Advantage, Republican; advantage, George W. Bush.

Yes, it appears that some new Americans will register Democrat when they can, but it also appears that Republicans have six more Bush years to reap a huge harvest of potential Hispanics. Considering that no one has ever claimed that Republicans even need a majority of Hispanics to win the Presidency, there is nothing but good news for Hispanic Republicans and bad news for those who pooh-pooh the President's obviously successful outreach to Hispanics.

Contreras's book, "The New American Majority, Hispanics, Republicans & George W. Bush," is available at **www.amazon.com**, **www.barnesandnoble.com**, and **www.iuniverse.com**

E-mail: **sdraoul@att.net**

DISHONORABLE POLITICS

Raoul Lowery Contreras
September 9, 2002

"Good Morning, this is Linda Chavez-Thompson, Executive Vice President of the AFL-CIO," is how she started her Democratic Party weekly radio address. This was, perhaps, the only truthful thing she said in the two and a half minutes the Democratic Party gave her. The question is, did she prevaricate because she's a Democrat, a Hispanic, or a Union propagandist?

For Example, she said, "President Bush has shown interest in a relationship with (Hispanics), but he hasn't shown interest in the politics that would really help our community. The president has interest in Latino votes, but no real interest in the lives of Latinos." Really?

Then she stated, "After Hispanic unemployment dropped to a record low during the Clinton Administration, it has climbed under President Bush, back up to 7.6 percent. That's 311,000 Latinos who have lost their jobs since the President took office. Recent layoffs have had a devastating effect on Latinos. In Arizona, for example, this year, 70% of layoffs were Latinos, when Latinos only represent 25% of the population."

In the first two years of the Clinton Administration (1993-1994 according to the Government), Hispanic poverty increased by the largest jump in history—20%. Her claim that Hispanic unemployment reached a historic low during the Clinton Administration is not relevant because Hispanic unemployment under Clinton was at least 62-75% higher than among "whites." Black unemployment was never lower than double of "whites" during the entire Clinton administration.

The AFL/CIO purposefully excluded Hispanics from union leadership for its entire history until Ms Chavez-Thompson came along. The AFL/CIO led the attack on free trade's NAFTA that American Hispanics overwhelmingly supported. Unlike the AFL/CIO, NAFTA has created hundreds of thousands of American jobs and business opportunities, especially for Hispanics.

As for the "311,000" Hispanics she claims lost their jobs since President Bush took office, did someone take them out and shoot them? Or did most just move on to other jobs? As for 75% of job layoffs in Arizona being Hispanic but that Hispanics amount only to 25% of the state's population, baloney. What their percentage of the population amounts to is immaterial. What their percentage of the work force and of those hired in recent years is relevant, but she doesn't mention those relevancies. Work force penetration is far more important than percentage of the population and every economist knows that, except those who wrote Ms Chavez-Thompson's propaganda.

Fact: Hundreds of thousands of Hispanics work in the American travel/hotel industry, which was devastated by the September 11th attack on America. Industry people declare that the industry is running at 30% less today than a year ago. In New York City, alone, 85,000 people—many of them Hispanics—lost their jobs after the attack.

Did these people lose their jobs because of Bush economic policies, or did the attackers cause the job losses? Have any of these "311,000" found new jobs? Most have and that would destroy her hatchet job on President Bush.

"If that's not bad enough, President Bush has also taken other measures that increase the problem of unemployment," she declared. But, Linda Chavez Thompson, there really isn't an unemployment problem, is there? The law defines "full employment" as four (4) percent. That means then, that (5.9% unemployment minus 4%=1.9% unemployment) there is little real unemployment for anyone.

Job losses caused by September 11th are the story, not President Bush, Ms Chavez-Thompson.

"Of course," she continued, "nothing is more important to future Hispanic prosperity than education. The children we teach today will be the successful business leaders and productive workers of tomorrow. But here, again, George Bush has failed. He provides no additional funding to help Spanish-speaking students achieve English-language benchmarks, and he wants to freeze funding for bilingual education, even though the number of children who need it is rapidly increasing." More misrepresentations.

What did her President Clinton do for bilingual education, a format outlawed under Clinton by several individual states? How much did he increase education spending? Did Hispanic national test scores improve under President Clinton? No. The education bill sponsored by President Bush is a quantum leap forward that truly helps Hispanic students.

President Bush's goal is that every third grader shall be able to read; no such goal was ever articulated in Clinton's eight-year Presidency. In President Clinton's first two-years, Hispanic poverty skyrocketed upwards and took the rest of the Clinton years to return to the level that existed when he became President. Under Clinton, Hispanic unemployment, wage and income levels never achieved parity with whites or even came close, according to Labor Department reports.

Ms Linda Chavez-Thompson, Executive Vice-President of the AFL/CIO union organization and official spokesperson for the Democratic Party, was not bound by politics to tell the truth. She was bound, however, by honor and she flunked that test.

Contreras's book, *"The New American Majority, Hispanics, Republicans & George W. Bush,"* is available at **www.amazon.com**, **www.barnesandnoble.com**, and **www.iuniverse.com**

E-mail: **sdraoul@att.net**

5

PRESIDENT BUSH, THE COURTS AND HISPANICS

UNDER GOD, BAJO DE DIOS"

Raoul Lowery Contreras
June 29, 2002

Three hundred and sixty nine days after President George W. Bush nominated two people to the 9th Circuit Court of Appeals who have not been given a hearing by Democratic Senators, two senior 9th Circuit judges ruled that the words "under God" in the Pledge of Allegiance are unconstitutional.

The Democrats have won a victory, won a Pyrrhic victory, a victory at too great a cost, perhaps.

Judging from the public outrage, and from the massive whining from most elected Democrats, the two judges, one a 79-year-old "senior status" judge and another a flaming septuagenarian liberal who is the husband of the head of the Southern California American Civil Liberties Union (ACLU) may have unleashed the dogs of political war. A war that may topple the dictatorship of the proletariat run by Democratic Senators Tom Daschle, the Senate Majority Leader and Judiciary Chairman Patrick Leahy.

Not only have these two men stopped most of President Bush's Court of Appeals judicial nominees in their tracks, but they have exposed the ugly anti-Hispanic bigotry that runs just below the surface of the Democratic Party, the same bigotry that runs in the strongest Democratic constituency against Israel and Jews.

Sure, the Democrats blah-blah to poverty and working poor Hispanics and kiss up to single women with gaggles of kids, but when the opportunity to truly support Hispanics comes about, they balk, instead, they support rich, white party hacks like Judges Breyer and Ginsburg of the Supreme Court. Neither of these undistinguished jurists seems headed towards the Oliver Wendell Holmes/Earl Warren Hall of Fame (both men were Republicans, by the way).

Not only did the Democrats totally ignore good Hispanic possibilities for the Supreme Court when they had two chances to put new justices on the Court during the Clinton Administration, they won't even schedule a hearing on President Bush's nominee to the D. C. Court of Appeals, Miguel Estrada, or for Bush's two nominees to the 9th Circuit Court, one of whom is a woman.

The two judge decision declaring "under God" to be constitutionally forbidden highlights two things: One, the paucity of good judges on the Court of Appeals—which Estrada's confirmation would partially cure; and, secondly, the emergence of Judge Ferdinand Fernandez as a judicial star, and a Hispanic one at that.

Judge Fernandez is a Californian. He is a University of Southern California and Harvard Law alumnus and a former California Superior Court judge. President Ronald Reagan appointed him the federal district bench. President George H. W. Bush appointed him to the Court of Appeals in 1989.

He totally squashed the spurious thinking of the two no more "under God" judges by calling their reasoning "picayune" and lacking in pure merit. That is, he pointed out that the Supreme Court decisions they quoted as the basis for their decision were quoted improperly. They used observations called "dicta" rather than the actual decisions on the litigated questions.

Observations—dicta-don't make law, they just are statements, observations, not law or precedent.

Those two words (under God), he wrote in his dissent, have no effect on establishing religion in the United States. He also pointed out that if this "under God" decision were to stand, patriotic songs like "God Bless America" would be banned from public stadiums or public schools. Then, he wrote, our "currency" which features the motto, "In God we trust" will be next.

Fernandez, then, is a hero to millions of Americans and must be ratcheted upwards on the list of four potential Hispanic Supreme Court nominees that President Bush will probably choose from as soon as an opening exists.

Certainly he is now the best known of the four potential Hispanic candidates. Miguel Estrada is now grouped with White House Counsel Alberto Gonzalez and 5th Circuit Judge Emilio Garza. The United States Senate has already confirmed Judges Garza and Fernandez twice for their district judgeships and for their Appeals Court judgeships.

I can't wait to see what Democratic Senators Tom Daschle and Patrick Leahy will offer up as excuses to keep either one of these two accomplished men off the Supreme Court.

Considering that the two Democratic judges named to the Court by President William Jefferson Clinton were confirmed by a Republican Senate, and that Judges Garza or Fernandez, or both might have to face a Democrat Senate, we have to hope that the current Senate obstacle course is dismantled by American voters in November.

(NOTE: 16 months after President Bush nominated Miguel Estrada to a seat on the D.C. Court of Appeals, the Senate Democratic run Judiciary Committee finally gave Estrada a hearing. Three Democrats displayed the finest McCarthyite tactics the Senate has seen in a generation. The prejudiced, racist Senators Schumer of New York, Patrick Leahy of Vermont and Dianne Feinstein of California unleashed the greatest racist display since those of Southern Democrat Senators when they viciously attacked Admiral Lewis Strauss, an Eisenhower appointee to the Atomic Energy Commission. Strauss' crime, he was Jewish.

Schumer wanted to know if anonymous charges about Estrada screening candidates for a Supreme Court clerkship were true in that did Estrada tell applicants they were too liberal and no liberal would ever get the job. Feinstein also made a big deal about the anonymous charges. The real racist kicker, however, was from Roman Catholic Leahy. He wanted to know if it was true that Estrada described an interview by three Puerto Rican Defense Fund lawyers as "Boneheaded."

Yes. Estrada told them, he used that word. He did so, he said, because one of the interviewers attacked him for not being "Hispanic" enough. Estrada was right in using that word. Personally, when anyone accuses me of not being "Hispanic" enough, I'm very likely to tell them they can take their left wing attitude and shove it up their "nose.")

6

HISPANIC VOTERS, EDUCATED & UNEDUCATED

HISPANIC SOUL

Raoul Lowery Contreras
June 10, 2002

When it comes to who Hispanics are, those Hispanics who represent the largest segment of Hispanic America, the best educated, the most productive, those who vote the most are simply not acknowledged by the media, and, sadly, by the minority of Hispanics who can't measure up.

For decades the media has focused on the economic lowest level of Hispanics, on their union activities, on their lack of education, on their dependence on government, on their gang activities, on their propensity to have illegitimate babies, on their whining and carping, ad naseum. Worse still is the energy these very people expend every day validating the views so many have of them.

Example: At a Los Angeles meeting of the AFL/CIO, a couple of handfuls of "Hispanics" paraded around wearing t-shirts whining about California Indian casinos. Why? Unions aren't able to unionize casino employees. Do these t-shirted protesters represent the Hispanic community, a community that has been employed by the thousands throughout California by their Indian cousins, or do they just represent unions?

Example: Proposition 187 passed in 1994 because so many Anglos and blacks voted for it-correct? No, it passed for three reasons, only one of which was hysterical and/or bigoted Anglos and blacks voting for it. Of the two biggest reasons, one was so many under or uneducated Hispanics didn't register to vote, or even vote if they could. The most important reason Prop. 187 passed was that over two million immigrant Mexicans in California had never bothered to become citizens despite being legally eligible for citizenship, some for years.

Example: The California public schools are, perhaps, the worst in the country. The less educated Hispanics in the community have not risen in anger to demand better schools and education for many reasons, but the most obvious reason is that they might not care. A rare exception may make it out of a public high school, into college and, perhaps, even medical, graduate or law school, but those cases are rare. The best high school graduation rates and college attendance and graduation rates are among those whose parents graduated from high school and went to college, not from those who whine, complain and dropped out of school.

Example: These under and uneducated Hispanics talk about "job training" as a panacea for their lack of employment, their underemployment, or their imprisonment, then complain when they aren't hired for jobs they aren't qualified for because they lack education. These lack an education available to every living, breathing human being in America, albeit not always a good one.

Counter-example: Of the 3,000-plus casino workers in the capitol of Indian gaming, San Diego County, hundreds are Hispanics, Hispanics who gladly work for good pay and benefits without being forced to join unions.

Counter-example: Hispanics have notoriously low voter registration and voting rates when one relates educational level to voting. The higher the educational level, the higher the voting rates. Thus, does a high school and college graduate Hispanic vote more than a 10th-grade drop out? Who, then, is more politically effective, the whiny unregistered Hispanic, or the educated Hispanic who registers and votes? Who is more valuable to the community? For the answers, examine the Proposition 187 votes.

Counter-example: Hispanic parents that can't countenance rotten public schools and ineffective union teachers enroll their children in private and parochial schools, no matter that they might have to work more jobs to afford such an education.

Jaime Escalante, the teacher immortalized by actor Edward James Olmos in the movie "Stand and Deliver," stated it best, a student, or his or her family, has to have "ganas" (desire) to overcome adversity, rotten schools and ineffective teachers. So it is in life, as well.

The Hispanic community's choices, then, are simple: On the one hand, the whiny under and uneducated Hispanic way without "ganas," and, on the other hand, the educated, productive Hispanic way—with "gamas."

The fact that educated, productive Hispanics outnumber the others almost three-to-one, according to the Census, is proof that such a way is available. Take your pick.

(NOTE: The American media is fixated on making Hispanics appear negatively in every way it can. There are several reasons for this crime against the fastest growing segment of our population. Number one is the lack of Hispanic reporters and editors throughout the media. If one examines all branches of the media, newspapers, television and radio, one finds less than three percent of all working media is Hispanic. Number two is the desire to lay off the real American underclass, big city blacks and rural Southern poverty stricken blacks and whites. Number three is pure ignorant bigotry. The media cannot deny these reasons for their incompetent coverage of the Hispanic community.)

7

THE CENSUS, CALIFORNIA AND LOS ANGELES

AMBUSH IN SACRAMENTO

By Raoul Lowery Contreras
May 30, 2000

When State Senator Art Torres ran for Insurance Commissioner against State Assemblyman Chuck Quackenbush, I voted for Torres. When State Senator Dianne Martinez ran against incumbent Insurance Commissioner Chuck Quackenbush, I voted for him because Martinez was one of the least qualified people I have ever seen run for public office.

Today, Art Torres is the paid, full-time Chairman of the California Democratic Party and must be reveling in Commissioner Quackenbush's troubles amid demands by almost every major newspaper in the state for Quackenbush to resign. Or is he?

The troubles come from the mistakes of civil servants in the Insurance Department. It was they who threatened insurance companies with phony fines amounting to billions of dollars even though they knew they couldn't make such fines stick. The threatened fines were for insurance company foul-ups, some intentional, during the processing of Northridge Earthquake claims. In a compromise strategy that called for the insurance companies to review every claim, a process that resulted in millions more dollars being passed out to claimants. With claim review, the companies were then allowed to make contributions to a new foundation set up to educate people about earthquake preparations.

Some money was expended to produce and disseminate public service announcements about the office and about how consumers can call on the Department for help. The ads, heavens to Betsy, featured the Insurance Commissioner. The Foundation's Board of Directors distributed funds to the Latino Police Officer's Association for scholarships; a group headed by Democrat Ann Soto, daughter of Democratic State Senator Nell Soto, in Los Angeles for more scholarships; the Urban league and other groups.

None of the $6-million left in the foundation's treasury has been distributed to earthquake victims, yet. A plan is working its way through that will distribute the money to victims.

But, now enters politics, Quackenbush is a Republican and Democrats control the State Legislature and the Attorney General's office. Subpoenas are flying, testimony is taken and Quackenbush is on the hot seat. People who received some of the money, like Democrat Ann Soto and her boss, L.A. County Supervisor Yvonne Burke, have fallen off the radar screen. They took the money, but are no where to be seen supporting Quackenbush.

Assemblyman Jack Scott, Chairman of the Assembly Insurance Committee, is on his high horse and kept Quackenbush and his aides on the hot seat for hours. Scott, who can hardly put a sentence together, receives campaign funds from the insurance industry. State Senator Jackie Speiers, a potential candidate for Insurance Commissioner, now wants to fry Quackenbush in her Insurance committee.

Alas, Quackenbush refused her inquisition and walked out of her committee the other day. Before he left, however, he blew her and her Democrats away with an E-mail written to one of her top assistants.

Assembly staffer Anne Mitchell wrote Richard Steffen, Speier's Chief of Staff: "DON'T WRITE A LETTER TO QUACKENBUSH ON ANYTHING." She wrote the capital letters to Steffen in response to a note from him. Further, she wrote, "We have to set him up first…he is very adept at warding off controversy—if we do not completely ambush him he will slide out of it."

Steffen admits to the e-mails. But, he says, "We're all political animals here whether we want to admit it or not."

Well, well, Steffen's admission places the entire investigation under suspicion. Or, as Assemblyman Rod Pacheco from Riverside states, "It's absolutely unconscionable…Doesn't that call into question the whole process?" Former prosecutor Pacheco is right on.

So, where are we now? We know for a fact that Attorney General William Lockyear has paid a secret visit to Commissioner Quackenbush to assure him that no criminal investigation is underway, or, perhaps, even pending. We know that Hispanic recipients of foundation settlement money are on both sides of the controversy. The Latino Police Officers stand by their grant, while Ann Soto in Supervisor's Burke's office hides. We know that Hispanic claimants will have money distributed to them from the settlement foundation as soon as third party reviews are completed. We know that Senator Jackie Speiers wants to run for Insurance Commissioner in 2002 and would rather not run against Quackenbush. We also know that Senator Jackie has also received insurance campaign funds, even as her committee oversees the insurance industry.

We also know that the Los Angeles Times has decided that Quackenbush has outlived his political usefulness and has gone out of its way to kill his political career by publishing article after article about Quackenbush's troubles. We also know that the Times went out of its way to destroy Senator Art Torres some years ago and was instrumental in his defeat by Quackenbush.

We also know that Sacramento legislative staffers have committed to "paper" damaging e-mails that admit to a "set-up" of Quackenbush to "ambush" him. They have succeeded, it appears.

With that, and assuming that Quackenbush will retire at the end of his term, Hispanics in California can once again target the office of Insurance Commissioner, as they have twice before, except this time, it may be the Republicans with a Hispanic candidate, term-limited Assemblyman Rod Pacheco. Will the Times zero in on former prosecutor Pacheco because he's a Republican, or because he's Hispanic? They will do one or the other, they've proven that with Art Torres and now with Republican Quackenbush.

(NOTE: Quackenbush resigned and went to live in peace in Hawaii because Democratic Attorney General Bill Lockyer couldn't charge Quackenbush with crimes without also charging the Democratic John Garamendi, Quackenbush's predecessor, for the same crimes. As it turned out, Garamendi ran again and was nominated by the Democrats for the same office. Though the above article named a Hispanic Rod Pacheco as a good candidate for the office, it turned out that Hispanic Republican Gary Mendoza ran for and won the Republican nomination for Insurance Commissioner. The former Commissioner of Corporations under Republican Governor Pete Wilson was giving Garamendi a run for the office he simply never expected.)

LOS ANGELES VOTES

Raoul Lowery Contreras
June 9, 2001

If my politically active grandfather were still with us, he would have winced at the election results from Los Angeles the other night. The Primary front-runner lost the general election for Mayor. The loser, Antonio Villaraigosa, the losers, Old Los Angeles Angelenos will survive, of course, just like they survived years of Mayor Tom Bradley's isolated version of running a city that was highlighted by his not speaking to the Chief of Police for 18-months before the Rodney King Riot. They will survive like they did for years of Mayor Sam Yorty, the Yokel mayor. They will not, however, ride the high road like they have for the past eight years under Wonder-Mayor Dick Riordan, Republican Dick Riordan, the Mayor who received 71% of the city's Hispanic vote when he was reelected four years ago.

They are sentenced to four boring years under a Mayor who was elected because his father was elected and reelected for forty years in an immature Los Angeles. Los Angeles segregated its Blacks and Mexicans into ghettos and barrios and ruled them with police batons wielded by a police force made up of transplanted white Midwesterners with no California roots. Los Angelenos will regret their boring choice.

While the "front-runner" was getting wiped out by suburban whites and ghetto Blacks and Westside moderates, City Attorney candidate Rocky Delgadillo organized a successful campaign for City Attorney making him the first Hispanic to win a citywide Los Angeles office in 129 years. Moderate Rocky Delgadillo is now the role model for future California Hispanic politicians. He set parameters that broke the long-time invisible barriers for Hispanic politicians. He was a successful pioneer. Antonio Villaraigosa is a losing pioneer. He came within 40,000 votes of becoming the first Hispanic mayor of Los Angeles in 129 years. Though he fell short, he gave this warning-Old Los Angeles is in its last throes. The New Los Angeles looks like Villaraigosa and the millions of Spanish-speaking people who call Los Angeles home.

Looking like Villaraigosa, however, is not like thinking like Villaraigosa. He is too left-wing for most voting Hispanics in Los Angeles or in California. People who politically think like Villaraigosa can get elected in small districts but have a rough time in large broad-based electorates. Rocky Delgadillo instinctively knows that and that's why he won. Moderation in public has its virtues almost all the time in almost every political district, city or state. Moderation in a city of millions also has its virtues, highlighted, of course, with victory.

Villaraigosa, then, can expect to be left behind, a historical oddity. He was the first serious Hispanic candidate for Mayor in the modern era. He will not, I think, be a viable candidate for mayor in the future. There are dozens of well educated, well heeled Hispanic politicians jockeying for early positions to take on the Anglo mayor elect in four years. The leader has to be the new City Attorney, Rocky Delgadillo. And, not all of them have fathered illegitimate children, or written stupid letters on behalf of imprisoned crack-cocaine dealers, or smoked dope and snorted cocaine. Some are women, some are Congressmen, some are state representatives, some are city council people and one is designated to be Treasurer of the United States.

Friend/Colleague Gregory Rodriguez recently wrote that moderation was the key to the Hispanic political future. Los Angeles proved that the other day. Left-wing union red flag waving lost, as it always will, if the electorate is large enough. The very liberal unions and radical Chicano politicians succumbed to the charms of the ultraliberal Democrats and huffed and puffed their support with money and big mouths. The average Angeleno or American who read the newspapers had to perceive that the grand City of Angels would become the Peoples Republic of Los Angeles governed by shops stewards of the Service Employees International Union.

Moderates like departing Republican Los Angeles Mayor Dick Riordan are living proof that moderates win it all. My grandfather would approve of a Hispanic political future based on moderation.

CENSUS SAMPLING, AN ISSUE NOT TO DIE FOR!

Raoul Lowery Contreras
September 27, 1998

It seems that the whiners among us have issues of the week to draw sustenance from that involve children, cigarettes, clean water, dirty water, dirty air, clean air and ghosts. Ghosts? Now the whiners want to count ghosts in the next census of the year 2000.

Yes, the census is upon us again and every Democratic Party hack in the country will be placed on the Federal payroll to help count the American people as mandated by the Constitution in Article I, Section 2, Paragraph 3, which states, "The actual enumeration shall be made within three years after the first meeting of the Congress of the United States, and within every subsequent term of ten years, in such a manner as they shall by law direct."

The problem, the whiners tell us, is that not all of us are counted every ten years. Black activists complain that not all Blacks are counted; Latino activists complain that not all Latinos are counted; homeless activists complain that not all homeless are counted. These three groups of uncounted have one primary characteristic, they are the poor and dispossessed and they usually "live" in the cities. Thus, we are told, not only are these groups deprived of congressional representation, but the federal dollars that follow population are sent elsewhere.

These people estimate that there might be 4,000,000 undercounted people, ghosts if you will, and that deprives cities some Congressmen. By the way, each U.S. Congressman represents about 600,000 constituents, thus we are talking about 6-7 Congressmen out of 435 representatives. In dollars, we are talking about some serious money, $3-4-billion.

So what's the big deal? A few people disappear when the Census counters come to their neighborhood in order to avoid being talked to; a few people don't respond to Census questionnaires—so what? At most, a half-dozen Congressmen represent the right number of people. They just don't represent the "right" people. The dollars are spent, though not on the "right" people. The cities want cash, the activists want the money and the half-dozen Congressmen.

So, how do we handle this problem? The activists, the Democratic Party and President Clinton want the uncounted counted in some way so they can spend the money, elect more Democrats and give the President another issue. The Republican Party says no and points to the Constitution and to the word "enumeration", which means to count, not to guess.

Specifically, President Clinton wants to place into being a system where counts are projected by "sampling". This is a system designed to use mathematical and computer calculations to "estimate" the uncounted and to include that estimate into the total census "enumeration". Thus, something like 90 per cent of the American population will be actually counted and something like 10 per cent will be estimated. So desires President William Jefferson Clinton.

Two Federal three-judge panels have said no to the President and the Supreme Court has already announced that they will take up the matter in November. The Republican Congress has repeatedly told the President No to sampling and has not voted the money necessary to set up the sampling system. President Clinton has warned that he will veto any appropriation bill that contains money for the Census that doesn't include money for sampling. The President thinks he can shut down the government on this issue and embarrass Republicans. The President thinks he can turn this into a racial and ethnic issue by turning Blacks and Hispanics against Republicans. The President thinks he can win this issue. Can he do any of these things on the issue of "sampling", can he? No. It simply isn't a do or die issue. Only six potential congressmen are involved and they would go to New York City, Chicago, Los Angeles and Houston.

The other 429 Congressional districts would not be affected. Blacks might gain a seat or two, Hispanics a seat or two and the other seats would be shared with suburban areas, so it isn't a matter of do or political die.

For Black and Hispanic activists to start the partisan anti-Republican rumble and how they are going to punish them for not counting ghosts is silly and whiny. Never mind that "sampling" is unconstitutional. Of course, the Constitution never stopped these people, so why should it now. Rather than conjure up political strife and Presidential vetoes over a stupid issue like "sampling", why don't the whiners get behind the Republican-sponsored Puerto Rican statehood. If Puerto Rico does send Democrats to the House and Senate, wouldn't that suffice to enlarge representation for Blacks and Hispanics as Puerto Ricans are certifiably of both minority-types.

Sure, those apportioned seats would come from New York, Chicago and other eastern cities, but so what? Under "sampling" Blacks and Hispanics would lose representation in some areas to gain in others. Certainly, the White-suburbs aren't going to lose, Presidential-vetoes notwithstanding, there are more votes in the suburbs than in the inner-city. Even the Census Bureau says so and that wouldn't change with "sampling".

REAL PEOPLE, NOT GHOSTS

Raoul Lowery Contreras
March 6, 2001

The political fight of the year is shaping up between those who want to conjure up people that may or may not exist and those who read the

United States Constitution and understand it. The fight is over "sampling" a process the Hispanic left is pushing and that the Hispanic center and right are fighting.

"Sampling" is a process developed to account for the physical undercounting during the Census, the census conducted last year. Sampling people declare that about 4-million people were not counted in the 1990 Census and that most of those people were of some minority persuasion or another.

Black activists claim Blacks weren't all counted in the 1990 Census. Hispanic activists claim Hispanics weren't all counted and they do so with some justification. The Census itself says it undercounted the Hispanic population by 4.99 percent. However, they claim that the undercount has been cut to 2.85 percent.

The claim is these people weren't counted because people don't want to be counted, so they aren't. Illegal aliens, for example, hide from census takers because they avoid all government contact, say activists.

The effect of this alleged under-count is in two forms—dollars and political representation. Both of these potential effects are serious enough for places like Los Angeles to announce that it will sue the government if sampling isn't used to artificially build up the numbers of the city so it can get more federal money and, perhaps, a new congressman or two. Every major urban area in the country will probably join LA in that suit, for lots of money is involved, millions of dollars.

Politically, Congressional seats are being snatched from Pennsylvania and other Rust Belt areas and transplanted to California, Arizona, Texas and Florida. In California, it appears that a new Hispanic district will be carved out in the Los Angeles area. New congressional seats also mean more electoral votes for President.

The Supreme Court ruled in 1998 that "sampling" numbers cannot be used for congressional reapportionment, but has left open the question of "sampling" numbers being used to allocate federal dollars. Nonetheless, there are people who are fuming over the forthcoming decision by the Commerce Secretary on whether to use "sampling." A Census Bureau committee of civil servants has recommended that actual raw numbers be officially used by the government, not 'sampling numbers."

Democrats benefit from waving a magic wand and creating people from numbers for most of the invented people will be in heavy urban areas, areas where they predominate. Republicans benefit from using real numbers of people because phantoms can't vote. With "sampling," phantoms would be represented by more Democrats in Congress and in state legislatures.

Thus, no phantoms will be allowed by Republicans in the census count to be released in April. Using the civil servant's recommendation, Secretary of Commerce Dan Evans will announce that raw numbers only will be released. The Constitution will be served, not the Democratic Party.

The Constitution is clear about the census. It says: Article 1, Section 2- "The actual Enumeration shall be made within three years after the first meeting of the Congress of the United states, and within every subsequent Term of ten years, in such a Manner as they shall by law direct."

The words "actual Enumeration" are the stumbling blocks for Hispanics of the left, their Black and liberal allies and cities like Los Angeles. The words "actual Enumeration" mean actual count to Hispanics of the center and right. The Supreme Court thinks so also.

Politics is what's at stake here, for the "sampling numbers" will be used to allocate dollars, but will be prohibited from use in drawing up political districts—and, of course, creating new Democratic congressmen.

The real factor involved here is how we govern ourselves. We have developed the greatest country by living by the Constitution. It means what is says and it must mean what it says. The words "actual Enumeration" mean just that, not a guess, no matter how "scientific."

We can allow the Constitution to bend, but it must not break.

The fight over "sampling" is important to the preservation of the Constitution. Adding in another batch of invisible Hispanics will have little benefit to the country's political makeup. The fighting must end with the Hispanic center and right prevailing, for if they don't, the Constitution will be one step closer to being useless.

That is far more important than a few imaginary Hispanics being counted when they don't really exist except in the gleeful imagination of the Democratic National Committee.

(NOTE: The new Bush Administration refused to use sampling and, as predicted above, cities and states went to court, supported by whiny Blacks and Hispanics of the leftist persuasion. They lost in the courts. Of course, the country was stunned, surprised, blindsided by the Census Bureau when it announced that there were over 32-million Hispanics in the country, not counting those on the island of Puerto Rico. What a laugh! The whiners were routed by the facts. There was no need for ghosts, there were real Hispanics to be counted, four or five million more than was expected.)

SHORT, LONG FORMS AND "...OTHER PERSONS"

By Raoul Lowery Contreras
April 1, 2000

One in six Americans have received the "Long Form" from the Census Bureau that asks a gazillion questions about each person in the USA. Among these people, we have many complaining, whining and declaring their own unlawful actions to boycott the "Long Form" for a number of reasons, but race is foundational to the whining and complaining.

Everywhere, I see or hear people complaining about the "Long Form" and even about the "Short Form's" questions, particularly on race. I see it in Letters to The Editor, I hear it on radio talk shows and see it on television.

My eyes and ears provide certain data to my brain that allows me to make some observations about the complainers. They are mostly White suburbanites. The louder ones, Whites we normally associate with a race mentality we thought was dead, are making the most noise. They claim privacy is their rational for protesting, but gleefully use credit cards for their store and computer shopping giving away their privacy rights to merchants, banks, mailing houses and political parties.

If they are so concerned about privacy, do they have a clue as to what's on their driver license magnetic information strips? They claim they don't want "Big Brother" government knowing everything about them, but they have permitted their Social Security account numbers to be usurped by court clerks and grocery checkers and made into an ipso facto national identification number. They claim the government may use the "Long Form" information in some nefarious way to violate them, somehow and that's why they object to the "Long Form" or even the "Short Form" the Census Bureau is using.

They point to recent revelations that the Census Bureau fed information to the War Department in 1942 that assisted in rounding up Japanese Americans (and Japanese nationals) for re-location to concentration camps throughout the West. They do not acknowledge that such assistance wasn't even necessary.

All the War Department had to do is pick up the phone and talk to Chiefs of Police or Sheriffs in California, no more than 100 phone calls altogether, to find out where these suspected traitors lived. I was only a kid during World War II and I knew where each Japanese descent person lived in my neighborhood. All the Army had to do was give me a Tootsie Roll and I could have pointed out each Japanese person, personally.

So, what are these people afraid of, bad government? Mal Gobierno, as we say in Spanish. Aren't these the same people who massively rush the polls every election in percentages that approach a high-tide 60%? These people don't want the government to know how many television sets there are in their homes, or how many cars they have, or how many kids they have in college? Wow! That is dangerous information, for sure.

And, aren't these the same people who complain about the race questions on both the short and long forms? "I'm an American!" they proclaim. It isn't anyone's business whether or not I'm white or Black or mixed, or non-Hispanic White or Black, or of Mexican or Asian descent, they haughtily say. With, however, the exceptions of a few Hispanic/Latino people arguing about what they call themselves and an isolated Black person, most complaints come from Whites. Why?

As the White proportion of the country's population decreases, they've done an about face and object to race questions they used to love and live by. Why, the original Constitution called for "enumeration" (Census) by race using the term "three fifths of all other Persons (Negroes)."

So, any argument that race hasn't been an integral part of our every decade census is nonsense.

How hypocritical it is now for American Whites, who lived by the "one-drop" of Black blood makes one Black, period, to object to Census racial queries that attempt to quantify people by what they classify themselves as. This is "racial classification" and that that is wrong, they say. After almost four hundred years, they are now color blind, they say. Sure.

There are myriad federal/state laws prohibiting official discrimination and racism. Congress, the courts, legislatures and local sheriffs have been the traditional instruments of official racism. Now, with scientific data from Census forms, these institutions can atone for past sins against the soul and idea of America, despite whimpering suburbanites, and enforce the laws of the land.

With scientific population information, the kind our new color-blind" Whites object to, they can enforce all of the laws, for all of the people regardless of color, skin shade or drops of Indian, Black or blood of "other Persons." Is that bad government?

ONE HUNDRED, TWO HUNDRED MILLION

By Raoul Lowery Contreras
January 17, 2000

New Year's Eve in the United States a hundred years from now may be celebrated by almost 600-million Americans, more than double our population today.. That, according to the newest Census Bureau population projections, are based on current numbers. In 50 years, the Bureau projects a population of 404-million, with 98.2-million being people of Hispanic origin. Hispanics are expected to be 24 percent of the total population then, in contrast to only 12 percent today.

Caramba!

The Census Bureau breaks down the projected 2050 American population as follows: The Asian population is expected to triple from the current 10.9 million to 37.6-million; the Black population is expected to increase by 70-percent from the current 34.9 million to 59.2 million, or a slight increase from its 13-percent of the total American population to 15-percent; the Anglo (non-Hispanic white) population is expected to increase from 196.1 million to 213 million, a 9 percent increase that will, however, reflect a shrinking percentage of the total population, which is 72 percent today, but will only be 53 percent in 2050.

Astoundedly, the Census Bureau projects that in one hundred years, year 2100, there will be 190 million Hispanics in America, one in three Americans. Anglos will barely outnumber Hispanics in that year with 40 percent of the population, down from today's 72 percent.

What does this all mean? Well, it means that projections are based on today's ethnic and racial definitions and they may change through assimilation in the future. It also means that these projections may be pie-in-the-sky feeble efforts that mean little. For example, the current 2.9 birth rate of Hispanic women will undoubtedly fall in future years as more and more Hispanic women learn the lesson of Mexico City women whose birth rates have been halved in recent years to less than their American counterparts, Hispanic American women. In other words, the projections may assume too much.

As noted, the longer immigrant Hispanics, especially those of Mexican origin, are in this country the less Spanish they speak, the less cultural they tend to be and their names morph from Jose to Joe, from Maria to Mary and Jesus to Jessie. Thus, ethnic lines will blur far more than they do today, causing nothing but problems for the Census takers of 2050 or 2100. Census takers in those years might be befuddled by guys named Gary, Jonathon, or Joshua with surnames like Garcia, Martinez or Contreras. One beneficial factor of this growing population and assimilation is that Hispanics won't have to change their names out of shame or bigotry like Emilio Estevez Sr. (actor Martin Sheen) or guys named Martinez that wind up Martin, or Valenzuela that wind up like Rock and Roll pioneer Richie Valens.

Two projections are meaningful, however. That is that the number of seniors will increase significantly from the present 34.6 million to 82 million in 2050—a 137 percent increase. Can Social Security withstand such an onslaught? Probably not. Can Medicare withstand such an assault? Definitely not.

The second meaningful projection of the Bureau is about the foreign born that total 26 million today—10 percent—to 53.8 million in 2050, 13 percent, a percentage still lower than the highpoint of foreign born early in the 20th Century when the foreign born reached almost 16 percent. They keep coming, thank God, for without these immigrants we would shrivel up and die as a country like Japan and Germany are destined to do in coming decades.

The combination of immigrants and young Hispanics will be of huge value to an America with a median age (half above and half below) of 40 years of age. In other words, the work force will be made up mostly of Hispanics and immigrants. Blacks, Asians and non-Hispanic whites will be minority segments of the work force. It is these "minority" workers who will pay Social Security and Medicare taxes, if the current system is maintained or doesn't go broke. It should be noted that after seven years of William Jefferson Clinton's Presidency, we have not solved the gigantic upcoming financial problems of the Social Security and Medicare systems.

So, welcome to the Millennium. Medicare and Social Security are flailing and failing. Clinton didn't lift a finger to save either one. And, now, both systems will have to be saved by immigrants and Hispanics, all 100 or 200 million of them in the years 2050 or 2100, take your pick.

Caramba!

RAPE IS A POLITICAL ACT

Raoul Lowery Contreras
August 28, 2001

The Florida presidential election fiasco notwithstanding, people have died for the right to vote, to have their vote count and to elect people of their choice.

In this year after the Census, as mandated by the United States Constitution, politicos of both political parties are busy carving up the country to affect who is going to be elected to most offices in the country for the next ten years.

Democratic friends and political compadres of Hispanics are raping them, sodomizing them and the leftwing Hispanic loves the attention, despite the pain. Contrarily, Republicans are busy in Virginia creating a Hispanic legislative district that will enable Hispanics to elect one of their own for the first time ever in Virginia. More telling is the fact that Virginia Republicans have even recruited a viable Hispanic Republican candidate to run for the seat.

In California, where Democrats control both houses of the legislature and the Governor's office, Democrats are busy protecting their incumbents, no matter the effect on Hispanics. For example, in San Diego, the third Hispanic to win office to the state legislature from a "Hispanic" district watches helplessly as a large number of Hispanics are stripped from his district. Thousands of Hispanic Democrats are handed over to an elected openly lesbian "white" liberal Democrat in an effort to raise her Democratic registration to guarantee reelection.

Unfortunately for Democrats, their effort to help one Democrat at the expense of another runs into the federal Voting Rights Act. That law does not allow districts to be drawn that cut any community's ability to elect a candidate of their choice. Thus, a high-Hispanic registration district that has elected Hispanics three out of four candidates in recent years cannot be stripped of Hispanics for partisan political purposes.

So say the Mexican American Legal Defense Fund (MALDEF) and the California Latino Redistricting Commission (the Commission), both based in Los Angeles.

The San Fernando Valley of Los Angeles is a flash point as far as the MALDEF organization is concerned, according to the group's redistricting expert, Amadiz Raul Velez. The Commission's expert, Alan Clayton, a longtime LA union politico and redistricting expert, agrees with Velez.

What is happening in the San Fernando Valley is that the Hispanic population of that area has doubled and tripled in recent years. The area has elected an Hispanic LA City Councilmen, Hispanic state assembly and senate members but not a single one to Congress. In fact, Democrats are so strong in this area because of Hispanic Democrats, the local congressman, liberal white and Jewish Democrat, Howard Berman, has been reelected without Republican opponents in recent years. This is the quintessential safe incumbent Democrat district.

Congressman Berman, however, knows that a 60% Hispanic registration district will eventually develop a Hispanic Democrat who will run against him in a primary race and beat him with Hispanic votes. So what does he do to save his political career? Rape, he politically rapes his own Hispanic constituents. So goes the political whispering in the back rooms of the legislature.

Berman's brother is drawing new district lines. Will he draw lines that result in a Hispanic voter diaspora in order to protect his brother, or will he follow the law and court definitions to keep a 60% Hispanic district intact?

Watching the Bermans is MALDEF and it is ready to go to court if the Bermans move one registered Hispanic voter into nearby congressional district, two of which are represented by Democrats Adam Schiff and Brad Sherman who need more Democrats and would welcome Hispanic Democrats. Its theory is that by cutting Hispanic registration in a 60% Hispanic district, the ability of Hispanics to elect one of their own is diminished, and that, they posit, violates federal law.

Also watching is Clayton's Commission. He describes what the Bermans are alleged to be doing as "cracking." He points to the Berman situation and to San Diego's Assemblyman Juan Vargas' potential loss of Hispanic constituents as classic examples of Hispanics being sucked dry of their political support.

Being a loyal union veteran and Democratic behind-the-scenes Democrat operative, Clayton doesn't make the logical political leap that this writer can: i.e., the Berman Democrats are raping Hispanics to benefit white, liberal Democrat incumbent congressmen.

As we enter the once-in-ten-years exercise of political self-protection, Hispanics can look at California and see rape. Or, they can look to Virginia, where the powers-that-be are taking care to see that Hispanics have a real political voice. Or, they can look to Florida where Hispanic districts elect Hispanic congress people, Hispanics that replaced liberal white Democrats.

CALIFORNIA'S VANISHING HISPANIC POLITICAL POWER

Raoul Lowery Contreras
September 6, 2001

Elected members of the State Legislature and precious incumbent Congressmen and women are breathing heavily at the prospect of taking advantage of a helpless Hispanic population. It is called gerrymandering for partisan purposes.

Let's look at what the Assembly and State Senate Democrats propose to do to the Hispanic population of California, a population that amounts to 32% of California:

Almost half—18—of the proposed 40 Senate districts have smaller percentages of Hispanics than during the past ten years. The losses range from -0.05 to 16.92%; with eight (8) having losses higher than 4%. Are Hispanics expected to elect more Hispanic State Senators under this plan? No.

An example: the 23rd District—where 10.86% new Hispanics are moved into the district, bringing the district to 10% Hispanic, enough to make district safe for Democrats, but not enough for Hispanics to win a Democratic primary.

The only good example of Hispanic gain—the 40th District—adds Imperial Valley and the Coachella Valley by a 60-mile, hundred yard corridor to San Diego's South Bay. The plan takes 16.92% Hispanics away from geographic contingent areas and adds 17% to district tailor made for Denise Moreno Ducheny, former member of the Assembly. The district looks like a 150-mile "U" separating San Diego Bay and the Colorado River.

In the Assembly, the Legislature has produced districts that lose Hispanic population in 41 of the 80 Assembly seats. That is a remarkable feat.

The real attack on Hispanics by the Legislature comes in the new congressional districts it proposes. More than half of the proposed 54 California congressional districts (29) lose Hispanic population under this plan. This is a remarkable feat. The losses range from -0.13% to -24.64%.

The most egregious Hispanic loss comes in Democratic incumbent Howard Berman's district (the 26th) where he loses 24.64% of his Hispanic population, with almost all being transferred to Adam Schiff's district (+31.85%). This transfer is designed to protect Berman from future challenges by successful Hispanic Democratic politicians Assemblyman Tony Cardenas, LA City Councilman Alex Padilla or State Senator Richard Alarcon.

The second most egregious loss comes in moving 15% Hispanics from Duncan Hunter's 52nd District into Susan Davis' 49th District, enlarging her swing district's Democratic registration by adding 17.6% more Hispanics. This move is the direct opposite of the Mexican American Legal Defense Fund's (MALDEF) plan that would have added Imperial Valley to Mary Bono's district in the Coachella Valley, thus uniting a substantial Hispanic population with similar characteristics that might someday elect a Hispanic to Congress.

The "creation of a Latino district" in Los Angeles by the legislature is a sop for Hispanics who value their partisanship more than their community (although it pretty much sets up former mayoral candidate Antonio Villaraigosa or State Senator Richard Polanco to run for the new seat).

MALDEF is now talking suit against the Legislature because it feels the Legislature has violated the federal Voting Rights Act by slicing and dicing the Hispanic population in such a sway as to do permanent damage to their right to elect representatives of their choice.

They are not alone. Orange County's LULAC (League United of Latin American Citizens) joins the fray decrying Orange County districts being drained of Hispanics to shore up LA Democratic incumbents at the expense of Orange County Hispanics.

In Los Angeles, a "California Redistricting Commission," made up of veteran Democratic Hispanic politicos, also feels the Legislature has violated the Voting Rights Act and says it will register a complaint with the U.S. Department of Justice. As to whether or not it joins a MAL-DEF lawsuit, the guess is that their Democratic loyalties will overcome their alleged "passion" for Hispanic representation in the Legislature and Congress.

MALDEF, on the other hand, has re-expressed its view that the two new congressional seats of Berman and Bono are grounds for a lawsuit under Section 2 of the federal Voting Rights Act. It appears that MAL-DEF will file a lawsuit on the congressional districts. I don't see any compromise between parties here. They also might file on the Assembly and Senate plans.

Someone needs to openly challenge the Legislature on the plans to redistrict the state. Be it MALDEF or LULAC, or just plain citizens, someone must.

Hispanics are moved around to protect Democratic non-Hispanic elected officials. In the process, Hispanics lose power and the ability to elect one of their own, or even to influence Republican representatives who feel no obligation to a handfull of Hispanics. That may cause celebration in the offices of Democratic Congressmen Howard Berman, Adam Schiff, Maxine Waters, Dianne Watson and Susan Davis, but it will not cause joy in the homes of a couple million or so Hispanics who have basically been disenfranchised by the Legislature.

IS IT FAIR?

Raoul Lowery Contreras
February 8, 2002

The George W. Bush White House announcement that President Bush and Mexican President Vicente Fox will meet on March 22 is very good news.

Better yet, their continuing discussions on the "regularization" of Mexican nationals in the United States illegally are digs at those in the country who hate all-American words like "amnesty," fairness, and equity.

In California, the issue of illegals and any benefits they are taxed for has become an issue in the race for Governor, again. The issue has two minor Republican candidates on the negative side and front-running Republican Richard Riordan, the former Mayor of Los Angeles, the second largest Hispanic city in the Western Hemisphere, on the right and positive side.

Specifically, Riordan questions the fairness of denying certain humanitarian benefits to people who work and produce in the USA, regardless of their legal status.

Is it fair? That was the question Supreme Court Chief Justice Earl Warren asked those groundbreaking years he ran the court. Is it fair?

Is Richard Riordan right in bringing the fairness question into the debate? Or, are those who ask, what part of illegal don't you understand, right?

Fairness is the right word.

Take, for example, the California farmer. Is it fair to deny the California farmer the work force he needs to plant, care and harvest the very food the country eats in the absence of Americans willing to do that work? No. Without those illegal workers, how will food arrive on our tables? How would farmers survive? What would happen to California's largest industry, agriculture?

On the other hand, is it fair to deny Americans those farm jobs, those hundred thousand jobs throughout California? It would not be fair if there were 100,000, or even ten Americans seeking those jobs. There aren't many Americans who want that work—at any price, at any wage in this year of our Lord, 2002.

Would it be fair to pay farm workers $20.00 an hour? Of course it would. But can a farmer pay that kind of money to hundreds of men and women during a harvest? Sure, if we are willing to pay more for our food. Would it be fair to charge us more for our food than we now pay? Look at Japan and Europe, they pay more for food than we do for they have fewer farmers and farm workers. They have to buy food from us, food produced by our farm workers, the mostly illegal very productive farm workers.

Fairness? "If we could find a way to move a substantial portion of the current illegal flow from Mexico into legal channels via some kind of temporary-worker program and combine that with a new cooperative law enforcement arrangements with Mexico, we could benefit the U.S. economy, we could substantially reduce illegal immigration," Immigration and Naturalization Service Commissioner James Ziglar told reporters in Washington last week. "And," he continued, "it could enable the Border Patrol and other law enforcement agencies to focus on the bad guys coming across—not on the flow of people who just want to get into this country to work."

Contrarily, Steven Camarota, research director for the Center for Immigration Studies, an anti-immigrant hotbed, says, without any real world proof, "The bottom line here is Mexican immigration generally makes poor people poorer without creating significant economic benefits."

He says this with a straight face as he eats the fruits and vegetables illegals bring to his table, wears the clothes they make in Los Angeles and eats the finger licking good chicken they process in Arkansas and North Carolina. Gourmets eat the mushrooms illegals pick in Pennsylvania, the Vidalia onions they harvest in Georgia, and the fine corn-fed beef they dress in Nebraska, Kansas or Iowa.

Who's right; who's fair? Camarota's not; minor Candidates for Governor aren't; Richard Riordan, James Ziglar and George W. Bush are. That's why March 22 looks like a very important date for millions of people, Americans included.

(NOTE: Bill Simon pulled off a huge upset to snatch the Republican nomination away from Richard Riordan. He proved to the world that any rich boy can get a law degree if Daddy pays enough money for it and any rich boy can get a job in the U.S. Attorney's office if Daddy is important enough. He also proved that a rich Daddy can leave enough money behind to keep sons rich. Simon proved among other things that he is the dumbest candidate to ever run for office in California. Former Reagan honcho Lynn Nofziger declared that Simon "is too dumb to win."

Just weeks before the election, Simon was being pummeled by Democrats for being a crooked businessman who has swindled the United States Government and former partners. Simon had no defense, he was being sued by the Bush Administration.

Simon's TV answer, he gave "millions to charity." As for losing the race to the worst and most crooked governor in California history, the Republicans sigh. Simon wouldn't even have been in the race if Secretary of State Bill Jones had not tripped over his tongue when he withdrew his early endorsement of George W. Bush in the Presidential race and endorsed Arizona Senator John McCain. Jones, with Bush support, would have raised $50-million and defeated Davis without breaking a sweat. Because Jones acted so stupidly, he lost the White House, thus he lost the primary to a totally dumb political novice.)

THE DEATH OF THE CALIFORNIA GOP
Raoul Lowery Contreras
August 16, 2002

The long slide into political oblivion of the California Republican Party that started 20-years ago when Republicans won the governorship with a bland Long Beach lawyer will be complete this November 5th Election Day.

The slide accelerated when Republican Governor Pete Wilson blithely blamed all immigrants for the state's budget deficit he inherited from the bland Long Beach lawyer/governor whose name few can remember. It jumped into high speed when the mossbacks Pete Wilson anointed to run the state Republican Party pumped $300,000 into a petition drive that resulted in the illegal proposition 187.

The thrashing of Republican Dan Lungren by Governor Gray Davis in 1998's election appeared to be as low as California Republicans could sink, but it wasn't even close. Only one Republican managed to win a statewide race that year. None will probably win this year.

State Democratic Chairman Art Torres infuriated California Republicans when he declared that Proposition 187 (and its Republican Backers) was the "last gasp" of "white (redneck) America." How true.

Despite spending millions in California, Candidate George W. Bush, hardly improved the disastrous results of the state's 1998 election and it wasn't even his fault.

The fault lay with those political morons who had been running the California Republican Party after the halcyon days of Richard Nixon and Ronald Reagan.

First, they refused to accept that the Long Beach lawyer, Attorney General George Deukmejian, didn't beat the black mayor of Los Angeles because he was brilliant or even competent, he won on simple racist reflexes. The mayor was black and a majority of Californians refused to accept the color of his skin. This fact is important because Deukmejian's campaign guru never understood that and is back.

Secondly, Governor Wilson's crusade against all immigrants, though later refined specifically to illegal aliens, alienated the bulk of California's fastest growing population, the Mexican origin slice of the state.

Thirdly, the enthusiastic support of Proposition 187, a highly dubious effort fueled by rabid anti-Mexicans, of the state Republican Party drove away hundreds of thousands of Mexican Americans, including many who had climbed into the state's middle-class. Professor Bruce Cain of UC Berkeley reports that Mexican American men were reregistering Republican at a 50% rate before Proposition 187. That ended with Proposition 187.

Fourthly, and finally, California Republicans got sassy and rejected the two term mayor of Los Angeles, an anti-abortion Roman Catholic millionaire Richard Riordan who appeared poised to smash Democratic Governor Gray Davis into oblivion. Instead, they nominated an unknown son of a brilliant former Nixon Cabinet member, a Roman Catholic William Simon Jr. from New Jersey.

Given the smelly Davis campaign contributions that appear to buy contracts and special favors from Governor Davis, he should be 20 points behind in the polls and rushing into a multi-million dollar defeat at the hands of the proven former Mayor of Los Angeles.

Cavemen fanatic supporters of Bill Simon labeled Mayor Richard Riordan a RINO (Republican In Name Only) and were joined by $10-million Gray Davis campaign dollars. Both sides exulted in Simon's primary victory. Purity is what the Simon fanatics demand and such will bring the worst defeat in California history, come November.

Simon's proven and documented business failures, negates his platform of a businessman running the state. Simon convinced a jury that he ran a crooked business and awarded millions of dollars in fraud punitive damages to Simon's business associate, a convicted drug dealer. Simon used tax shelters that are legally questionable. Simon hired Deukmejian campaign manager, Sal Russo, to run his campaign. Simon just fired almost his campaign staff to "conserve" campaign money for television ads.

What fun we had when Democrat Kathleen Brown ran out of money weeks before her defeat by a risen-from-the-political-grave Governor Pete Wilson. Now, the empty wallet is Republican Simon's.

Empty also is the integrity of Simon and his ersatz campaign staff. Simon brings defeat and disgrace to the once-mighty Republican Party that gave the nation Republicans Earl Warren, Richard Nixon and Ronald Reagan.

All we have left is the Party of George Deukmejian, Pete Wilson, Dan Lungren, William Simon Jr. and his rabid anti-Mexican supporters who, every day, are smaller and smaller in number and will soon be as powerless and extinct as the California Republican Party.

"The New American Majority: Hispanics, Republicans & George W. Bush" by Contreras is available at barnesandnoble.com and amazon.com bookstores

8

MEDIA IGNORANTS,
O'REILLY AND LIMBAUGH

IGNORANCE OR BIGOTRY

Raoul Lowery Contreras
June 28, 2002

There is monstrous fraud being perpetrated on unsuspecting Americans by media people they trust. Newspaper editors sometimes inadvertently defraud the public when they publish letters to the editor that are not factual and feed the current hysteria about people from south of the Border.

Example: FoxNews star Bill O'Reilly is the most uninformed national television personality currently working. He recently stated that illegal aliens make up 25% of our prison population and that most of their crimes are violent ones. Wrong, O'Reilly!

As of May 31, 2002, the California Department of Corrections reports 160,000 inmates serving time in the state's 33 prisons and 38 prison camps.

Fact: The Immigration and Naturalization Service (INS) has official holds on 19,891 California inmates, or, in percentages, the INS suspects that 12.4% of California inmates MAY BE illegal aliens. Mr. O'Reilly, 12.4% is not 25%. Furthermore, California reports that less than half are in prison for crimes against people, even fewer for crimes of violence. California, of course, has the highest number of illegals in the country.

Considering, Mr. O'Reilly, that there are reputed to be more than 6-million illegals in California 19,891 amounts to a tiny, tiny .003 percent.

Where in the world does O'Reilly get his get his information? Even in the federal prison system, the vast majority of Mexican nationals in prison are there for smuggling, not violent crimes, nor for even being in the country illegally.

Example: Radio talk show host Rush Limbaugh of the "Excellence in Broadcasting Network" perpetuated the greatest national fraud of all in 1994 when he declared that California's Proposition 187 was all about welfare. Limbaugh, of course, never read the proposition's text.

Fact: He was unaware that the proposed law denied "non-emergency" medical care to any child, including citizens, in every hospital in the state, including private ones, even though the parent was willing to pay cash for medical services or had medical insurance IF, either parent couldn't prove legal residency to hospital clerks.

Fact: Because he never read the text, Limbaugh was unaware that the proposition mandated that any child, U.S. citizens included, be expelled from school if either parent couldn't prove their legal residence to school secretaries.

Example: Newspapers are full of articles, op-ed pieces and letters to the editor that proclaim that Hispanics drop out of school in great numbers and are flooding the labor market with uneducated illiterates that will never escape poverty.

Fact: National editors associations report that less than 3.5 percent of working press people, editors and reporters, are Hispanic, a deficiency that leads to ignorance of facts that are critical to understanding the Hispanic population.

Fact: In 2001, 103,795 Hispanics graduated from California high schools, according to the State Department of Education, an increase of three-percent over the year before and 28% more than in 1994.

Fact: In 1994, the four-year high school drop out rate among California Hispanics was 26.5 percent, while the Black drop out rate was 29.1 percent.

Fact: By 2001, the Hispanic drop out rate had dropped by almost half, to 15 percent, while the Black drop out rate was cut by a third to 19-percent.

What we have, then, is false information being drubbed into the heads of unsuspecting people that skews their view of the fastest growing segment of the country, Hispanics.

To combat this misinformation, intellectual and media alliances must be organized by informed people willing to buck the high and mighty media types like O'Reilly, Limbaugh and the newspaper editors who—out of ignorance, or bigotry—allow lies and misstatements to appear in their shows or newspapers without proof, or documentation.

Facts are facts, except when O'Reilly, Limbaugh and newspaper writers conjure up misinformation out of ignorance or bigotry.

(NOTE: Neither O"Reilly nor Limbaugh have ever presented an original thought or idea. Both are ignorant of their surroundings and rely on less-than-qualified researchers to provide them with words they do not even understand. Limbaugh tries to convince us that he writes his own books, while most professional writers laugh their heads off. As for O'Reilly, who knows if he writes his own words. If he does, he demonstrates even more inadequacies than Limbaugh.

9

GUILT BY THOUGHT, BY AN AMERICAN GESTAPO

THE GESTAPO AND KGB—ANAHEIM, CALIFORNIA

Raoul Lowery Contreras
September 10, 2001

The good citizens of Anaheim (aka Disneyland), thought that Gestapo secret police techniques were buried in the rubble of a defeated Germany in 1945. When those techniques emerged in Mississippi in the Sixties in the form of White Citizen Councils, we thought we buried them again with enforcement of federal civil rights and liberties laws.

The Gestapo (and Soviet KGB) technique was, of course, neighbor spying on neighbor, secret police surveillance of suspects uncharged with real crimes and secret dossiers kept on people suspected of anti-government and/or un-American activities.

White Citizen Councils of Mississippi used sheriffs and local cops to spy on people suspected of perfectly legal pro-civil rights activities, be they white (liberals, of course), or Black (Communists, of course). Voluminous secret records were kept. Courts have recently ordered the opening of those 40-year old records. Shockingly, those records disclose that some current elected officeholders were once mucky-mucks in the White Citizens Councils.

These highly illegal, un-American techniques have been resurrected, again, from the ashcan of history by cops, in, of all places, Anaheim, California.

Using the same methods it uses to track organized crime, illicit drug networks and street gangs, the Anaheim police department, under direct orders from police Chief Roger Baker, has embarked on a massive secret police campaign to track the activities of five (yes, FIVE) Hispanic activists. Complaints about police brutality and activities in and against the Hispanic community appear to be the "crimes" causing the Chief to order the secret activities.

Anaheim, unlike neighboring Santa Ana, hasn't become a Hispanic majority city but rather remains a traditionally "white" Orange County city that reflects a traditional white Orange County attitude of hostility towards people who look different.

Organizational charts have been created by Baker's cops that link these five Hispanic activists to Hispanic community groups, which then extends the surveillance to groups organized to better the community, to distribute food, to train job seekers, to register voters, etc.

Chief Baker gave a report on this activity to the Anaheim City Council in a secret meeting, according to the Orange County Register. This "closed" briefing was closed, officials told the Register, because pending litigation was discussed. Sure. The meeting violated state open meeting laws, period, and, thus, was illegal.

In fact, Anaheim City Manager Jim Ruth stated-through a spokesperson, of course—that the charts were developed to "identify any possible group bias." Group bias? Chief Baker says that all the information was developed from public sources such as newspapers. Sure. Baker says the charts were developed after the City Manager asked him for information to respond to Hispanic complaints about the police department. Sure.

It is one thing for Hispanic activists and columnists to scream about quasi or ersatz legal surveillance and investigation of non-criminals, it is another for a police professional and a city mayor to view these activities with reservations.

"I personally am uncomfortable with any police agency compiling unnecessary information about citizens," says Anaheim Mayor Tom Daly. Score one for the Mayor.

Retired Anaheim police Captain Marc Hedgpeth goes further: "To my knowledge just looking at the report, I can't think of a time when we ever used a link analysis process to deal with people who are not suspected of any kind of criminal conduct." Hedgpeth was the final competitor for the Chief's job when Baker was selected. Perhaps, Anaheim city officials will now reconsider their choice and ease Baker into retirement before the onslaught of lawsuits begin.

There are some who approve of this activity, or would have federal police issue parking tickets on our streets, or have local cops illegally pretend to be federal immigration officers, but mixing constitutional responsibilities doesn't work. This Anaheim case is a perfect example of far more than police harassment. It is extreme violence by local cops against the federal Constitution and ordinary people. It must stop.

Complaints against police are not un-American or illegal, secret police tactics are.

(NOTE: The most frightening specter in this writer's memory is the idea that local police can exercise their investigatory abilities on their own bosses, the citizens of their community for political reasons as in the case of Anaheim. Moreover, the idea that local cops can investigate and arrest California residents who are of Mexican origin simply because they look Mexican is totally repugnant. This was one of my issues with Proposition 187 in 1994. One section of the Proposition would have mandated that local police arrest and hold anyone they suspected of being illegally in the country or even anyone in their custody until the suspect proved they were in the country legally, or a citizen. Any and all local sheriffs and police chiefs would, according to 187's author, set the guidelines, individually, for what documents might or might not be acceptable on a local jurisdiction basis. In other words, California would have been the only state in the United States where each individual person would have to carry papers proving legality, not to federal immigration officers, but to traffic cops.)

10

DEMOCRATIC RACISM TOWARDS MEXICANS AND THEIR TRUCKS

BIGOTRY IS SPELLED D-E-M-O-C-R-A-T

Raoul Lowery Contreras
August 23, 2001

Not since the 1950s, Sixties and 90s has racism towards a single group been so ubiquitous as it is today. Unlike those crisis years, Democrats are leading the way in promulgating the current race riot against Mexicans.

Fact: Democrats in the House of Representatives, led by their leader Richard Gephardt and his assistant David Bonior, have built a wall of racism against the United States following the law and allowing Mexican trucks to operate outside a 20-mile commercial zone along the border.

Fact: Democrats in the United States Senate, led by their leader, Tom Daschle, have imposed restrictions on Mexican trucks that even American trucks don't have to meet.

In other words, if Democrats do have their way, Mexican trucks will have to operate under more stringent regulations than trucks from either Canada or the United States. Why? Are they inherently unsafe, more so than American or Canadian trucks? No, no, no. Anyone who says so is lying. But, lying is not new to racists, for racists must lie.

Am I saying that Gephardt, Bonior and Daschle are racists? Yes, and they prove it every day. These men led the fight against the North American Free Trade Agreement (NAFTA) with Mexico—using lies and misrepresentations. They totally supported President Clinton in implementing the death penalty for Mexicans in the deserts and mountains of Arizona and California under Operation Gatekeepr. They come with lukewarm support for regularizing Mexicans in the country illegally and declare that any such program shouldn't be restricted to Mexicans only. Lastly, their opposition to NAFTA's trucking provisions and their support of discriminatory rules on Mexicans only is total proof that these alleged American leaders have only the basest motives in mind.

President George W. Bush has threatened to veto any bill that contains racist discrimination against our next-door neighbor Mexico. He should, just to teach these racist politicians that they can no longer get away with their campaign against Mexicans.

What's amazing is that these people were on the right side in the 50s, and 60s when the targets were Blacks. They and people like them created and supported civil rights laws that protected Blacks and their rights to equality and voting. In the early 1990s, these men were on the right side when Republican Governor Pete Wilson campaigned hard against Mexican immigrants and supported the infamous and unconstitutional Proposition 187.

Politics, however, are comical sometimes. Faced with the danger that President Bill Clinton might lose in 1996, after his party was wiped out in 1994 when Republicans smashed through to control the House and Senate, these men succumbed to politics and supported operations on the border that have resulted in hundreds of deaths. Gephardt,

Bonior and Daschle sacrificed hundreds of men and women so that Clinton could claim to be tough on the border.

Concurrently, they led the way in supporting Clinton in his betrayal of NAFTA by not even setting up an infrastructure to check Mexican trucks for safety and then allowing them to operate as per NAFTA.

Commerce is being ravaged by these men and Americans are paying higher prices so these men and their labor union supporters can smirk their way through press conferences by claiming safety issues are the reason to keep Mexicans from operating on American highways. There are very few safety issues. A phony Clinton-run study in Laredo of Mexican trucks allegedly found that over 40% of Mexican trucks were found to be unsafe—THAT IS A LIE! The issue is not pickup trucks as were examined in Laredo, but 18-wheel highway trucks. What was that percentage, Mr. Clinton, Mr. Bonior, Mr. Gephardt and Mr. Daschle? Wonder of wonders, no one knows. Because those trucks weren't examined and compared to similar American trucks, there is no honest basis to use the Clinton truck safety study for anything but toilet paper.

In California, the Highway Patrol reports that after inspecting over 600,000 Mexican trucks crossing into the United States, 23% were cited for safety or paperwork violations while, at the same time, 22% of American trucks were cited for safety or paperwork violations.

One should notice that none of these three Democratic leaders cites the California statistics. They might fall on their faces if they do, for it is Republicans George W. Bush and Senate Republican Leader who point out that discrimination against Mexicans is discrimination. Discrimination on the basis of national origin is racism, pure and simple.

When Congressman Gephardt and Senator Daschle run for President in 2004, Americans of Mexican descent must remember them and their 1990s support of death for Mexicans and bigotry against Mexicans in 2001. As for David Bonior, Michigan Mexican Americans need to remember him and his slashing attacks on Mexicans when he runs for Governor.

Gephardt, Bonior and Daschle lead the Democratic Party; they are bigots against Mexicans and, by inference, against Americans of Mexican descent. If the Democratic Party really cherished its Mexican American supporters, it would throw these three out of the Party. As it won't, we must remember on Election Day and do as labor leader Samuel Gompers used to say—Reward our friends and punish our enemies.

(NOTE: David Bonior was humiliated in defeat in his run for Michigan governor. President Bush won the argument and Mexican trucks are rolling through the border after safety checks that are the same as American or Canadian trucks. As most trade between Mexico, the second largest trading partner of the U.S. and the USA is by truck, this Bush win has serious and positive economic consequences.)

FAIR AND BALANCED?

Raoul Lowery Contreras
February 10, 2001

I was beginning to believe the Fox News Channel's claim of being "fair and balanced." I was beginning to believe that Fox is totally superior to other 24-hour news channels. But then they slapped me back into reality with the most one-sided, wrong and untruthful news report I have ever seen on national television. Subject: Mexican trucks on U.S. highways and American trucks on Mexican highways. Mexicans were the real subjects, of course.

Background: The United States, Canada and Mexico negotiated the North American Free Trade Agreement (NAFTA) in 1992-93. Both houses of Congress approved NAFTA in 1993 for implementation on

January 1, 1994. One segment of NAFTA involves trucking between the three countries, allowing trucks from all three countries to work in the other two. That portion of NAFTA was not to be implemented until December of 1995, two years after the agreement went into effect. President Clinton, however, bowing to union pressure from the Teamsters Union has blocked the entry of Mexican trucks into the U.S. Conversely, the Mexicans blocked American trucks from operating in Mexico. The Mexicans filed a formal complaint to a board set up by NAFTA and the two American, two Mexican and one British panel members have just unanimously found that the U.S. has violated the NAFTA agreement on trucks. President Bush has indicated that he approves the NAFTA provision on trucking.

Hardly any of these facts came out in the Fox News report.

Another rarely known fact is that Mexican trucks have been allowed to operate within a "commercial zone" up to 50-miles from the border in the case of San Diego and that literally thousands of commercial trucks operate on San Diego streets and freeways every day. This has been the case for fifty years.

Fox News said that "many" Mexican trucks weren't safe. Where did that information come from? Did they quote any official agency report? No. In fact, the California Highway Patrol—in charge of inspecting Mexican trucks—reports that 23% of Mexican trucks they inspect have safety problems. They also report that 22% of American trucks they inspect fail safety inspections.

Now that we are all aware that Mexican trucks operate in the U.S. by the thousands in "commercial zones" along the 2,000-mile border, did Fox News give us an accident count of those trucks on U.S. territory? No. Did they give us a casualty report of those killed and injured by Mexican trucks on U.S. territory? No. If Mexican trucks are so unsafe and lethal, why didn't we hear any statistics from anyone on the situation? Why was there no one from the California Highway Patrol or the

United States Department of Transportation on Fox news reciting public information? Why, Fox, why?

Perhaps if Fox News had read the transportation section of NAFTA it would have known that Mexican and Canadian trucks operating under that section must be insured to American standards. In practice, that means policies with American companies. Why were no insurance experts on the Fox News report telling us how insurance companies rate trucks and rigs for safety before they insure them and their drivers?

As a media person, I have to wonder about Fox. What happened to the Fox motto of "fair and balanced" insofar as the subject of Mexican trucks operating in the United States? We saw a Teamster representative complaining about low Mexican wages for drivers and on alleged Mexican safety issues. No one questioned him on how strenuously the Teamsters lobby for less enforcement of safety regulations and how they fight almost every proposed safety regulation.

Why would Fox produce and air such a one-sided and incomplete report? Well, this report follows on similar one-sided and incomplete reports aired on the O'Reilly Factor that airs on Fox News every evening. O'Reilly totally drops the ball on the subjects of Mexico, illegal aliens from Mexico and the border between Mexico and the United States. Mr. Bill O'Reilly, for example, calls for the use of American military troops on the border despite that being illegal under the Posse Commitatis laws passed by Congress 124-years ago. The military cannot be used to enforce civilian laws. Illegal aliens violate civilian laws and their crossing the border is not a military invasion.

Nonetheless, O'Reilly's hysterical reports and comments color the actual situation and add to a frenzy that has little basis in fact. Illegals from Mexico don't shoot Border Patrol Agents as a rule, it's the other way around. Illegals from Mexico don't shoot property and ranch owners along the border, it's the other way around. Illegals are shot and killed for drinking water out of cattle troughs. Mr. O'Reilly and his Fox News Channel don't seem to know these things.

If they do, as in the trucking issue, Fox is doing the country a great disservice. I say that because bad news reports perpetrate bad influence and bad policy. That has been the argument of news purists and conservatives for decades; that has been the argument of people who seek the truth. Given reports on Fox about Mexicans, Mexico and, now, trucking between the United States and Mexico, I sadly report that the Fox News Channel has apparently sold its soul to the evil Gods of bigotry and untruthfulness.

(NOTE: Fox's Roger Ailes has constructed a fine network. Unfortunately, he has hired some people who are dumb and stupid and are so because they are television people, not real journalists. O'Reilly is the quintessential TV journalist who can't find his tail with both hands. His inability to search out truth and facts is highlighted in almost everyone one of his issues and presentations. Ailes should be ashamed that his Network isn't that much different from the others and they are all lacking in truth and open mindedness.)

HISPANICS AND WOMEN NEED NOT APPLY

Raoul Lowery Contreras
September 30, 2002

The Democrats talked retired Navy man John Herrera into running against Republican California state Assemblyman Mark Wyland in a district where Democrats are outnumbered two to one. They talked 77-year old Democrat great-grandmother Sarah Lowery into running against Republican state Assemblyman Jay LeSeur who has a two to one Republican registration.

Other than talking these two into running, the Democratic Party has abandoned them to overwhelming Republican/Independent registration.

Other than opening a rent-free donated campaign office in a Democratic city, Escondido, the Democrats won't do anything on the serious money front to help these two. There will be no union-sponsored or trial lawyer million-dollar fundraising events for these two.

When one of these candidates sent a letter to 50 incumbent or retiring Democratic State Assembly members—all with fat campaign funds, some as large as half-million dollars—asking for help, nothing. One incumbent mailed a return-postage paid envelope with his state-paid-for business card and nothing else, nothing. The other 49 incumbents didn't even send their business cards.

Without real money, these candidates are voiceless

Where is Governor Davis? Where is former vice-President Al Gore? Where is Senator Joe Lieberman? Where is Democratic National Chairman Terry McCaulife? Herrera and Lowery are Hispanic candidates, yet nothing from Hispanic Democratic groups so far. A tiny Latino Democrat group has scheduled a fund-raising dinner at $75.00 per that may net $4-5,000 to be split between 8-candidates. All in all, these two have had no help, no money and other than "aren't you good loyal Democrats," nothing.

Contrast that with the seismic changes in the Republican Party. Former Montana Governor Mark Racicot, the Republican National Chairman, charmed a group of interested citizens on Wednesday night and reached out to ask for their support of Republican Hispanic candidates, including statewide Insurance Commissioner candidate Gary Mendoza; congressional candidate, Maria Guadalupe Garcia (running against Congressman Bob Filner), and Oceanside City Council candidate, Rocky Chavez.

Joining Governor Racicot was the White House's Deputy Assistant to the President and Director of Inter-government Affairs, Ruben Barrales.

Circulating through the crowd of a couple of hundred people were invitations from the San Diego and Orange County Lincoln Clubs to a fundraising luncheon on October 8th that will raise money for each and every Hispanic Republican candidate on our San Diego County ballots (one in Imperial County, two in Orange County, and Republican John Sanchez running for Governor of New Mexico, as well).

There has never been a mainstream Republican organization fundraiser for Hispanic candidates in San Diego County—ever. The traditionally all-White, Protestant San Diego Republican Party is joining the national Republican Party in reaching out to the fastest growing group of people in the country, Hispanics, some Protestant, but mostly Roman Catholic.

Compare the plights of Democrats John Herrera and Sarah Lowery to those of Hispanic Republicans that will be saluted at the luncheon and financed with its proceeds. No comparison.

While this is occurring, Democrats pulled out their stilettos and attacked Miguel Estrada in his hearing before the Democratically controlled Judiciary Committee that is essential to President Bush's nomination of Estrada to the Court of Appeals.

Democratic Senator Dianne Feinstein, the quintessential California Girl who married money, asked stupid questions od Estrada based on "anonymous" charges published in the left-wing Nation Magazine, the flag bearer of the American ultra-left.

Democratic Senator Leahy of Vermont asked why Estrada labeled the Puerto Rican legal Defense Fund's interviewers of Estrada as ignorant and "boneheaded." Estrada replied that one of the three interviewers challenged Estrada with declarations that Estrada wasn't Hispanic enough to suit the Puerto Rican Legal Defense Fund.

New York Democratic Senator Schumer demandehd Estrada's legal memos he wrote while working as a career lawyer in the office of Solicitor General. Never mind that each and every Solicitor General of the past thirty years wrote the Committee a letter denouncing such a request. Despite President Clinton's Solicitor General praised Estrada and is supporting his nomination, Schumer kept up his demands.

California and national Democrats seem to have gone out of their way this year to post a symbolic sign "Hispanics and Women Need Not Apply."

In Washington, Democrats use stalking horse Puerto Ricans to accuse a brilliant, Democrat-recommended Miguel Estrada of not being "Hispanic" enough because his family was middle-class (as if one has to have been poor to be a real Hispanic). They use "anonymous" accusations to smear Estrada, then ask for Hispanic support.

Perhaps they might fare better with intelligent Hispanics if they dropped their class-warfare and McCarthy—like (anonymous and unproven) charges they use like verbal graffiti to destroy any Hispanic that isn't of the plantation variety they desire.

(NOTE: Local Democrats blew a fuse when the local version of this article appeared in San Diego's North County Times. Ms Erin Emblem quoted Herrera, Witt and Lowery in a counter op-ed piece that this writer was totally wrong in specifics. Unfortunately for her, however, my version was and is true. I should know, Sarah Lowery is my mother and I personally handled her campaign funds; I personally wrote her fund raising letters to prominent Democrats and wrote a letter to the labor union honchos asking for help for this life-long Union member. No help was forthcoming. As for Herrera and Witt, their campaigns were made of fools gold for their districts had never elected a Democrat. The local Democrats did sponsor a $75-a-plate dinner that was attended by 240 people and that raised about $12,000 in net campaign funds. However, when that post was split up among all the candidates, each received less than $1,000—enough to buy 2702 stamps, enough exactly to reach 1.8% of the total households in their districts. Big deal.)

Contreras's book, *"The New American Majority, Hispanics, Republicans & George W. Bush,"* is available at **www.amazon.com**, **www. barnesandnoble.com**, and **www.iuniverse.com**

E-mail: **sdraoul@att.net**

11

RACIAL HATRED

HATE IS PUNISHED

Raoul Lowery Contreras
June 22, 2001

Will they never learn? They, are White supremacists. They think they are superior to "mud people"—like me, like those of Jewish faith, like people of the African American persuasion. One of them was just sentenced for conducting a terrorist campaign against Jews, Mexican Americans and Jewish houses of worship.

Alexander James Curtis, 25 (son of a public high school teacher), of Lemon Grove, California a working class suburb of San Diego (where I lived in the late 50's and early Sixties) was sentenced by U.S. District Court Judge John C. Coughenour to three years of supervised probation and five years of random searches of Curtis after he is released.

Curtis pleaded guilty March 16 to three felony counts of conspiracy to commit civil rights violations. He admitted that he and three others in his group waged a terrorist campaign based on the victims' race or religion. Racist literature throughout the East San Diego County (including my Mother' condo entryway) and spray-painted slogans with Nazi swastikas on a Jewish house of worship in Poway (a prosperous San Diego Suburb) and another in the San Carlos area of San Diego (where homes appraise at $250-300,000) were among the hate crimes committed by these young men with poisoned minds.

For the benefit of those who oppose "hate crime" legislation, especially those in this readership, let's use Mr. Curtis' crimes as examples of what "hate crimes" are, for there are many who disbelieve the concept of hate crimes and laws (and court decisions) that have criminalized such actions.

Spray-painting Nazi swastikas on a house of worship is designed not to insult Jewish people, but to terrorize them psychologically, to cast fear among them. Such actions don't relate to a mugging, an armed robbery, or any physical attack on any individual—true. But, to the Jewish community, it is a blow to the collective psyche and, that is a profoundly criminal act. It is KRISTALLNACHT, Crystal Night, Germany, 1938. History records that the persecution and slaughter of Europe's Jews by the Germans began with defacing Jewish temples.

Sending threats of a physical nature against public officials is a crime against the entire community, the very community that elected these officials and whom they represent in government. Curtis and his co-conspirators did just that. Specifically, Mr. Curtis threatened Congressman Bob Filner (D-Chula Vista) because he is Jewish. He threatened La Mesa Mayor Art Madrid, a Mexican American and the only such ever-elected Mayor in San Diego County because of his Mexican origin.

These are hate crimes and they must be punished. Punished not for their racist and White supremacist thoughts and views, but for how they manifested their views and thoughts. In other words, actions count, actions are punishable.

A few years ago, Fallbrook (California) racist/White supremacist Tom Metzgar was convicted of burning items on private property without a burn permit in the Los Angeles area. Of course, the burning item was a large Christian cross and the burners, Metzgar included, were rump KuKluckers (KKK) burning the cross to protest "mud people," Blacks, Jews and to honor the superior White race. Metzgar was convicted for an illegal cross burning that violated community laws against burning without a permit in a fire-sensitive area. Metzger was confined for six months in the LA County jail.

There are people who protest such crimes and sentences as a violation of "free speech," but are they? Someone once said that "Your right of free speech ends when your fist hits my nose" and that applies to synagogue's defaced with swastikas. Curtis and his thuggish friends are free to think about painting swastikas on synagogues, but they cannot be permitted to deface them. That is a crime against humanity, not just Jews.

In sentencing Curtis, the Federal judge made an interesting observation that White supremacists like Curtis, Metzgar and people who think like them, and people against hate crime laws, should think about extensively: "Mr. Curtis, you're living proof that the white race is not superior."

RACISM, THE CANCER AMONG US

Raoul Lowery Contreras
July 21, 2002

There are people around us who just don't get it. No matter how many commentators write about the deep-rooted cancer of racism, there are those who simply refuse to accept that such exists and that it undermines the very essence of 21st Century America.

Case in point: The incident in Inglewood, California, where a white police officer was videotaped assaulting a 16-year-old black boy. The officer was indicted by a Los Angeles County Grand Jury for assaulting the teenager under the color of authority.

The specifics of the incident were that the 16-year-old was seen handcuffed and face down on the ground. The large officer picked up the boy by the belt and slammed him face down on the trunk of a car.

Moments later the officer slugs the boy in the face. These are video-taped facts. What happened before this tape was made is not seen, but is recorded on a security tape of the gas station where the incident took place. The security tape was certainly seen by the Grand Jury.

The indicted officer's attorney says the officer slugged the boy in the face because the handcuffed boy grabbed the officer by the "testicles." The videotape does not substantiate that allegation in any way. The officer is not seen wincing or grimacing in pain, nor, simply stepping back from the boy's hands. The officer is not telling the truth. His partner was indicted for filing a false report.

The question is: Did this incident occur because the officer is white and the boy is black? What we have is a police officer assaulting a hand-cuffed arrestee, and that's against the law, no matter the races involved.

Concurrently, in San Diego a white young man is shot and killed at the beach at 2:30 a.m. by a black suspect and whites spill their guts in public decrying the attention devoted to the white Inglewood cop and the little attention being paid to the black suspected murder.

Example: Letter to the Editor, San Diego Union—"It's a sign of the times: When a white cop in Inglewood bops an unruly black kid on the head a couple of times on camera, it's all over the news for weeks. Certainly it wasn't the right thing for the cop to do, but the kid wasn't badly hurt. Yet all we hear about is the white cop and the black kid. Activists fly in from all over the country decrying the incident. In contrast, a couple of weeks later, when a suspected black gang member shoots and kills a completely innocent white college kid whose bike he has stolen, your story is relegated to the B-section. Only near the end of your story is the race of the perpetrator briefly mentioned. The next day, your follow-up report, also in the B-section, reference to the race of the suspected perpetrator is omitted entirely. What's going on here? Is it OK to talk about race when it's white on black, but not when it's black on white? You can't have it both ways. TODD STRIBLE, San Marcos"

The trouble with this simpleton letter is that it reflects so many whites around us. They simply don't get it. A police officer who assaults a handcuffed prisoner is a criminal. If the officer is of one color and the prisoner another, there is a high likelihood that race may be involved, but race doesn't matter as the act itself is criminal.

If a gun-carrying criminal shoots someone while committing a crime, race usually has little to do with this crime. To assume a gun toting criminal is a "gang member" because he or she is black is also racist and deserves short shrift. That would be like assuming the indicted Inglewood white cop is a Ku Klux Klan leader because he is white and he assaulted a black kid. Or, better yet, to assume that all whites are Ku Klux Klans people because Ku Klux Klansmen are all white.

12

RACIAL PROFILING

GOOD RACIAL PROFILING

Raoul Lowery Contreras
May 9, 2002

Racial profiling has reached a level of acceptance in our society that allows me to use it as a tool.

These crimes are occurring as this is written and read.

Fact #1: Vandals deface acclaimed famous Mexican American murals on the San Diego Bay bridge supports with, of all things, spray paint. These criminals aren't graffiti "taggers," they are racial criminals who signed their defacements with misspelled insults and attacks on Mexicans.

Fact #2: Vandals deface acclaimed giant Mexican American murals on the sides of old water tanks that house the Centro Cultural de La Raza (Cultural Center of the Mexican People) in San Diego's Balboa Park with insults and attacks on Mexicans.

Fact #3: Vandals build pipe bombs and place them in a number of rural mailboxes in America's Heartland, some of which explode and injure innocent Americans. The bombs are accompanied by anti-government messages.

Fact #4: Birmingham, Alabama, prepares for the ultimate criminal trial of one of the most infamous criminals in American history, a bombing killer of five little Black girls in a church bombing in 1965.

Using the currently accepted tool of racial profiling, let us discuss who committed these crimes.

From the misspelled words on the mural defacements and the incoherent messages that accompanied the Heartland pipe bombs, we can deduce these people are not educated. In other words, we probably find school dropouts are the perpetrators.

From the targets of the crimes in San Diego and Birmingham, we can deduce that the criminals are not Mexican or Black.

From the anti-American government messages found with the planted pipe bombs, we can deduce that the perpetrators don't understand our political or governmental system, or the Constitution, or reject all out of hand, thus placing themselves outside our system.

From the use of bombs, we can deduce that there are philosophical links between the Birmingham bombers, the Heartland bombers and people like the Oklahoma City bombing conspirators, one of whom is in jail for life and another who has been executed for that monstrous mass murder.

So, what have we here? We have disaffected, uneducated people who have a number of things in common. At their base is race hate of Blacks and Mexicans. They hate America and its system of laws, government and the Constitution. They believe in skulking about in darkness and defacing cultural art and planting death-dealing bombs. They are all over; they are in Alabama, California, Iowa and everywhere in the country. They are all cowards.

What we have here are uneducated school dropouts, probably unemployed with few, if any, marketable skills, probably raised by abusive alcoholic school dropouts and, probably members of, or wannabes of, WAR, the White Aryan Resistance of Fallbrook's infamous race hating Tom Metzger, or of Louisiana's former Ku Klux Klanner, David Duke.

Did I mention that all the evidence suggests that these criminals are all White, as are their WAR and KKK heroes? Did I mention that these people live in a world that yelling fire in a crowded theater is perfectly acceptable as is the midnight defacement of art or the bombing and killing of innocent children and adult?

If I didn't, let me so state now. We must hunt down these criminal cowards and throw them into deep dark prison cells from which they can never emerge again to threaten America.

(NOTE: The only perpetrator of the abovementioned crimes is, of course, a punk white young college man from the upper Midwest who apparently was upset because he couldn't smoke marijuana legally. In all he planted about a dozen pipe bombs in several states during a cross-country odyssey fueled by marijuana.)

13

AFFIRMATIVE ACTION

A BLACK AND WHITE CENTURY

Raoul Lowery Contreras
May 21, 2001

A hundred years ago, Negro men and women, now known as Blacks or African Americans, were not allowed to work in any job, or go to school or college without the specific concurrence of the white community and its power structure. Thomas Jefferson's, "Among men there is a natural aristocracy of talent and virtue" simply didn't exist outside the white community. It didn't want competition from former slaves and their children and grandchildren.

A hundred years ago, complete subjugation of the black community for the benefit of the white man was the norm and there was nothing American Blacks could do about it. They formed groups like the National Association for the Advancement of Colored People (NAACP) and the Urban League, but little changed.

One Black Republican managed to get elected to Congress but all U.S. Senators were white males and each and every member of the House of Representatives, but the one Black, were white, almost to the man, male.

This was the American system a hundred years ago, ninety, eighty, seventy, sixty, fifty. forty, twenty, ten, five years ago, and today. There was some progress in softening the edges of Jim Crow job discrimination, and against discrimination in higher education, but not much.

Affirmative Action came to the country. Affirmative Action was designed by lawmakers to prohibit the hiring of incompetents over better-qualified people, skin color notwithstanding. It also applied to contracts by the federal government and several states in a formula that allowed minority and women owned firms to be certified as such and to be eligible for work set aside for such firms.

The United States Supreme Court ruled in the Baake case that race could be a factor in college admissions, but lower courts have ignored that case and instituted a ban on Affirmative Action anyway. Then came a case from San Jose in which a more experienced white woman was chosen for a job over a less experienced and less skilled white male and the male went to court. Then came a case in which a state law giving some preference to minority owned firms for state work was hauled into court by a white male-owned firm because the white male thought he was being discriminated against.

Suddenly, much of the progress made in recent years to overcome the legacy of a century ago has come to a halt. Of course, during these years, women made significant strides, though they are still frozen out of the highest echelons of corporate America. Blacks comprise only 3% of the Fortune 500 executive corps, thus miniscule progress has been made there in a hundred years. Discrimination in business is so deeply imbedded in American culture that few notice.

The most noticeable attack on Affirmative Action occurs in, of all places, higher education. Yes, academia. Yes, the university.

It started, of course, in California in a 1995 move by University of California Regent Ward Connerly to do away with Affirmative Action at the University. A Black man, Connerly carried Governor Pete Wilson's water on the issue as Governor Wilson was secretly preparing a run for the Presidency. This clever political ploy failed Wilson, but succeeded in the Board of Regents. The University of California officially dropped Affirmative Action and Black and Hispanic student bodies shrunk.

Needless to say, other states took notice and soon lawsuits were being filed in Texas (Hopwood) and in Michigan to overturn alleged racial admission preferences. In Texas, the plaintiffs won a Circuit Court victory, but were foiled by Governor George W. Bush's ten-percent admissions plan that allowed the top ten percent of any graduating class entry into the Texas public university system.

In Michigan, two federal judges decided on opposite sides of the issue. The issue argued by the University of Michigan was that racial preference in admission guaranteed "diversity" in the student body. It further argued that "diversity" was absolutely necessary for a future society that will not be an almost all-white society like it was a century ago.

The opposite argument is that "diversity" is simply not a compelling enough reason to discriminate against some white students. These arguments will be presented to the Supreme Court in future months. We do not know how the Court will rule.

I do know one thing, an officially commissioned study in 1925 by the United States Army concluded scientifically that Blacks could not fly airplanes. In 1954, the Supreme Court ruled that "separate but equal" schools were inherently unconstitutional and unequal. In 1962, President Kennedy ordered U.S. Marshals and Army troops into the University of Mississippi to enroll one Black man. In 1969, new President Nixon found three fourths of all schools in the South still segregated by race.

In 2001, we find white lawyers, white students and white professors arguing that fewer Black students in college and law and medicine schools won't have deleterious effects on American society in the future. Such arguments a hundred years ago perpetuated the great American crime of racial economic and educational segregation. Is this déjà vu all over again?

(NOTE: Ward Connerly has sponsored a successful petition drive to place his Racial Privacy Initiative (RPI) on the March, 2002, ballot. RPI would eliminate all little boxes on state employment and academic applications that request the applicant's race. His argument is that we are supposed to be a "color blind society" thus no citizen should be forced to identify himself by race. Connerly is nothing but a front for the most racist elements in California. Racists fund him and support him. No legitimate organization in California supports Connerly. Fact: Tom Wood, the originator of Affirmative Action's Prop. 209 in California opposes the RPI for myriad reasons, the most important of which might be that how are we supposed to quantify discrimination if we have no data? We are nowhere near being a "color blind society" in California or the nation. No matter what fantasy world Connerly lives in.)

14

IMPEACHED PRESIDENT WILLIAM J. CLINTON

TWO WRONGS DON'T MAKE A RIGHT

Raoul Lowery Contreras
May 31, 1998

Twenty years ago, we non-Southerners had to tolerate the butchered "Nookeh-lehr" from the lips of a former small Southern state Governor who was temporarily and unsuccessfully filling the Oval Office of the President. The context was that his ten-year-old daughter, Amy, was worried about "nookeh-lehr" confrontation between the United States and Soviet Russia.

Today, we have another former Southern small state Governor working in the Oval Office at the White House. He does so among seven Independent Counsels investigating his appointees, two Justice Department criminal investigations of fund raising and his waivers of laws pertaining to export of hi-tech secrets to Communists in China, and three separate federal Grand Juries taking testimony and evidence regarding an alleged intimate sexual relationship with a 21-year-old intern and the more important perjury, subornation of perjury, bribery and obstruction of justice charges. Busy, busy man.

And, now, the largest democracy in the world, India, tests "Nookeh-lehr" weapons as a political weapon by India's newly elected right-of-center government against it's mortal enemy, its ethnic and genetic twin peoples, in next door Pakistan. Not to be out-cojoned (coh-honehd, more testicled), Pakistan tests its own "Nookeh-lehr" weapons. Wow!

What does our President have to say about all this "Nookeh-lehr" hanky-panky in Asia between twin peoples, albeit enemies because of religion? On May 28, 1998, the leader of the free world, the most powerful man on earth, the kisser-on-the-lips of young women not married to him, appointer of crooks and liars (allegedly), host to Chinese Communists in our House, the White House, told us—in the most intellectual and profound words ever uttered by an Ivy League graduate—"Two wrongs don't make a right." Presidential!

WOW! What insight! What confidence! What policy! It sort of reminds me of how Jimmy "Nookeh-lehr" Carter reacted when the Soviet Communists invaded Afghanistan—he couldn't believe that the Soviets were capable of such an affront to world affairs, to US policy and the United Nations Charter. He never did figure it out.

Today, Bill Clinton, who is ill-equipped to deal in world affairs and is bogged down by all the investigations swirling around him, is wandering through the wilderness of foreign affairs like a child.

Moreover, lacking the comfort of Monica Lewinsky, his young doyenne (a 21-year-old woman uniquely skilled by long experience in some field of endeavor) and faced with the obvious judicial hostility of District Judge Norma Holloway Johnson, appointed by Jimmy Carter, of his silly "executive privileges", William Jefferson Clinton is paralyzed.

Is this what all those "soccer moms" wanted when they voted for Clinton with their "I'd do him" hormones instead of their brains? Did they want a President more focused on 37-nocturnal White House visits by Monica Lewinsky than by "Nookeh-lehr" tests by mortal enemies India and Pakistan? Do remember that Clinton's Central Intelligence Agency and other intelligence agencies, all headed and run by Clinton appointees, had no warning—that we know of—of the tests by India.

So much for a popular, sexy President. Sexy, of course, to women who voted for Clinton in large numbers while men voted for opponent Robert Dole. Women are for peace, we are told, in contrast to men who are too macho for the political tastes of women. Women are more capable, we are told, of making rational political decisions. Men, you see, elected Richard Nixon and he bombed—quite legally by the way, Cambodia; they elected Ronald Reagan and he bombed Libya's terrorist dictator; and. they elected George Bush who brilliantly led us in the Gulf War against Iraq.

Neither Nixon, or Reagan or Bush were caught by surprise in "Nookeh-lehr" affairs, however. They took care of business. We breathed easier when Nixon went to China and sundered the Communist world in two; when Reagan tossed the Soviet Empire into the "ash can" of history and the Berlin wall came down; and, when George Bush's Army swept through the Arabian desert. These men took care of business and that is exactly what the men and women who elected them wanted.

In the President from Arkansas we have a befuddled man obviously over his head on "Nookeh-lehr" affairs, just as we had with Jimmy Carter. He does well with a 21-year-old groupie intern but is ignored by Prime Minister Sharif of Pakistan. He does well with "soccer moms" but fails with serious people. He does well with fellow lawyers who swoon in his Presidential presence but is slapped around in the courts by his and fellow Democrat Jimmy Carter appointees.

He does well, allegedly, in Oval Office affairs with Ms Lewinsky and at least one other Clinton groupie, but he fails in "Nookeh-lehr" affairs. A "Nookeh-lehr" confrontation by enemies who have fought three wars since 1948 is what's involved here. The face off is in an area where one in six people on this planet live—and this President doesn't have a clue. "Two wrongs don't make a right", he righteously declares. And, the boys in India and Pakistan continue to build nuclear weapons, willy nilly

The only improvement since Jimmy Carter's ineffectual days in the White House is that this President doesn't pronounce nuclear, "Nookeh-lehr."

PRESIDENT WILLIAM J. CLINTON AND A JURY OF HIS PEERS

Raoul Lowery Contreras
January 8, 1998

It's a good thing that Black prize-winning author Toni Morrison's declaration that she considers President William J. Clinton "Black" is but a flight of rhetoric and fancy, for if he really was Black, he would be removed from office, for he wouldn't have a jury—the U.S. Senate—that would be of his peers.

If he were Hispanic, he would be bound for Hollywood by now, for he would not have a jury of his peers, either. But, he does have a jury of his peers, for the U.S. Senate is composed of all White people, mostly White men. This, of course, is contrary to the normal judicial process in which most criminal defendants are poor, whether White or Black, usually uneducated and usually with skin-color darker than the jury pools, the prosecutors and judges.

From the pro-Clinton precincts we hear complaints that the 13 House of Representative-appointed case "managers" are all-White Southern former federal prosecutors, but, their facts are deficient. Henry Hyde (Illinois) isn't from the South, James Rogan (California) isn't either, George Gekas (Pennsylvania) and Chris Cannon (Utah) aren't either, neither is Wisconsin's James Sensenbrenner.

We also sense desperation on the part of pro-Clinton precincts when the subject of witnesses comes up in preparation for the Trial of The Century. Why? Even the lowliest, uneducated criminal crack-for-ten-dollars seller knows that some witness must testify against him if he is to be convicted. Ah, but, they say, the Starr Report is sufficient for the Trial. This, of course, is just the opposite position taken by the 16-pro-Clinton, Democrats of the House Judiciary Committee who constantly complained and whined that no witnesses were called for their hearings.

The whole Trial scene resembles shifting tides with Republicans on one side one day and the Democrats taking the same position a day later as Republicans shift to another position. Much depends of whether or not the 100-Senator supported bi-partisan Gramm-Kennedy plan and calendar is implemented and adhered to by Democrats, not just a handfull of swing Republicans. It depends on whether or not witnesses are allowed by 51 Senators. Can the Senate, White House and "Managers" work deals without corrupting the Trial?

Questions: If a potential or actual juror in a criminal trial at the local courthouse announced that he would never vote to convict the defendant—in this case the President—that juror would be dismissed, but not Senators, it seems; If a judge ruled that prosecutors couldn't produce any witnesses, wouldn't the prosecutors be handcuffed? Wouldn't the "jury" be handcuffed? Would justice be served with these handcuffs? No.

Not long ago, we were confronted with an enraged White community when a multi-racial jury could not find accused murderer O.J. Simpson guilty. Critics of the Simpson jury insulted our collective intelligence by charges that Black jurors ignored evidence and witnesses, and did so because they and the accused were Black, as was the chief attorney for Simpson. Ok. So how do we label the Democrats, the Congressional Black Caucus and the Democrats of the Hispanic Congressional Caucus who all declare that they will stick to the President "No matter what", no matter the evidence, the testimony and no matter what the President even admits to, as long, of course, as he's "sorry."

I submit that these stick-no-matter-what people are disingenuous violators of the Constitution and the most partisan achichincles (ah-chee-chee-nklehs, backside-kissing, parasitic, party-blinded gofers for the Man) in American history. Who ever heard of a trial without witnesses? Perhaps in Nazi Germany or the Soviet Union, but not here. Who ever heard of a trial in which prosecutors couldn't introduce evidence and testimony that they didn't use in the Grand Jury (The House of Representatives)? Who ever heard of a trial that was confined to two days for prosecutors to make their case, as was proposed by the President's lap-dogs in the Senate? Who ever heard of a national trial, the Trial of The Century, a trial so rare only two have occurred in history, that is judgment pre-ordained by a minority of 45 people, in direct violation of democratic principles and the United States Constitution?

The President has a jury of his peers, i.e., educated White folks, mostly White men, who can snap their heels together, salute, ignore any evidence, declare their loyalty to the Democratic Party and President and behave like a bunch of partisan morons, all 45 of them. The President is truly fortunate he isn't a Black President, as Toni Morrison would like, for how often does a totally White jury exonerate a Black defendant, regardless of evidence?

CAN THE COUNTRY SURVIVE IMPEACHMENT OF THE PREZ?

Raoul Lowery Contreras
October 4, 1998

"My country tis of thee…Sweet land of liberty"

For the second time in a generation, Presidential impeachment is in the air, in Washington and in the country. The Constitution tells us in Article I, Section 2 that the House of Representatives "shall have the sole power of impeachment." And, Section 3 states, "The Senate shall have the sole power to try all impeachments."

Section 4 of the Constitution defines reasons for impeachment; to wit: "The President, Vice President and all civil officers of the United States, shall be removed from office on impeachment for, and conviction of, treason, bribery, or other high crimes and misdemeanors."

Unfortunately, in President William Jefferson's 1998 United States of America, few people know what a Constitutional impeachment is and, thus, the pollsters, who probably don't know either, are flooding the media with poll results indicating that the "people" don't want to see President Clinton "impeached."

Impeachment is defined in my Webster's Ninth New Collegiate Dictionary as "A. to bring an accusation against, B. to charge a public official before a competent tribunal with misconduct in office." That is the exact definition the Founding Fathers meant when they wrote the Constitution. They didn't, however, define "high crimes and misdemeanors." That was left up to the Congress.

The Congress defined them when it impeached, tried and did not convict President Andrew Johnson after the Civil War and when the House Committee of the Judiciary wrote Articles of Impeachment against President Richard Nixon in 1974.

We are now embarking on the path of impeachment of President Clinton with his adulturous affair with Monica Lewinsky as the base for an investigation of subsequent admitted lies and assorted other alleged felonies by President Clinton.

There is a phalanx of possible grounds for impeachment that were referred by Independent Counsel Kenneth Starr to the House in a report that millions of people have read. Additional thousands of pages of testimony and documents, plus a video of the President testifying before a Federal Grand Jury, have been released for the people to read and study. This information, alone, is historical and without precedent. The American people are overwhelmed, in fact, with information.

The questions are: Did the President lie in a January Federal court-ordered deposition in front of the judge in charge? Did the President lie in front of the Grand Jury on August 17th? Did the President, directly or indirectly, tell, order, suggest or even imply that any potential witness in the same Federal court action or any potential court action lie, dissemble or shade the truth? Did the President use Federal employees, resources and others to deny, lie about and distort the truth? Did the President lie to the people of the United States?

Then, the question is, if any of these charges are true, do they amount to impeachable offenses?

Democrats trying to save their election-day necks are arguing that these charges don't amount to impeachable offenses. They say the Republicans are just fishing to embarrass the President and are trying to stretch out any Congressional inquiry for as long as possible, considering that President Clinton has but two years and some months left in his second and last term. Some Democrats complain that the superior numbers of Republicans will carry the day and an inquiry will go forward because the Republicans are so partisan. They complain that the Republicans are unfair and are out to embark on a witchhunt.

The Republicans counter with—they are only following the Democrat's model from the Nixon Watergate Impeachment Inquiry of 1973-1974. Democrats are trumped.

The Inquiry goes on with support from enough Democrats to make the Inquiry "Bi-partisan." The first vote taken by the full House was 363 to 63 to release all of the evidence by September 28th that Ken Starr turned over to the House. All 63 of the No votes were Democrats, all of the Democratic leadership and two thirds of the Democrats voted with all Republicsns on the matter of information release.

The official Inquiry will come and it will take time. The country will suffer, not from the process, but from Democratic whining and crying about the process of impeachment and partisanship. They will accuse the Clinton-haters among the people of being part of a right-wing conspiracy to bring the President down. They will so accuse the

Republican Party. They will accuse all except the one person responsible for the tortuous thousand national cuts, President Clinton.

Regardless of how the official Inquiry turns out, regardless of whether or not the House votes for the impeachment of President Clinton and regardless of whether the Senate convicts the President if he is impeached, the United States of America will survive, even if the man responsible does not. We have survived much more than l'affaire Clinton.

> **"Mine eyes have seen the glory of the coming of the Lord.**
> **"He is trampling out the vintage where the grapes of wrath are stored.**
> **"He hath loosed the fateful lightning of His terrible swift sword.**
> **"His truth is marching on."**

FREE-THINKING HISPANICS ARE RARE IN CONGRESS

Raoul Lowery Contreras
August 10, 1998

The stereotypical Mexican or Puerto Rican peasant stands, straw hat in hand, eyes glued to the ground, humbly responding "Sí PATRON, to his master, the master of his hacienda, his life, and his world. We've seen this scene in countless Hollywood and Mexican movies. Some of us have seen it in real life and been pained by the experience of our humble paisanos.

We saw this scene in Washington just minutes ago when 17 Mexican American and Puerto Rican Democratic congressmen met with embattled President William Jefferson Clinton, alleged perjurer, obstructionist of justice, suborner of perjury and adulterer and pledged their support of him "no matter what." These guys (including one woman) look and sound like Mexican fascistic ruling party (PRI) supplicants in the extreme. They sound like PRI dinosaurs; they sound like PRI thugs.

Whatever they look and sound like, they demonstrably do not represent the entire Hispanic population in anything, much less the bleeding President's affaire'd Monica. After all, they don't represent all Hispanic congressmen either.

They didn't, for example, unanimously support the most important Mexican-American issue in recent history, the North American Free Trade Agreement. Several sold out to the AFL/CIO and opposed it. Two Cuban-origin Congressmen voted against it because they don't approve of the Mexican/Cuban connection.

Of the 17-Clintonistas, not a one of them voted for welfare reform, claiming that welfare reform would hurt Hispanics. Clinton signed the Republican bill anyway. All of them voted to raise taxes on Middle-America despite the deep wounds it inflicted on October 1, 1993 on the poorest of the poor. What? Yes, Clinton, the 17-Clintonistas and the largest tax increase in history plunged the American Hispanic into more poverty than it had experienced in decades. In fact, for the first time in memory, according to the Clinton Labor Department, the percentage of Hispanics in poverty outnumbered the Black poor.

IT'S THE POVERTY, STUPID!

Consider this: From 1987-1992 (The Reagan-Bush years), including the worst recession in 50-years, the number of Hispanic-owned business increased 300% and ran 75% greater growth than non-Hispanic business formations did during the same time. Moreover, because of the momentum built up during those years, it appears that the rate continues. Huge immigration from Mexico and other south-of-the-Rio Grande countries brought many poor to America. One would have thought that Hispanic poverty would have increased during those years reflecting immigration, but it didn't. During the Reagan-Bush years, the poor immigrant numbers were matched by former poor immi-grants bursting into the middle class, leaving poverty behind..

The poverty level remained constant despite voluminous immigration. Until, that is, Clinton became President. Hispanic poverty surged 20% in the first three years of Clinton.

Nonetheless, retiring California congressman Esteban Torres says, "No matter what, we stand with the President to the end." This sounds like a Mexican PRI thug politician standing by fraud and felony for the sake of "party". Torres, a former United Auto Worker union official, is not alone. Harvard-trained California Congressman Xavier Becerra says, "The President we believe is doing the right thing."

Unfortunately, many people in the media and thus the population think that these 17-Clintonistas represent the entire Hispanic popula-tion in the U.S., all 30-million of them. Not true.

They don't represent anyone who agrees with this article, or who shares a Spanish-surname with me. Nor do they represent the scores of His-panic Republicans who are running for public office throughout the country. Nor, I think, do they represent all Hispanic Democrats. Democrats usually hold back on criticizing President Clinton, even when they suspect he is lying and has committed "high crimes and mis-demeanors". But, reason dictates that they hold back full-endorse-ments of a President under fire until all the facts are on the table.

It seems to me that Torres, Becerra and the other 15-Hispanic Demo-cratic Congressman have betrayed their oath of office to "protect and defend the Constitution against ALL enemies, foreign and domestic" by pledging their total support to a man who might have committed egregious felonies, plus betrayed his wife and daughter by sexually involving himself with a twenty-one-year-old girl.

That's why I posit that they have forsaken their constitutional responsibility. They are part of the unique 435 people who may be required to call into question Presidential actions that might be illegal in impeachment proceedings. The evidence is forthcoming from the Office of the Independent Prosecutor and must be dealt with by these very people who are proclaiming their fealty to the President, "no matter what."

A closed-mind on a political question is one thing; a closed-mind on a legal or impeachment question is another. It sounds like these men and woman will vote no on impeachment, if it comes to that, in the words of Congressman Torres, "NO MATTER WHAT..."

And, "no matter what", they make it sound that all Hispanics support the President during these self-induced troubles. They don't, "no matter what."

THE NATION IS LARGER THAN PRESIDENT WILLIAM JEFFERSON CLINTON AND LARRY FLYNT

Raoul Lowery Contreras
January 20, 1998

The coup d'état was carefully planned to take over the government of the United States from the big winners of the Presidential election of the previous year. The conspiracy was led by a handful of Congress people and the Congressional Black Caucus. The year, 1974.

Fortunately for the country, the Black Congressional Caucus and a gaggle of ultra-liberal New York City congressional representatives led by Elizabeth Holtzman, who combined to keep President Richard Nixon from appointing a Vice-President, failed. Felon Vice-President Spiro Agnew lost his job in a plea bargain for bribery. If they had succeeded, they would have denied the country a Vice-President for an impeached and removed from office President Nixon and the Presidency would have revolved to a Democrat, Senator Carl Alpert, thus completing America's first coup d'état and reversing the greatest electoral sweep in the country's history when Richard Nixon carried every state in the country except for Massachusetts. So says now a high-ranked Democrat lawyer for the Senate of 1974.

The conspiracy failed. This time the conspiracy of the day in Washington is highlighted by the shocking resignation of Speaker of the House designate, Robert Livingston, on the floor of the House just an hour or two before President William Jefferson Clinton's political career took a hit from which he might never recover, a solid impeachment vote of 228 to 205. Beverly Hills-based Larry Flynt, publisher of Hustler Magazine, is the chief conspirator to destroy America. He offered a million dollars to anyone who could prove sexual dalliances with Congress people and other high government officials.

Flynt aside, the President's hit came as a result his reckless behavior dotted with instant sexual gratification with a young woman just slightly older than his own daughter. Then, dozens of lies and cover-ups, plus a gigantic obstruction of justice by the President and his confidants, including Vernon Jordan, erstwhile Washington hot shot lawyer and the ever loyal sexual fixer for the President, and personal secretary Betty Currie, have all combined to bring the President to the brink of being removed from office.

"Mission accomplished", Jordan reported to President Clinton when he landed a good job for an unqualified Monica Lewinsky in the capitol of the world, New York City. Clinton's secretary Betty Currie collected subpoenaed articles of evidence from Lewinsky—on whose orders?—and hid them under her bed. Looks to me like jail time is forthcoming for Vernon Jordan and Betty Currie.

After the impeachment vote of 228 for and 206 against on Article One and a pure bipartisan vote of 221 for and 212 against on Article 3, the country lurched through the end of World War III against Iraq and listened to the President claim that Iraq's forces and potential had been "degraded" by at least "a year." VICTORY, Arkansas-style.

Just before he declared VICTORY over Iraq, the just-impeached President Clinton declared that he wanted a "reasonable" and "fair" resolution of his problem in the Senate before a Senate trial that is required by the Constitution. Funny as this was, funnier was his declaration for an end to the "politics of personal destruction." Or, as everyone in politics knows, POLITICS ARKANSAS-STYLE.

Since Clinton declared for the Presidency as a junior varsity Democrat in 1991 when Republican President George Bush was riding high, he has brought the slash and burn politics of Arkansas to the fore. Copying his historical mentor, Louisiana's larger-than-life Huey Long, dictatorial and ultra-corrupt governor and U.S. Senator, Clinton even tried to gather a round-robin letter in the U. S. Senate some months ago hoping to get 34 U.S. Senators to sign that they would never vote for removal of Clinton from the Presidency—no matter what. Long did that in Louisiana when he was impeached and he beat the rap with such a letter. Clinton, of course, failed in his copy-cat version of Long's letter.

So now, we are faced with a trial in the U.S. Senate in front of the staid and sober 100 men and women who run statewide to win office, rather than little volatile districts of 600,000 like the men and women who impeached the President. What will they do, these 100 men and women? Who knows?

But stirring up dust and mud in Washington is porno publisher, Larry Flynt of Hustler Magazine. The million-dollars he put out as rewards has already destroyed Representative Robert Livingston, now resigned Speaker-to-be and shuffled the House Republican leadership into new and untried hands. Flynt says he has more dirt on as many as ten Congressmen and that he will publish all this material in a forthcoming issue of his skin mag.

In a few words, thus, the government of the United States is in the hands of two men: One, whose career was destroyed by arrogance, deceit, lies, an unparalleled satyr-like appetite and a big-mouthed teeny-bopper-like Monica Lewinsky; and the other, a multi-millionaire publisher of double xx-rated pornography. What a country!

PART II

A HISPANIC VIEW OF THE POLITICS OF IMMIGRATION

15

THEY CAME TO FIGHT FOR AMERICA

WAR, DEATH AND CHOCOLATE
May 24, 1998

The train from El Paso, Texas, to Los Angeles was full of men in uniform. Sailors, soldiers and Marines, warriors all, were going to the Pacific to fight Imperial Japan. In November of 1943, the United States had been warring 23, almost 24-months.

I was on that train. I spoke not a word of English. For, you see, I had just crossed the border from the country of my birth, Mexico, to live in the country of my citizenship, the United States of America, a country at war with the greatest of all evils. I didn't know any of this then because I wasn't even three-years-old.

What I did know was that warriors laughed when I made funny faces and warriors gave me chocolate when they laughed. Thus, using the impeccable logic of an-almost-three-year-old, I wandered throughout the train making funny faces and making warriors laugh. I was full of chocolate the entire trip.

> *HERRERA, SILVESTRE S.*, Private First Class, U.S. Army, near Mertwiller, France, 15 March 1945. Born-El Paso, Texas. Medal of Honor citation…he made a 1-man frontal assault on a strongpoint and captured 8 enemy soldiers. Pvt. Herrera again moved forward, disregarding the danger of exploding mines, to attack the position.

He stepped on a mine and had both feet severed, but despite intense pain and unchecked loss of blood, he pinned down the enemy with accurate rifle fire.

"COMMIES INVADE SOUTH KOREA" was the newspaper headlines on June 25, 1950. I knew there was a war on that day, because my ice cream bar that cost a nickel the day before had doubled in price. At nine-and-a-half I knew that war brought higher prices, because I remembered WW II ration coupons and higher prices right after the war.

> **OBREGON, EUGENE ARNOLD**, Private First Class, U.S. Marine Corps, Seoul, Korea, 26 September 1950. Born—Los Angeles, California. Medal of Honor citation—Pfc. Obregon observed a fellow Marine fall wounded…Armed only with a pistol, he…dashed from his covered position to the side of the casualty. Firing his pistol with one hand as he ran, he grasped his comrade by the arm with his other hand…dragged him to the side of the road…when hostile troops began advancing…(Obregon) placed his own body as a shield in front of him and lay there firing accurately and effectively (with the wounded Marine's carbine) into the hostile(s) until he was fatally wounded…

I rode my bike past the little corner grocery store on the way to the 5th grade every morning. There, that morning, the newspaper headline screamed 'TRUMAN FIRES MACARTHUR." I turned and raced home to awake my father screaming my first political statement, "that son-of-bitch Truman fired General MacArthur." President Truman had fired our Korean War commander. My second political statement was my "I Like Ike" button in the 8th grade in 1952. Candidate General Eisenhower promised to "Go to Korea" to end the stalemated war. I knew he would if he won; he won and he did.

My first day in college was four months before I turned 18. When that birthday came, I left the house for my eight o'clock class, like I did every day. I came home later than usual, just as my three younger brothers and parents sat for dinner.

My Mother, noticing a little extra gusto in me, asked, "How was your day?" I replied, "Fine." Are you sure, she asked, "Yes, the day was very, very good." Why was it so good, she asked. "Because I joined the Marines today."

> ***JIMENEZ, JOSE FRANCISCO***, Lance Corporal, U.S. Marines Corps, Quang Nam Province, Viet Nam, 28 August 1969. Born-Mexico City, Federal District, Mexico. Medal of Honor citation—L/Cpl Jimenez reacted by seizing the initiative and plunging forward toward the enemy positions. He personally destroyed several enemy personnel and silenced an anti-aircraft weapon. He slowly maneuvered to within 10 feet of hostile soldiers who were firing automatic weapons...In the face of vicious enemy fire (he) destroyed the position...He continued to press forward...(until) he was mortally wounded.

All three of my Drill Instructors fought in the Korean War that ended just six years before the day I walked into Marine boot camp. They survived. 33,629 Americans were killed and 8,000 more were missing in Korea. Many of my boot camp sergeants and officers fought in World War II, as well. They survived. 293,986 Americans were killed.

In the toughest Boot Camp in the world, I had a question: Could I measure up to those who were fighting and dying for me when I was a little kid making faces for chocolate, or calling President Truman a son-of-a-bitch? How many of the Marine sergeants and officers around me lost friends on the islands of Guadalcanal and Tarawa or some anonymous numbered hill or the Chosin Reservoir in the place called Korea?

Later, I would study battles at Yorktown, Gettysburg, Little Big Horn, Belleau Wood, Iwo Jima, Normandy, Monte Casino, Inchon and Khe Sanh where Americans died. I salute them every day, every single day.

I wonder this Memorial Day how many of those laughing boys in uniform on the train I rode from El Paso to Los Angeles 23-months after Pearl Harbor, died for freedom, died for me.

16

RACIAL HATRED OF MEXICAN IMMIGRANTS

THE MEXICAN BORDER LOVE CONNECTION

By Raoul Lowery Contreras
July 16, 2000

Men in their sixties normally leave the work force behind, collect their retirement checks and Social Security, go fishing, play golf or ride their motor homes into the sunset. There are some men who don't have these opportunities, however.

Andres Ramos Diaz, 66, works at a nursery in North San Diego City, a stone's throw from the best high school in the county and multi-million dollar homes. He and a few other Mexicans live in a canyon (small valley), in plywood shanties. No rent makes the hard life worthwhile for the men get to send almost all their earnings (after taxes) home to Mexico, to their families. Some of the men, like Ramos Diaz, live just a few miles away in Tijuana, Mexico, but live in the canyon during the week in order not to go through a difficult commute.

There is no television, nor comfortable dens, fireplaces, toilets or soft sofas. This life is difficult for youthful Mexican workers, even for the illegals who come and go. These Mexicans are legal workers in the USA. Of course, their living quarters aren't exactly legal in McGonigle

Canyon and the City comes by from time to time to report the shanties to the private owners of the land.

Just six years ago, McGonigle Canyon was a place where some 750 mostly Mexican people, including 100 children, lived in plywood shacks. According to Lola Sherman of the San Diego Union/Tribune, the Canyon also had two restaurants, a grocery store and a medical clinic. Catholic priests drove into the "village" and offered mass, even married people in McGonigle. Then, the hammer fell and the City went in to the Canyon and leveled the "homes" of almost a thousand people. With an army of television cameras and reporters on hand, the City was careful and made sure no violence occurred.

If only the City had continued to make sure no violence was directed at innocent Mexicans, legal residents and legal workers, here in the good old USA. On the day after this year's 4th of July celebration, July 5, there were no San Diego Police, or Border Patrol "Agents," or any of Janet Reno's finest around when some 6-8 shorthaired non-Hispanic whites drove into the Canyon.

With their vehicle, they chased Ramos Diaz and three other men (one 68-years-old), shooting the men in the back with pellet rifles. The shorthaired "white" men jumped out of their fashionable Sports Utility Vehicle and with clubs and pellet rifles assaulted the four men, sending one of them, the 68-year-old, to the hospital. No arrests have been made.

That, however, may change soon. The quintessential driving American force has entered the picture and we might expect some action soon. Money, fifteen thousand dollars ($15,000), has been offered in rewards for information leading to the arrest and conviction of these shorthaired non-Hispanic whites. The reward comes from the local Crime Stoppers ($1000), $4,000 from Latino leaders and organizations, $5,000 from the Anti-Defamation League and another $5,000 from non-Hispanic San Diego City Councilman Byron Wear.

We won't call these young men, "Skinheads" for now because we don't have them in custody, but why am I not surprised that the attackers were described by their victims as young Anglo men with short hair, mostly blonde.

In Texas, two non-Hispanic whites are being charged with murder of Mexicans for the crime of trespassing on private property. The fact the Mexicans were illegals has nothing to do with the charges of murder, for murder is murder. The last time I looked "deadly force" is not authorized for the simple act of trespassing

In Arizona, a place were a Border Patrol "agent" was found not-guilty of murdering an unarmed Mexican by shooting him in the back, then letting him bleed to death, armed "ranchers" are "arresting" illegals as they cross the border and handing them over to Border Patrolmen. Apparently the "ranchers" have strayed off their properties and stopped cars on public highways—at gunpoint—and called in the incompetent and ineffective United States Border Patrol.

Like Texas and McGonigle Canyon, violence is close in Arizona. In Texas, the murderers are being prosecuted by Governor Bush's criminal justice system. In McGonigle Canyon, police are investigating and looking for the attackers. In Arizona, Time Magazine idolizes the ranchers. In California, extreme and fanatical Mexican-haters, supporters of Pat Buchanan for President, a handful of about 250 people (out of 32-million people), honor anti-Mexican, anti-immigration hysteria on the 4th of July.

Fanatic Mexican-haters parade around Los Angeles on the 4th of July, honoring gun-toting "patriot Arizona ranchers" and the next day, two-hours away by Interstate-5, shorthaired non-Hispanic white males attack Mexicans legally in the country for the crime of being Mexican, even 66 and 68 years-old defense-less Mexicans. Is there a connection?

(NOTE: Six teenaged boys from the $300-400,000 Rancho Penasquitos housing area, and the sons of upper-middle-class, educated households were arrested for the assaults. One of the boys is the son of a Cuban American Naval officer. They were charged as adults and were the test cases for a new California law that permitted such minors to be charged as adults. They lost in the State Supreme Court and pleaded out their felonies. They all received jail time and probation. Their parents all settled out multi-million dollar lawsuits. The city was enraged at the assaults and everyone was satisfied with the jail time and the money that changed hands. None of the Sixtyish Mexican men will ever have to work again and the six boys, now young men, will live with felony convictions the rest of their lives. There was no connection with the anti-immigrant fanatics of Los Angeles and Glenn Spencer. The boys stated they did it to have fun. The anti-illegal fanatics justified the attacks by, "Boys will be boys.")

THE WICKED WITCH OF THE WEST AND ILLEGALS

Raoul Lowery Contreras
May 20, 1998

They use the World Wide Web; radio talk shows; letters-to-the-editor; writers quote them in books and articles; and, now they're using an old-fashioned billboard. They are small in numbers but noisy.

The billboard sits alongside Interstate 10 just inside the California border. The billboard is sponsored by the woman who screenwriters had in mind when they wrote about the Wicked Witch of the West. She is Ms Barbara Coe, founder of the California Coalition for Immigration Reform (CCIR) and the mother of the Save Our State Initiative otherwise known as the constitutionally stillborn Proposition 187.

The billboard reads:

"WELCOME TO CALIFORNIA, THE ILLEGAL IMMIGRATION STATE... DON'T LET THIS HAPPEN TO YOUR STATE CALL TOLL FREE (877) NO ILLEGALS"

Let's examine the problem here. Yes, there are illegals in California, probably more than in the rest of the country. Yes, there are probably five-million or more illegals in the country and many of them are from Mexico. Yes, most illegals work and they generally work at dirty, low pay jobs in the cities, or at back-breaking jobs in the fields, orchards, slaughter houses or poultry factories. Yes, it's illegal for employers to hire them. And, yes, illegals are illegal because they haven't spoken with an Immigration officer on entering the U.S. They, however, are not here in a vacuum.

Given all this, do they steal jobs from Americans? How many blonde, blue-eyed suburban boys does the reader see picking strawberries, peaches, or walnuts? How many Black inner-city kids does the reader see picking lettuce, grapes, or oranges? How many blonde or Black kids do we find in hot, miserable restaurant kitchens? How many Black or blonde kids do we find working in slaughterhouses, or in the poultry factories in Arkansas? How many do we see digging ditches, pouring concrete and hanging drywall? And, it doesn't matter who used to do these jobs, it only matters who does them now and who will do them in the future.

Now, do these jobs need to be done? Do clothes have to be cut and sewn? Of course they do. Surprise, hi-tech industries need low-pay workers as well. In a three-year long study of future demand for low-pay jobs in our economy, Dr. Wayne Cornelius of the University of California at San Diego concluded that our hi-tech, highly-productive economy will need low-pay, low-skill workers for as far as the economic eye can see.

Given that, where do we get these workers? Consider San Diego County, we have 3-per cent unemployment and our hi-tech industry, alone, has five-thousand job openings. In the country there are 120-million or so people working and perhaps 2-million or more jobs available every day. There are an estimated 346,000 good-paying hi-tech jobs going begging in the U.S., according to the LA Times. If every single illegal is working and there are still two or more million jobs open every day, who is being deprived?

Any argument that certain low-skill uneducated Americans are being deprived doesn't hold water either, for we have the statistics that show March unemployment in California was slightly over 5-per cent for Whites and double that for Blacks. Right in the middle of these percentages are Hispanics and Asians. As most illegals are Mexican or Asian and if all illegals were working and taking jobs from Americans, no Hispanics or Asians would be unemployed amd more Whites would be unemployed, but that isn't the case. Besides, these numbers co-exist with huge shortages of teachers, police officers, hi-tech workers and of convenience store clerks, etc..

Jobs are going begging, even with hundreds of thousands, maybe millions of illegals around. So, "THEY KEEP COMING", to quote one of California Governor Pete Wilson's high-class TV campaign ads, for jobs. The number of available jobs demonstrates that we need them, for they will do work no one else will, no matter the pay—unless you can see the suburban blonde boy or the inner-city Black boy on his hands and knees for ten hours a day picking strawberries. Can anyone see our precious teenaged daughters (mine's 21) forsaking the malls to work in badly-lit, unventilated, un-air conditioned fire-trap clothing factories ten—twelve hours a day sewing, making the clothes for other girls to buy in the malls?

The Wicked Witch of the West would have us believe that there are plenty of Americans around to do necessary work. She would have us believe that jobs are being stolen from Americans. Can she prove that? No, and neither can anyone else.

If the Wicked Witch of the West and her fellow-traveler-anti-immigrants really had the best interests of California and the country in mind, their billboard at the state line would read:

**WELCOME TO CALIFORNIA,
WE HAVE PLENTY OF DIRTY JOBS...
PAY $200 FOR A WORK PERMIT
AND GO TO WORK LEGALLY,
WE NEED YOU!**

A CRYPTO-RACIST SPAWNS HATRED

By Raoul Lowery Contreras
August 7, 2000

When too many non-Hispanic white (Anglo) teenagers were sent to prison for marijuana possession, Anglo state legislators responded quickly to California's Anglo majority. They changed the law to make possession of one ounce or less of marijuana a ticket offense, an infraction with no jail time. That is the War on Drugs.

When more people drove faster than 55-miles-per-hour on America's highways, the speed limit went up to 70-mph. Changing the law is common when too many people, certain, chosen people, violate existing law.

When special interests run the White House, the American President violates the law whenever he pleases. For example, in 1846 President Polk sent American soldiers to invade Mexico, all to draw Mexican fire. Goals: bully a weak neighbor, steal California and the Southwest, all to extend slavery. Congressman Abraham Lincoln objected vehemently to President Polk's immorality and duplicity.

More recently, The Kennedy Administration covered up a sexual dalliance between a beautiful East German Communist spy and President John F. Kennedy. Another Kennedy dalliance with a Mafia moll was covered up for years. The Nixon Administration (1969-1974) violated wholesale laws and the Constitution, not for money, as in President Harding's administration, nor to cover up illicit sex as in William Jefferson Clinton's administration, but to "combat" a security threat to the United States by free love Anglo teenaged dope-smoking hippies.

Law and order is a squishy proposition under the best of circumstances.

For example, I am criticized for "encouraging" illegal aliens from Mexico. Not true. Yes, I support illegal aliens because I don't want them to die or be injured for the singular purpose of wanting to pick our crops, wash our dishes, or be our bus boys. I hold that view for all people, of all races and nationalities, no matter where they are or want to be. I don't encourage anyone to cross the border illegally. I encourage honest work, honest. This is a conflicting juxtaposition.

The real question is, do we need these people to work in this country? The answer is a resounding irrefutable yes! Thus, if we need the workers and they are willing to work and employers are willing to hire them for honest work—what is the problem?

This is the true free market. Willing employers and willing workers are at the core of our free enterprise system. If, therefore, anyone interferes with that system, they are interfering with the core of America. Such people are subversives of the worst sort, for they rip into the finest economic system in the world for reasons other than economic, say, "law and order," ethnicity and/or race.

I totally support our American system of free enterprise. I support people willing to work and people willing to hire them. Between these two legitimate economic parties exist laws that simply don't work, laws written by people who haven't a clue about free enterprise. Our former Guest Worker exchange program with Mexico was killed by pressure from Cesar Chavez and the AFL/CIO unions for the benefit of a union, not farm workers, or farm owners, nor the country. The entire illegal alien problem we have today can be laid at the feet of Cesar Chavez, the AFL/CIO and John Fitzgerald Kennedy, who killed the program through his Labor Department to pay off labor unions.

As stated, law and order is a squishy proposition. Bad laws make bad order. People with bad motives to match bad laws support bad laws. America revolted and expelled the British because of bad laws.

One Mister Doug Bell writes in a letter to San Diego's North County Times that I am "invincibly ignorant of the threat to our nation's democratic pluralism and culture posed by continued mass immigration from Mexico, and also of the growing irritation, disgust and even hatred of Americans not by the senseless violence of teenage boys in (San Diego) or by the courageous Arizona ranchers protecting their land and our border, but by the galling ethnocentric double standards of crypto-racists like Contreras."

Whoops, his hatred is now my fault, not the 150 years of Mexicans being treated like dogs by many in this country. John Steinbeck had it right 60 years ago. For pointing out how badly native-born Mexican Americans were treated in his California, White Californians shunned Steinbeck for his expose of the deep racism he saw all around him. I pick up the struggle and Mr. Bell and his people blame me for their hatred. They blame me for hatred decades long and old. What a laugh!

Bigots choke with anger because I defend free enterprise, and because I defend people who want to work and people who want to hire them. Bigots choke with anger because I defend Mexicans. Bigots choke with anger at the mention of my name. I say change the laws that keep honest workers from working, honest employers from hiring and the American free enterprise system from functioning properly and freely.

Change bad laws now! By the way, it is a badge of honor to be criticized ("crypto-racist") for supporting honest hard working people without a voice of their own.

17

GUESTWORKERS

THE GUEST WORKER NEED

Raoul Lowery Contreras
February 21, 2002

The dumbest misrepresentation of reality since President Clinton stated he never had sexual relations with "that woman," Monica Lewinsky, is in these words by Ira Mehlman, paid spokesman for the Federation of Americans for Immigration Reform (FAIR):

"We (FAIR) don't see any evidence of a labor shortage that would warrant a guest-worker program," stated Mehlman, who continued that there was no evidence to support legalizing undocumented immigrants. He made these statements in response to a reporter's inquiry after a farm Worker's Union spokesman demanded that American farmers support a legalization program for undocumented farm workers.

Now, let's examine this FAIR position as expressed by Mr. Mehlman.

The State of California has studied the farm worker force in California and concluded that 90% or so were born in Mexico. The federal Labor Department estimates that half of the nation's 1.7 million farm workers are illegal aliens, mostly all from Mexico. That estimate accounts for about 850,000 illegal alien workers. The Census Bureau is now estimating that there "might" be 8-9-million illegal aliens in the country. Of those, Border Patrol arrest statistics indicate that 20% might be women and children. Thus, as many as 6.4 million illegals of the male persuasion might be in the work force, mostly, in fact working, working in every state and locality of the country..

Subtract out those illegal workers and what might we find in the labor market? How about CHAOS?

Specifically, let's look at San Diego and Orange Counties in California (the 9th and 10th largest counties in the country). Both counties have unemployment rates around 4%. In both San Diego and Orange Counties, estimates have well over 120,000 illegal alien workers in each county.

Thus, if they weren't here, approximately ten percent of the existing work forces would disappear, as would their economic production. The tourism and hospitality industries would collapse for everyone knows that few, if any, of the busboys and housekeeping staffs of hotels are legal. Everyone knows that restaurant dishwashers and many waiters and waitresses aren't legal. Everyone knows that landscaping company staffs are rarely legal. Everyone knows that most "criadas" of children, nannies to the English, in California, Arizona, New Mexico, Colorado, Texas and myriad other places are rarely legally in the country. And, everyone knows that almost every single farm worker one sees working in these states is rarely legally in the USA.

Everyone knows this except Ira Mehlman, paid spokesman for the anti-immigrant FAIR.

Mehlman says that "legalizing" illegal workers would encourage more illegal immigration. Is he right? No. No one comes if there are no jobs. Jobs are the magnet. If there are jobs, then, there must be a labor shortage, for there can be no other conclusion.

The data Mehlman and FAIR say doesn't exist, does exist and exists in every county where there are any illegal immigrants. Count the number of jobs, then subtract the estimates of illegal aliens in that market-place and one will almost always come up with negative numbers. It does not take a rocket scientist to figure out the situation. But, then again, neither FAIR nor their spokesmen ever look at real facts, nor are they rocket scientists.

Let's make it clear: If there are illegal aliens working in a community, there is, logically, a labor shortage, or they wouldn't be working. If half of the nation's farm workers are illegal aliens, that means there is a labor shortage of almost a million people willing to do farm work. Now, what part of that doesn't FAIR and Ira Mehlman understand?

A RESIDENT IS A RESIDENT

Raoul Lowery Contreras
February 4, 2002

A prison convict gets a $100,000 heart transplant and nothing is heard from citizens who decry certain children being educated. In contrast, note the hue and cry from those who object to the University of California/California State University System charging normal tuition to California residents, no matter their "legal status."

But, what the heck, the convicted criminal is a "legal" resident of California. Never mind that he is a convicted felon—he is "legal." Because he's legal, his children are allowed to go to school, get medical benefits, attend college with lower tuition, receive financial aid and scholarships and receive all the welfare benefits they can find. Never mind that the convict is costing us $40,000 per year in keeping him behind bars and that he doesn't pay taxes. He and his fellow "legal" resident prisoners cost us billions of dollars. In fact, studies show that the average felon costs us $100,000 in losses and insurance claims per before he even goes to prison. And, please, 85% of our state prisoners are "legal residents" or citizens, not illegal aliens.

And, I see no one calling for denial of schools, food stamps, welfare assistance, medical assistance, college scholarships and financial aid, in-state tuition at the State University, driver's licenses, et al., for children of the 85% of California state prison inmates who are "legal" residents.

I do see a United States Supreme Court decision (Plyler v. Doe, 1982) that clearly stated that all children required by law to attend school must be educated no matter their "legal" resident status. The decision also stated that this country does not punish children for the sins of their fathers.

It specifically noted that children couldn't choose the country they live in, nor were they guilty of any crime if their parents sneaked them across the border. In the Plyler decision, the court also observed that illegal aliens were "persons" (they breathe, don't they, asked Justice Brennan).

The Court, despite having the opportunity to change Plyler when Proposition 187 was challenged in the courts, showed no interest in doing so. The Supreme Court could have faxed a note to the Federal district court ordering it to send the 187 case directly to it, but it didn't. It didn't because there are not five votes on the Supreme Court to overrule the Plyler decision, period.

Given, then, that children from Kindergarten through 12th grade have normal access to schools, why shouldn't the same kids have normal access to the University? Specifically, why should youngsters who attend California schools for three years and graduate from them pay the same tuition as someone from Arizona who has never paid a nickel in California taxes?

Kudos to California and Texas for making such access the law.

Remember this, a youngster who attends California schools for three years and graduates from one is a resident and a California taxpayer, as well. Graduates from Arizona or Alabama high schools are not until they have lived in California for a year.

It doesn't matter if the kid was brought into the country illegally. A resident is a resident. Resident tuition is for taxpaying state residents. Nonresident tuition is for students who didn't attend state schools and didn't pay state taxes. Immigration or citizenship status has absolutely nothing to do with the question

GRADUATES WITHOUT HOPE

Raoul Lowery Contreras
May 28, 2001

What are we to do about illegal aliens? If they are Arab princesses smuggled into the country by a U.S. Marine boyfriend, they are allowed to stay to avoid embarrassment for the Immigration and Naturalization Service (INS). At the very moment that the princess was walking across the border into Mexico to finalize a pre-arranged deal to reenter the country legally, 16 Mexicans were dying of thirst in the Arizona desert.

What's wrong with that picture?

Dead bodies strewn across the desert by evil gods, helped by coy-oh-tehs, smugglers who abandoned the 16 without water, are not a pretty picture. Neither is the thought of people so desperate to get to America that they are willing to endanger their very lives. Neither is the thought of those who object to lessening the problem of illegal aliens by passage of a simple, yet thorough, guest worker program.

Let's see—is it true that there are more illegals in the country than previously thought? It appears to be so. If so, can it be that much of the huge productivity increases (and prosperity) of the 90s can be attributed to these millions of hard working people that no one knew were even in the country? Maybe and probably true. Are detractors correct in claiming that illegals have taken away, or stolen, jobs from poor job-less Blacks? There is no data to support this claim. Are illegal aliens draining the public treasury? There is no data to support this claim that is accurate or based on facts.

Specifically, let's look at how illegal alien children are treated by our system. The pertinent and unchallenged law of the land on illegal children and education, was decided by the United States Supreme Court in 1982 (Plyler v. Doe). Illegal alien children are here through no fault of their own, the Court stated. They cannot be charged with their father's crime, the Court stated. These children are "persons" as stated in the Constitution's 14th Amendment and, thus, cannot be discriminated against by virtue of whether or not they are in the country legally. These children, then, can go to school from kindergarten through high school graduation.

But, what happens when they graduate?

California has passed laws prohibiting these kids from attending state public colleges paying resident tuition rates. One must keep in mind that if a kid graduates from high school and attended California schools for years, some for their entire lives, they always were considered "residents" as defined by the California Constitution. That is, if you lived in California for a calendar year, you were a "resident" for tuition purposes. That was changed in order to deem any such youngsters as "non-residents" so that they must pay "non-resident" tuition which is usually three or four times resident tuition.

Texas thwarted such deviousness by simply passing a law that Mexican nationals could attend Texas public colleges by paying resident tuition even if they actually lived in Mexico.

Enter Democratic Congressman Howard Berman from Los Angeles. He has introduced a bill into Congress that would define "resident" for college tuition purposes as anyone who graduates from high school in the United States and can prove that he or she attended school for the previous four years, for a total of five consecutive years. This is a good bill and deserves support of all who relish education and support kids who want education.

Let's look at the logic of the bill. If a kid is in the country for five years before he or she graduates from high school, are they any different than their schoolmates who were born here and graduate in the same class? No.

The difference is but one little piece of paper, a birth certificate. For example, is this illegal alien kid a taxpayer? Yes. Are his parents taxpayers? Yes. Are they residents, parents and kids, of California? Yes. Are they "legal" residents? No. If they are taxpayers and live in California aren't they plain and simple residents? Yes. Thus, they should pay exactly what "legal residents" pay, no more, no less.

Their tax dollars help support the public college system. To deny these kids who want to attend college equal treatment is illogical and, in fact, criminal. Their parents have mightily toiled to help propel California into the forefront of all states and most countries economically. Their parents have paid every tax the reader pays. Their parents have been insulted and defamed by their critics, even as some lie dead in the Arizona desert.

On the other hand, the princess watches her story in a made-for-television movie, gets her "green card" despite breaking dozens of immigration laws and her smuggler husband got a "Do not go to jail card" from the Marine Corps. Any other Marine would spend years in jail for what this young man did, but then what would Hollywood do with that story?

The former Marine and former princess will live happily ever after in Las Vegas just north of were Mexicans die coming to America—like the princess, illegally.

(NOTE: The Princess married, then divorced the former Marine and returned home to the Middle East, unharmed at last reports despite her claims of potential harm from her Arab Muslim family if she was not allowed to stay in the United States. After the divorce, her former Marine boyfriend dropped out of sight, hopefully embarrassed beyond measure for his teenaged silliness and so-called love affair.)

IS PRESIDENT BUSH "VOMIT"?

Raoul Lowery Contreras
January 27, 2002

Ernesto Gutierrez rises before dawn six days a week in Tijuana, Mexico, and starts an hours-long commute to one of the richest communities in America, Rancho Santa Fe. On San Diego's northern border, Rancho Santa Fe's average home has many bedrooms, acres of land and a value in excess of $2,000,000.

Gutierrez has been making that legal commute for 19-years to work at a gas station in Rancho. He credits good pay, good customers and good employers for his longevity. Though he spends little time with his family, what with not arriving home until 8:30 or 9:00 p.m., his children make it worthwhile. He proudly talks about his 18-year old son who is studying to be a lawyer; his 15-year old aspiring to medicine and who goes to work every Saturday with his father.

On the other side of the country, President George W. Bush proposes to cut eligibility time for food stamps for immigrants in half to five years. Until 1996, legal immigrants were eligible for food stamps without a waiting period. President Clinton signed the anti-immigrant bill he supported that was passed by a hysterically anti-immigrant Republican Congress. Attackers of the Bush proposal claim to be conservatives, but are not really, but rather, just plain anti-immigrant fanatics.

"It's plain to see that the president has chosen to steal a page from the Democrats' playbook," said Rep. Tom Tancredo, chairman of the House Immigration Reform Caucus (less than 50 adherents).

"His attempt to expand our political base through surrendering to the Hispanic vote is usually the Democrats' job. Votes can't be bought with welfare," states Tancredo, R-Colo.

President Bush plans to restore food stamps to legal immigrants who've served in the U.S. military, or those who have been in the country—and paying taxes—for at least five years.

"This is election year pandering to ethnic voting blocs, plain and simple," charged Dan Stein, executive director of the Federation for American Immigration Reform (FAIR), which advocates immigration limited to small numbers of whites-only. Michigan doctor John tanton founded FAIR with almost a million-dollar contribution from the Pioneer Fund, a non-profit foundation organized by American Nazi Party founder, Harry Laughlin.

"The sensible political thing to do is to cut immigration levels and change the immigration policies that allow far too many (non-blonde, blue-eyed) people to settle here who lack the skills necessary to make it on their own," Stein says, despite empirical data that proves him wrong. Many studies prove that when "refugees" from places like Africa (Blacks) and Bosnia (Whites) are deducted from immigrant status, welfare usage among real immigrants is below that of native born Americans.

Here is more Blah, Blah: "That Amnesty Proposal—Ruling Class Returns To Its Vomit (Again) by Sam Francis." Francis, who claims to be an American, writes: "With the unemployment rate pushing 6 percent and Ford announcing it will close four plants in the United States and lay off more than 21,000 workers, a light bulb flashed on somewhere in the nether depths of the Bush administration."

Francis: "Not only is the Stupid Party (Republicans) reversing its own achievement in welfare reform but also it's encouraging even more illegal immigration by aliens who will now have an incentive to gain amnesty, live here for the requisite length of time and get food stamps. By now it ought to be clear that the Republicans have entirely abandoned even the pretense of representing the American working and middle class voters who gave their party landslide victories in the 1970s and '80s. In their place, the Republicans plan to capture the elusive butterfly of the Hispanic vote.

Recent surveys conclude that 89% of Hispanics support the President and more Americans believe that the "Stupid Party," the Republicans, can defend the country better and provide better economics than Democrats. It appears that Mr. Francis and his gang are wrong again, "Vomit" and all. Proof: Ernesto Gutierrez.

(NOTE: The "elusive" Hispanic vote elected George W. Bush President, not Sam Francis and his candidate Pat Buchanan. As for food stamps, just how many immigrants come here for food stamps, Mr. Francis? Tell us. Show us. Prove it. Francis emotes about the "American working and middle class voters" who gave Republicans "landslide victories" in the '70s and '80s. Weren't they the same people who abandoned President Bush, the 41st? Weren't they the very people who gave us William Jefferson Clinton in 1992 and Jimmy Carter in 1976? Yes, they were. Despite their lack of support across the board, Bush was elected, elected by Hispanics.)

IS FAIR FAIR?

Raoul Lowery Contreras
February 13, 2002

Once again, the paid mouthpiece of the Federation of Americans for Immigration Reform (FAIR) has hit the editorial pages with another attack on this writer. They would never level such an attack if my name was Smythe, but it is not.

Dan Stein, a former Reagan Administration official and now highly-paid President of FAIR writes: "Demagogues can be found at the fringes of every political debate and the one that surrounds U. S. immigration policy is no exception. One of the most strident of these demagogues is Raoul Lowery Contreras, an open-borders advocate whose invective and blatant misrepresentation aimed at those who oppose him is featured…"(fill in the name of this newspaper).

Further, Stein writes, "The overwhelming majority of advocates for reduced immigration are motivated by this belief that mass immigration does not serve the long term interests of the nation or its citizens. However, many Americans are hesitant about expressing opposition to mass immigration because there are those, like Contreras, who instead of using persuasion, they try to silence their opponents. The unfortunate result of the human response to unpleasantness is that demagogues win."

Notice, please, that Stein mentions not a single specific, nor any proof that challenges any position I take.

Let's see if he can dispute these facts:

By an amazing coincidence, the numbers of immigrants annually entering the USA happen to match the number of children who were aborted twenty years before. Are immigrants filling a natural vacuum?

Economic data from Europe and Japan indicates that these areas and countries therein are contracting economically because their populations are aging and there are fewer young workers to replace the elderly and to support their welfare states. Japan is an economic basket case. It doesn't allow any immigration.

The American population is rapidly aging every day, week and month and only immigrants can replace it in the workplace and marketplace. In fact, isn't a disaster in the making when "baby-boomers" retire in a decade or so?

American workers are the most productive in the world and have become more productive in recent years as immigrant workers became more numerous. Coincidence?

Fed Chairman Alan Greenspan credits immigrants with keeping inflation down for a decade because they are productive and don't put wage pressure on the economy.

Federal income tax filings of FAIR report that the Pioneer Fund (a non-profit) founded by Harry Laughlin, founder of the American Nazi Party, provided the start up funds of almost a million dollars to FAIR founder Dr. John Tanton. Is this fact name calling?

The Pioneer Fund that provided the start-up of FAIR finances research into such esoteric studies as trying to relate black male penis size to crime rates. No respectable university accepts research funds from the Pioneer Fund, but FAIR does and has.

The New York Times reports that the Immigration and Naturalization Service has the highest percentage of employees convicted of crimes of any federal agency. These crimes include bribery, forgery and murder, sexual harassment and rape of immigrants.

The beef and poultry packing industries of the Midwest and South rely on immigrant labor, as do the very towns and states they exist in. Iowa, for example, is rapidly losing population as its native "white" population leaves for greener economic and social pastures, leaving ghost towns behind. The only people moving to Iowa are immigrants, mostly Mexican immigrants. The Iowa governor claims 250,000 jobs are going begging. Immigration critics conducted a survey and declared the Governor wrong. There are only 90,000 jobs going begging in Iowa.

President Ronald Reagan signed the illegal alien 1986 Amnesty act (sponsored by California Republican Congressman Dan Lungren) that foreshadowed the current efforts to "regularize" or "normalize" some of the illegals who have lived and worked in the country for years. State and local governments offer "amnesty" regularly for tax cheats and scofflaws. Why, then, are there objections to amnesty for illegals who work, pay taxes and live in the country?

President George W. Bush, many Congressmen of both parties, the AFL/CIO labor unions, the ecumenical churches, business and agriculture are campaigning for some sort of normalcy for these people who are taxpaying residents and working people. I agree with them wholeheartedly.

Need I point out that these facts are irrefutable and incontestable? So, who, in the final analysis is the demagogue, me, or Dan Stein of FAIR? Who is the demagogue, me, or the founder of FAIR, Dr. John Tanton, who was so labeled by Linda Chavez when she resigned from the very job Dan Stein now holds? Who is the embarrassment here, me, or Dr. Tanton who was so labeled by America's most trusted newsman, Walter Cronkite, when he resigned from FAIR's board? Are Chavez and Cronkite stupid open-border advocates, or demagogues?

Stein and FAIR object to my labeling them the "usual suspects" on immigration, but until they can refute the facts, they have motivations that are highly suspect. In fact, they are racist to the core and they prove it every time they open their mouths to espouse the slime they do. What's funny, is I just referred to them as the "usual suspects," not racists like they imply.

18

CRITICS, THE CENTER FOR IMMIGRATION STUDIES (CIS) AND GEORGE BORJAS

IMMIGRANTS AGAINST IMMIGRATION

By Raoul Lowery Contreras
July 31, 2000

When the Nazi Master Race people constructed death camps through-out Poland and Germany 60 years ago, inmate-police-functionaries enforced Nazi camp rules. They were called "kapos." Often, it was Jews policing Jews.

Today, a Cuban refugee immigrant, Dr. George Borjas, is the academic point man for the country's anti-immigrant movement. We have an immigrant demanding the demolition of American immigration policy, a demolition based on race and ethnicity.

Borjas (John F. Kennedy School at Harvard University), a former faculty member at the University of California, San Diego, is the academic messiah of the anti-immigrant movement in the United States. The movement is today's Know-Nothing Party that based its entire existence in the 1840s and 1850s on opposing immigrants and Catholics. Like the Know-Nothings, Borjas ignores facts in making policy suggestions, suggestions that become the ultimate "truth."

In his book, "Heaven's Door: Immigration Policy and the American Economy" Borjas states that current immigrants are less educated/skilled than native-born Americans. That statement is wrong. He uses Census data that includes illegal aliens, people the entire world knows are less educated and eager for farm work. RAND Corporation economist Jim Smith destroys Borjas with a study that found, "The median years of schooling for the LEGAL immigrants, 13 years, is a full one year higher than that of the U.S. native born."

Borjas, using Census data, claims that earnings of immigrants NEVER reach the level of the native-born. That is not true. According to economist Harriet Duleep of the Urban Institute and National Science Foundation senior analyst Mark Regets, immigrants have faster and larger wage growth (6.7 percent) than the native-born (4.4%) and any early negative difference in wages mostly disappears after ten years.

Borjas' argument is entirely bogus, by the way. According to Stuart Anderson, director of immigration policy for the United States Senate Immigration Subcommittee, Borjas deceivingly subtracts self-employed immigrants from his wage studies. Anderson, writing in Reason Magazine says, "If, out of 100,000 immigrants, 60,000 started restaurants and software firms, and 40,000 worked as waiters, Borjas would count only the wages of the 40,000 waiters. Moreover, if 10,000 of the waiters later started their own successful restaurants, Borjas would remove them from the calculations of immigrant earnings growth, thus further biasing the results downward." He doesn't do the same in stating native-born income. In other words, Borjas' immigrant wage calculations are intentionally misrepresented and miscalculated.

Borjas claims that immigrants are fiscal liabilities, based on his faulty interpretation of the massive study of the National Academy of Sciences (NAS) in 1997 that made such a claim insofar as California was concerned. Wrong, again, Borjas!

Ronald Lee, a UC Berkeley economist who prepared the NAS study told a U. S. Senate committee that the study did not reflect the true situation because of computer model problems. He says, "As for the fiscal impact of legal immigration, with the appropriate assumptions, a dynamic analysis would likely show that 49 of the states come out ahead, with the 50th, California, a close call."

Borjas and his adherents declare that immigrants cost us money. They don't.

Borjas states that immigrants don't add much to the American economy and do only when they lower native-born wages by accepting lower wages for traditional American jobs, like ditch digging and janitorial work. He further posits that immigrants would just as likely succeed in their own countries if they stayed there. Stuart Anderson writes in Reason Magazine, "In fact, immigrants come here precisely because oppressive political or economic policies block them from succeeding in their own countries. Anderson is as right as Borjas is wrong.

Further, Borjas ignores immigrant induced productivity, immigrant business formation and immigrant performance of jobs native-born refuse to do at any wage because, Borjas says, "They are difficult to quantify." Really?

The heaviest and most deceitful charge that Borjas makes is that the little educated native-born class suffers lower wages because of immigrants. That is blatantly untrue. Borjas claims that the true measure of this is the emigration of native-born from states that experience heavy immigration. But, Columbia University economist Francisco L Rivera-Batiz has proved that theory wrong. His studies show that where out migration can be measured, it is generally college educated who leave, not the-less-than-high-school class. In California, for example, there was a quantifiable out migration of college educated when the defense/ aerospace industry collapsed as the Cold War collapsed. What did that have to do with immigration?

Borjas thinks immigration should only be on a point basis of education and skills, but admits that if his imaginary point system was implemented, "most likely, the predominance of Mexican immigrants. will decline substantially."

Aha! So that's what is at the bottom of Borjas' proposed policies. In fact, he admits, if his point system was implemented, his own mother couldn't have immigrated to the USA from Cuba and she couldn't have brought four-year-old George Borjas with her (His education would have been an immigrant "cost").

Borjas takes us back to the same motive of the Ku Klux Klan in the Twenties and the German Nazis in the Thirties, race and ethnicity as policy. Borjas cannot escape his own words, nor can his supporters and sycophants

A STUDY BY BIGOTS

Raoul Lowery Contreras
July 16, 2001

Great news! The Washington, D.C. based Center for Immigration studies has released a study that unwashed, uneducated, thieves of American jobs AKA Mexican immigrants have lowered wages for the uneducated, unwashed, high school drop-out native-born Americans.

The Center's report is buttressed by immigrant and anti Mexican professor George Borjas. His views: Mexican immigrants may stay in poverty for a "hundred years" and may not assimilate or catch up to native-born Americans for a "hundred years." Reveling in this study and its findings. Borjas and the Center declare that Mexican immigrants cannot be compared to previous immigrant groups.

Why? They don't really answer that question in their study other than to point to some statistics that some Mexican immigrants never assimilate, never get educated and never rise above poverty. They also state that American consumer prices aren't lower because of cheap labor immigrants and that the cost of public services to these people is higher than the native-born, thus, they cost us money.

These exact conclusions about Mexican immigrants, to be precise, Mexican immigrants in poverty, were the same conclusions reached a hundred and fifty years ago by White Anglos Saxon Protestants when the whiff of the great unwashed millions of Irish Roman Catholics preceded their landing in New York, Boston and Baltimore. Given their lack of education, lack of good farming experience, lack of self-government and democratic skills, it appeared as late as 1900 that the Irish Americans would never rise above poverty, despite being in the USA for generations.

According to "THE IRISH IN AMERICA," in 1900 a German American 10 year old was 100 times more likely to graduate from high school than a similar Irish child. According to the Census, a California born Mexican American child is more likely to graduate from high school than a Scotch/Irish child in Appalachia. The center, its Research Director, "Dr. Steve Camarota (Italian?), and Cuban born Dr. George Borjas, forgot to mention these two salient facts in their news conference.

They also forgot to mention that Dr. John Tanton, also founder of the viciously anti-immgrant Federation of Americans for Immigration Reform (FAIR), founded the very Center that "conducted" this study. Tanton founded FAIR and this Center with money he raised from the Pioneer Fund (according to IRS documents). Harry Laughlin, founder of the American Nazi Party in the 1930s, founded the Pioneer Fund. The Fund supports research intended to prove racial inferiority of Blacks. For example, no accredited university will accept money from the Pioneer Fund since it funded a study of the relationship of penis size to criminality.

So, what can we conclude from the study, the Center for (anti) Immigration Studies, Dr. John Tanton and "academic" George Borjas? From the low road this study took, we can conclude that, in fact, Mexican immigrants are doing quite well when compared to previous immigrant groups. They can be compared to the Irish, who took a hundred years to mainstream, and the Italians who took three or four generations to mainstream.

The difference is that Mexican immigrants are getting far more education than the Irish did in their first 80 years in the country, or than the Italians did in their first 60 years in the country. There are perhaps a half million Mexican immigrants and children and grandchildren of Mexican immigrants attending college in California alone this year. That is definitely a greater number than all Irish immigrant college educated young people in the entire 80 years between 1840 and 1920. It is probably a greater proportion of the entire immigrant population between 1890 and 1920, the historical peak of European immigration. This is a good comparison because the bulk of Mexican immigration has occurred in the past thirty years.

Two other barometers contradict this study and George Borjas. After thirty years in the country did 30% of Irish immigrant citizens or Italian immigrant citizens register as Republicans like 30% of Mexican immigrant citizens have in California (according to a study in 2000)? No. After 30 years, were there enough Irish immigrant or Italian immigrant business founders around to count? No. Nonetheless, Hispanic businesses are being organized at three times the national average, today, with about 35% being organized by immigrants from Mexico.

Where, then, are we after this study was released? We are better off than ever. Mexican immigrants work hard, leave poverty faster than any immigrant group in history, put food on our table, work more productively than American high school dropouts and are helping their children become better educated faster than any immigrant group in history, sans Eastern European Jews and current Asian immigrants.

The Center for Immigration Studies prefers to study the lowest economic rung immigrants it can find, the least educated and to pretend this is a zero sum population. It predicts, with Gerorge Borjas cheer leading them on, that Mexican immigrants will never succeed and, thus, must be kept out.

The facts, however, don't bear them out. One salient fact is that similar groups to the Center made the same statements and declarations about the Irish, the Italians, the Jews a hundred years ago and look how history has proven them wrong. History will prove the Center and Gorge Borjas wrong, as well. Actually, it already has.

GIVE US YOUR SKILLED ARISTOCRATS, PLEASE...

Raoul Lowery Contreras
January 10, 2002

George Borjas, Cuban immigrant and current "intellectual darling" of the vociferous anti-Mexican, anti-anybody-but-white-immigrant not-so-secretive cabal takes another swipe at the very immigration policy that allowed he and his penniless and unskilled mother into the United States.

In a Washington *Post* opinion op-ed piece, Borjas says, (I, like Borjas, born in Latin America, respond in parenthesis) "What types of immigrants should this country admit? (Those who are willing to work and contribute to the national economy and well-being, regardless of skin color and national origin, contrary to what Borjas wants.) Borjas, "And how many immigrants does it (the USA) want? (Enough to keep us growing economically and to keep from choking on low birth rates like Europe and Japan, countries that are slowly dying economically.)

Borjas: "While the United States has proven curiously cautious about addressing such questions, several other "nations of immigrants" (including Canada, Australia and New Zealand) have far more proactive approaches to immigration: They have devised systems that are designed to favor people who will contribute economically to the country and who will assimilate quickly." (Needless to say, none of these—"proactive immigration states"—are shining economic lights that lead the world in any category of economic and/or political accomplishment…As for assimilation, baloney, every immigrant group to the USA assimilates…Hispanics are assimilating—like Borjas—faster than any previous non-English speaking immigrant group.)

He continues, "What justification is there, after all, for a policy that entitles a newly admitted immigrant to be eventually joined here by her sister's husband's father's brother's spouse? Yet, this is precisely the entitlement now enshrined in U.S. immigration policy—a policy that stresses family connections more than economic or security issues." (Why does Borjas ignore the history of Italian and Eastern European immigrants, who would gather resources to send one young man to America, who, in turn, would send for family members every time a steerage fare of ten dollars could be spared? Borjas also ignores the fact that descendants of Polish Jews earn more money than anyone else in this country—Polish Jews who came with nothing, without skills and brought their relatives in one by one-that's assimilation.)

Borjas says, "I believe we should make more of an effort to control the flow of population into this country—and to select those people who will benefit the United States. We'll never secure our borders completely. But we should do all we can to make sure we understand why we admit the people we do. (When America restricted immigration to White Northern European Protestants almost exclusively—in 1922, the country tolerated an entirely evil race segregation system and heavily bigoted policies against Catholics and Jews, and maintained millions of Ku Klux Klan members and groups...Does Borjas even know that?)

He concludes with, "Supporters of a more liberal immigration policy have claimed that some immigrants do jobs that natives do not want to do. Sept. 11 proved them right."

Borjas betrays his education and American citizenship with such stupid statements. American immigration policy and immigrants had nothing to do with September 11, nor with the hundreds of thousands of immigrants, mostly from Latin America, who toil daily in the fields, in factories, in Midwestern slaughter houses or poultry processing factories throughout the American South.

Borjas advocates restrictions on immigration that were used in America when an all-White and almost all Protestant Congress slammed the door shut on Eastern European Jews and Southern European Catholics in 1922. The founders of the American Nazi Party using the same words—assimilation, for example—George Borjas uses, convinced that Congress to slam the door.

The Borjas formula of restricting immigration didn't work in 1922 and it won't work now, or ever, if this country is to grow and prosper. More importantly, Borjas' restrictive immigration suggestions are clearly designed to stop immigration of Latin American and Asian people escaping political oppression and/or economic stagnation for opportunity and freedom.

What this country needs is a hard working immigrant willing to sacrifice to make a better life for his family and the country with skills, educational level and national origin being secondary to the fire in the belly most poor uneducated immigrants to the USA have had for 200 years. Neither juvenile Borjas nor his mother had any education, nor could they speak English when they arrived in this country as penniless refugees from Communist Cuba. Borjas certainly rose above his refugee status, just like so many millions of immigrants before and after him.

Borjas does not make any historical case to limit immigration by skill and education, much less a convincing one. He does, however, disguise white-only racism, intentionally or unintentionally.

THE RISE OF UNAMERICAN KNOW-NOTHINGS

By Raoul Lowery Contreras
March 23, 2000

What kind of society would we have in the United States if each individual city in it could decide who was an American citizen? We would have a society like Switzerland. If so, the United States of America would cease to exist as a constitutional republic and as the greatest country the world has ever seen.

Yes, Switzerland allows towns to approve foreigners who apply for Swiss citizenship. There is no national naturalization process in the tiny Swiss nation as most civilized countries have. Imagine Boston Protestants voting to allow Irish Catholics to become citizens in the 1800s. Or, imagine white Southerners voting on citizenship for black people. Or, imagine further, Texans voting on citizenship for former New Yorkers.

Each person applying for Swiss citizenship must list salary, tax status, personal background and hobbies on the application for citizenship. Personal information includes racial, religious and ethnic information. Here lies the rub. In Emmen, an industrial suburb of Lucerne, 48 people were just turned down by the town's electorate for citizenship. Only eight people were approved. They were all of Italian backgrounds. Almost all those turned down were from the Balkans, Bosnians mostly. What is the ethnicity of most of Emmen's electorate? Guess.

The basic population of Switzerland is made up of German, French and Italian-origin people who speak four different official languages, German, Italian, French and Romanesque. Swiss demographics mirror that of Germany and Italy and, absent immigration, the population is aging and shrinking. Sounds like the United States, where German and Anglo backgrounds predominate, where our native-born population is not reproducing itself and is getting older by the minute.

From 1990 until 1995, for example, according to the Census Bureau, the median age of the United States increased from 32.2 years to 35.2 years and is closer to 40 than not today. According to NBC News, an American turns 65 years of age every 12-seconds.

According to the New York Times (Elizabeth Olson), this local voting on citizenship is a test of the political strength of the right-wing anti-immigrant Swiss People's Party. "This is Swiss direct democracy," declared party member Urs Ischi. Push-ahw! Baloney!

"Direct democracy" may make sense in New Hampshire, but the Swiss must be suspected of ulterior motives. Switzerland's People's Party is a growing hard-right-wing movement that scapegoats immigrants with ethnic hatred and dislike rising from the depths of their souls. The same political process is working in ostracized Austria.

This is not new to Europe, or to the United States. The Know-Nothing Party in America flourished (six governors) in the mid-18th century as an anti-Catholic, anti-immigrant party. Noted former Ku Klux Klanner, David Duke, today, runs for office every election as an anti-immigrant candidate. Duke and his compatriots are fueled intellectually by the likes of anti-immigrant writers Peter Brimelow (Alien Nation) and Harvard's George Borjas.

Imagine if David Duke's hometown could vote on who could become a U.S. citizen. What would Serbian Chicago do if a Bosnian applied for U.S. citizenship? Would Spanish speaking El Cenizo, Texas, welcome Mexicans applying for citizenship, as would predominately Mexican-origin El Paso, but cast aside Scotsmen or Swiss?

This is all pertinent to us because there are people in California, and other states, who would institute a form of local control of citizenship. Proposition 187 was passed by California in 1994, despite everyone's knowledge that it was unconstitutional on its face. Even it's supporters acknowledged a court test. That proposition was intended to set up a state system of immigration control in a total trashing of the United States Constitution. Immigration, naturalization actually, is a specific duty assigned to the Congress (Article 1, section 7—"To establish an uniform Rule of Naturalization…)

Specifically, Californians voted to expel children from school if they or their parents were "suspected"—not proven in a court of law—but "suspected" of being in the country illegally. The word "suspected" appeared several times in Proposition 187.

In 1994, I had the self-proclaimed principal author of Proposition 187, Ron Prince, on my radio show. I questioned him about the 187 provisions that mandated that all "law enforcement agencies" check citizenship of anyone under "arrest" which can mean stopped for a broken taillight. When asked exactly what documents would be necessary for proof of citizenship or legal residency to a beat cop, he answered that documentation would be up to each local chief of police or sheriff.

Switzerland, land of gnomes and watches, shows Ron Prince the way. Yes, let each locality unleash the forces of meter maids to check papers and report "suspected" illegals to a "higher authority."

This issue of locals overriding the United States Constitution would be laughable in light of the courts dismantling of Proposition 187. But

Mr. Prince and a small cohort of his anti-immigrants are trying to get "Son of 187" on the November California ballot.

Their efforts are not laughable, they are, like Swiss citizenship "direct democracy", unconscionable and, worse, they are, in a word, unconstitutional. If a law or proposed law is unconstitutional, it is un-American, as are the law's proponents, no matter how many people vote for it.

THEY KEEP COMING

Raoul Lowery Contreras
May 20, 2002

"They keep coming," the announcer intoned on behalf of Governor Pete Wilson's run for reelection in the most infamous of television commercials of the 1994 campaign. Wilson meant illegals from Mexico.

The Census Bureau report recently released states that "they keep coming." Most of them are legal, of course and most of them do not have college degrees. In fact, most are less educated than even our Appalachian poor of Kentucky, Tennessee, Georgia and West Virginia.

There should be, then, no shock that these immigrants might not make middle or upper class wages. The fact is that they are repeating the historical experience of all mass immigration peoples in the past.

It took the Irish Catholics four generations, 80-years, to even approach income and educational levels of the "English," the very people, mostly Protestants," who posted "No Irish need apply" signs throughout the country.

Next came the Italians who took almost 60 years before they were accepted into American society and approached the educational and income levels of the "English" who thought all Italians were "greaser" criminals. If not for Prohibition (1919-1933), the Italians would have been denied American status longer than the Irish. The reason: The Italians shot they way into American society and its economy under the leadership of, among others, Al Capone, Lucky Luciano and a man who died a few days ago at the age of 97, Joe Bonnano (Joe Bananas).

Joining the Italians were Polish and Russian Jews, though not as many as from Italy. But, they too were foreign and non-Protestant and drew the wrath of the "English." The U.S. Army reported that Russian and Polish Jews called up in the draft of 1917 (WWI) did not score very high in general intelligence tests all draftees had to take.

Without the benefit of Census reports to track those three immigrant groups, we can deduce certain facts from anecdotal evidence.

None of these peoples came to America well educated or well heeled financially. They came without English language proficiency. They produced large families. They were mostly Roman Catholic or Jewish. They all lived at the lowest rungs of the economy for years, 80 to 100 for the Irish.

These facts fit the current wave of immigration from Mexico and points south. Critics, however, insist that we are importing "poverty" and point to the current Census report that shows an increase of poverty in Los Angeles and Orange County as proof of their dire predictions.

These other groups also lived in poverty and certainly increased the poverty numbers of where they settled, so what's the big deal now? Besides, exactly what do the percentage increases (LA +28%, Orange County +44%) mean?

Let's see, if there were 100,000 people in poverty in 1990 and 128,000 in 2000, that's a 28% increase. If there were 100,000 people in poverty in Orange County in 1990 and 144,000 in 2000, that's a 44%

increase. Using any number will still produce the same conclusion. It is not the percentage increase that's important, but the raw numbers.

In San Diego, for example, there was an increase of 200,000 foreign born in the county, doubling the 1990 number. Now that's an important increase. The question is, however, did poverty double? No.

In fact, despite the best efforts of the United States of America, the only significant decrease in poverty occurred when the full power of the country was targeted at poverty in the 60's and Seventies. Nonetheless, the poverty level hasn't changed much in the past 20 years with most poor being Black, Hispanic and elderly white.

All things considered, however, our poor aren't that bad off when one considers the real poverty in most of the world. Raising the consciousness of what poverty really means is a study recently released that concluded that the country of Sweden, the Swedish people, are poorer than American Blacks; that the Swedish earnings and purchasing power are lower than the poorest Americans, the American Blacks.

So, though "they keep coming" from Mexico and points south, their economic lot is better than it was at home and the opportunities provided them by the USA's free enterprise system gives them opportunities even the highly advanced Swedes don't have. Only in America!

19

ODDBALL REPUBLICAN CRITIC-TOM TANCREDO

TANCREDO NICE, BUT UNINFORMED

Raoul Lowery Contreras
March 5, 2002

Republican Congressman Tom Tancredo of Colorado appears to be a nice man, a well-mannered man, an educated man who has only one minor defect he is, perhaps, the most uninformed man in the Congress of the United States on the subject of immigration. Either he is uninformed, or he is a blatant liar.

For example, in a long speech he delivered to an empty House of Representatives chamber that I watched live on C-Span on Tuesday, February 26th, he stated the following:

(1) That he sat next to a Mexican government official named "Levy" that is a Deputy in the Mexican Congress and a "citizen" of Los Angeles, California;

(2) That the Mexican government passed a law making dual-citizens of Americans who used to be Mexicans;

(3) That the Mexican government was trying to enact a law allowing naturalized American citizens who were formally Mexican citizens to be able to vote in both countries;

(4) That new immigrants, especially Mexicans, were not assimilating and becoming Americans;

Tancredo made these statements in, I believe, bad faith, for they are not true. If he knows they are not true, then he is a liar and should be cashiered from Congress for lying. If he doesn't know that they are not true, then he should educate himself, or resign from Congress for he might do more harm than good as an ignorant Congressman.

It is true that in the last Mexican Congressional elections at least one Deputy was elected to the Mexican Congress from Los Angeles, California, but that man is not a U.S. citizen. He is a Permanent Resident Alien not eligible to vote in American elections, but fully capable of voting IN Mexico, in person, for absentee balloting is not permitted in Mexico. Besides, no one can be a "citizen" of Los Angeles. Tancredo knew better than to so state, but misstated the facts anyway.

The Mexican government has not passed a dual-citizenship law of any sort. What they passed was a law allowing former Mexican citizens who have become American citizens to reclaim their property rights and the right to travel on a Mexican passport. Such Mexicans "Nationals" cannot vote in Mexican elections, for they are not citizens. They can own land along the coasts or borders of Mexico, rights denied American or other citizens.

There is absolutely no effort by the Mexican government to legalize voting in Mexico of American citizens of any sort, much less those of Mexican blood or former citizenship.

Tancredo's dumb statements about lack of assimilation and the "melting pot" idea do not stand scrutiny, but since when do ignorant or misstatements of fact ever stand scrutiny?

As the Congressman was misleading C-Span viewers, a report was being issued in Florida that was written by experts from the Universities of Florida and Miami that strongly concluded that Tancredo is wrong.

The book-length report published by the University of Florida's Bureau of Economic and Business Research concludes the following about immigrants in Florida who are mostly—Hispanic:

> That Florida's foreign-born residents are generally learning English at the same pace as immigrants early in the 20th Century (including Tancredo's grandparents who came from Italy);
>
> That they are paying their "fair share" of taxes (they are 16% of the population and pay 15% of state taxes);
>
> That they are becoming citizens and intermarrying with U.S. native-born;
>
> That they are catching up to average American income levels within 15 years of arriving;
>
> That the adult U.S.-born children of immigrants, especially Hispanics—have significantly better status than their parents, with higher occupational and income levels;
>
> That immigrants in Florida are relatively light users of welfare, though they have higher use of food stamps and Supplemental Security Income.

Concurrently, a study by the Urban Institute conducted by Michael Fix and Jeffrey Passel concludes: "(Public) Benefit use rates among U.S. citizen children in low-income immigrant families (i.e., in poor mixed status—meaning some citizens, or some immigrant and mostly Hispanic-Mexicans) were substantially lower than for citizen children of native-born parents in poor families."

So, if non-English speaking immigrants are matching Tancredo's grandparents in learning English and if their children are doing significantly better than their parents and if the use of welfare/public benefits is declining among immigrants, what is Tancredo's problem?

If, Tancredo is misstating the facts about Mexico, what else is he misstating? Is he ignorant, stupid, or is he a liar? Is one worse than the other?

EMPTY WORDS TO AN EMPTY CHAMBER

Raoul Lowery Contreras
September 16, 2002,

The capture of the "20th hijacker" Ramzi Binalshibh in Pakistan on September 11th belies the most ignorant congressman in the House of Representatives, the Constitution-trashing Colorado Republican Tom Tancredo.

48-hours before Ramzi Binalshibh was captured, Tancredo stood before C-Span cameras at the House Special Orders non-session decrying the lack of American troops on the Mexican border who could, if they were assigned there, stop illegal entrants from Mexico and other countries from entering the United States. Tancredo claims that among the illegals from Mexico are potential terrorists. He also claims that had troops been on the border, September 11th might not have happened.

His proof? His (and, coincidently, Geraldo Rivera's) proof is the fact that Iraqi Christians have come across the border into San Diego from Tijuana, Mexico, and asked for political asylum. In other words, all Arabs look alike and as Arabs were the September 11th hijackers, all Arabs are September 11th-like terrorists and murderers. Tancredo (and Rivera) actually thinks this way.

Just like Tancredo can't differentiate between good Arabs and bad Arabs, he has difficulty in properly assessing who is coming into the country from Mexico, legally or illegally.

For example, in his C-Span speech, to an empty House chamber, Tancredo stated that of the 1500 illegals crossing "every night" through an Arizona Indian reservation, a 1000 of them are smuggling illegal drugs. How does he know this? He doesn't quote official arrest statistics, or inside intelligence, any concrete evidence, or even any personal interviews. He just says so.

There are, he says, "terrorist cells" in Canada and Mexico and that those people can sneak into the country anytime to spread terror in the USA. While it is common knowledge in the intelligence community that there are "terrorist cells" in Canada, a result of extremely loose immigration and asylum policies, there is absolutely no evidence that there are "terrorist cells" in Mexico of Al Qaeda or Hizbollah, Al Fatah, or any other Arab/Muslim terrorist group. Tancredo says they exist and we are to believe him because he says so.

Relying on unproven statements, Tancredo wants to change American law and have our soldiers assigned to the border. The law prohibits the use of the American military forces to enforce civilian laws. Immigration laws are civilian laws, and always have been.

The law resulted from the occupation of the South after the Civil War. The good part was that occupation troops were sent home and prohibited from "occupying" America any longer. The bad part was that in that troop-less vacuum fanatical white supremacist terrorized and murdered Southern blacks for a century.

Tancredo now wants to assign American troops to the Mexican border to stop illegal immigrants and workers from crossing without permission. He advocates this because, as he stated, two-thirds of these Mexican illegals are involved in drug smuggling, and "large numbers" of

Arab illegals are crossing the border and they may be potential terrorists. Neither statement is true, or even provable.

Tancredo: "What will we tell the sons and daughters of people killed by terrorists recruited and trained by illegal aliens?"

What planet is this man from? What kind of happy tobacco has he been smoking? As fifteen of the nineteen September 11th killers were from Saudi Arabia and entered the United States legally through American airports, not illegally from Mexico, why look to Mexico?

The arrest of Ramzi Binalshibh in Pakistan destroys Tancredo's silly proposition. Binalshibh failed a number of times to secure a visa to enter the USA to "study" in flight school so he could presumably fly a hijacked airliner into the World Trade Center. He failed. Did he then use Tanredo's theory to sneak into the country to direct September 11th? No. Sneaking into the country is not in the terrorist lexicon. He apparently stayed in Germany where he was legal.

The arrest of five U.S. citizens of Yemeni backgrounds living in upstate New York, including natural born citizens, is more flesh and blood proof that Tancredo is off base.

At the very moment that American troops are thinly stretched in Afghanistan, the Philippines, Pakistan, Kuwait, the former Soviet Muslim Republics and soon, into Iraq, Tancredo wants to needlessly squander American power along the border.

He attacks President Bush for not sending troops to the border for "political and cultural reasons," i.e. (code for) Bush doesn't want to offend the very Mexican Americans Tancredo disdains. He completely ignores American history and law that rejects military policing of civilians. President Bush and Mexican Americans are right, Tancredo is wrong.

Our troops are masterfully equipped and trained to fight armies and terrorists, not work-seeking Mexicans who would gladly pay two or three hundred dollars for a Congressionally authorized work permit.

(NOTE: After the Buffalo terrorist cell was arrested, another cell was broken up in Portland, Oregon, made up of American citizens. Another blow to Tancredo's dumb theory.)

TODAY'S PAT BUCHANAN

Raoul Lowery Contreras
September 24, 2002

Tom Tancredo, ersatz Republican congressman from Colorado, recently had his house remodeled by illegal alien immigrants. Tom Tancredo leads the charge in Congress against illegal alien immigrants, particularly those of the Mexican persuasion. He claims he didn't know the workers in his house are in the USA illegally. Tom Tancredo has just learned a very good lesson, albeit very bitter one for Tancredo. Illegal aliens immigrants, touch all of our lives, like it or not.

While illegals were in the congressman's house, he read a Denver newspaper account about a youngster complaining about growing up in the US and not being able to afford college because he would be forced to pay out-of-state tuition. Why? His parents brought the youngster into the United States illegally.

What did Tancredo do when he read the story? He called the Immigration and Naturalization Service (INS) and demanded to know why they didn't deport the kid and his family(Jusus Apodaca and family). The family is Mexican.

Tancredo experienced immediate rejection by his Republican Party when staffers of the Republican National Committee publicly lambasted Tancredo. Staffers don't do that in public without permission and agreement from their bosses. The critics pointed out that Tancredo wasn't the Republican Party and that only President Bush could set the official direction of the Party, not a single suburban congressman.

What we have here is a congressman rejected by his own Party and who has irritated his hometown newspaper. The Denver newspaper heavily criticized Tancredo for turning his anti-illegal, anti-Mexican crusade personal, or that Tancredo tries to blame others for illegals working in his house.

What a laugh! Tancredo has just discovered that illegal alien immigrants are here all around us. They are here and they work for us all. Yes, they even work for ignorant (innocent?) congressmen.

He and his allies are also finding out that picking on kids doesn't work well. Tell me that a child who is brought here at an early age and goes to school from kindergarten through twelfth grade and graduates isn't a resident. Actually, tell it to Tancredo for states are lining up to pass laws declaring such youngsters residents for the purpsoe of college in-state tuition.

Concurrently, the Republican Party, knowing that history is with it and not Tancredo and his gang of a hundred in the House, has let the public know that Tancredo is not the Republican Party, that George W. Bush is. The President sets policy and most of his party goes along with it and tries to implement it into law. Party mavericks are just that, mavericks. Political mavericks usually stand alone, as the quintessential political maverick Patrick J. Buchanan did in the 2000 election. He garnered less than 1% of the total popular vote. Ironically, he stood for the identical issues that Tom Tancredo does today.

The President reaches out; Tancredo attacks. The President works to make sure America lives up to its history; Tancredo attacks. The President has an affinity for Mexicans; Tancredo attacks them. He attacks adult Mexicans and their children, attacking the children with a deep-seated gusto that reminds one of Patrick J. Buchanan and his "Jose." Buchanan would snarl at "Jose" during his campaign for President in 1996. "Jose," according to Buchanan is stealing America out from under good white people like Buchanan and Tancredo.

The President is the head of the Party, because he was nominated by the Party to be so. He won the Presidential election and is the only President we have. The President represents all people in the country, not just those who voted, or are citizens.

- Tancredo/Buchanan represents a handful of people.
- Tancredo/Buchanan is not the head of the Party.

Tancredo has illegal alien immigrants work in his house while he demands the INS deport youngsters who have been in the country since childhood. Tancredo has illegal alien immigrants working in his house while he attacks the President for not enforcing immigration laws and shutting down the border. If, however, the President could shut the border down and he could hunt down and deport more than 8-million illegal aliens, who would remodel the Congressman's house?

(NOTE: Republican U.S. Senator Ben Nighthorse Campbell, with the support of Colorado Republican Governor Jim Owen, introduced a bill inj Congress that will legalize Jesus and his Apodaca family. Tancredo objects. Public opinion polls taken in Colorado have fed Tancredo's political ego, but, as I pointed out to one such Tancredo fan, polls don't mean much, we are not run by polls, or by the mob. We are run by the United States Constitution and as a representative Republic that issues from that Constitution.)

Contreras's book, *"The New American Majority, Hispanics, Republicans & George W. Bush,"* is available at **www.amazon.com**, **www.barnesandnoble.com**, and **www.iuniverse.com**

E-mail: **sdraoul@att.net**

20

A CASE OF PREJUDICE- THE MEXICAN HATERS

HISPANICS AND MEDIA REALITY

Raoul Lowery Contreras
April 7, 2001

With all the good news about Hispanics swirling around, with the media finally paying attention to Hispanics, with the shock of Census 2000 stating there are 35-million Hispanics in the country, why does the media continue its mean and ugly ways of highlighting Hispanic negatives?

First, we are confronted with stories ad naseum about Hispanic teenage girls dropping out of school, about 30 out of a hundred. Worse, those drop-out numbers are topped by Hispanic teenage boys.

Secondly, ostensibly respectable Robert Samuelsen of Newsweek Magazine publishes an attack on Hispanic immigrants that parallels the arguments constantly floated by anti-immigrant fanatics like the Federation of Americans for Immigration Reform (FAIR) and its founder, John Tanton of Michigan.

It is a shame, he writes, that so many Hispanics drop out of school; that so many choose to live together in neighborhoods that average 40% Hispanic and calls that self segregation. He also regrets that so many Hispanic immigrants speak Spanish. He suggests they are not assimilating. By the way, the very same arguments were made against

German Catholic immigrants in the 1800s. Needless to say, German Americans are now the largest "ethnic" population in the United States.

On the first problem, the fault for Hispanic drop-outs belongs to parents. The largest reason for Hispanic girls dropping out of school is pregnancy. Teenage pregnancy is, of course, a stupid reason for anything. There are, I guess, some Hispanic cultural defects that make it impossible for mothers to educate a daughter on how not to get pregnant or how to disbelieve that handsome boy when he says he loves her.

Hispanic parents must, I repeat, must sit their daughters down and explain the stupidity of pregnancy before marriage. If that doesn't work, then, maybe, chastity belts should be resurrected from their historical graveyards. Sex before marriage is fine with me, but precautions must be taken.

The entire American culture is threatened by illegitimacy rates that are obscene (65%) in the Black community, 30% or so in the Hispanic community and a rising 20% among the Anglo community. These illegitimacy rates are a disaster—today, not years from now, as evidenced by climbing dropout rates, drug addiction, welfare and crime rates that are all astronomically higher among children who are raised without fathers in the home.

As for Hispanic boys dropping out of high school, that is sheer stupidity only topped by stupid pregnant Hispanic girls. The excuse of dropping out of school to help the family is baloney. I don't care what the economic circumstances are, there is no excuse for a Hispanic parent allowing a dropout. If the father doesn't make enough money, then the mother should go to work. If that is not possible, then the father should take a second job. If there is no father in the home, welfare, community and church help is available. As for single Hispanic mothers, children should and must not be penalized because their mother beds down with every Tomas, Ricardo and Enrique.

Hispanics must educate Hispanics that illegitimacy is universally destructive. Pregnant unmarried mothers must be shamed into changing their behavior. Hispanic males who father such children must be hunted down like rabid dogs and forced to pay child support, or go to jail. We must insist that individuals accept responsibility for their own actions. Individual responsibility is what we Americans are about. This is the one single characteristic that Hispanics must accept.

As for Samuelson's anti-Hispanic immigrant attack, Hispanics are doing well. Despite noted problems, Hispanic immigrants are entering the economic mainstream faster than any immigrant group in history. They are rushing into the middle-class status like no other immigrant group in history and doing it faster and in larger numbers. There is evidence that 30% of Hispanic Republicans are foreign born. There is evidence that Hispanic immigrants are starting businesses at record rates. That's assimilation. That's the future, Samuelson and Tanton's FAIR notwithstanding.

A THICKET OF LIES

Raoul Lowery Contreras
September 3, 2002

If a lie is told often enough, the lie will eventually be believed, maybe.

For example, the Mexican haters among us whine about George Washington's birthday celebration being shoved aside for Farm Worker Union founder Cesar Chavez. That is not true. They whine that Cinco de Mayo, a Mexican celebration of a military victory over France in 1862,has been substituted for Washington's Birthday. No jurisdiction in America has made Cinco de Mayo a holiday, or even talked about it. The Mexican haters are wrong.

Another lie these Mexican haters tell is that Mexicans have not been part of the construction of the United States. That is a lie. Mexicans and their Spanish forbearers created the cowboy culture and cattle economy of the West. There are no bucking broncos or cowboys in London, Sherwood Forest, or Glasgow.

Did Mexicans (and Chinese) build the railroads of the West? Yes or no, whiners? Did experienced Mexican gold miners teach rookie American gold seekers in California how to mine for gold? Yes or no, whiners? Did Mexicans teach Americans irrigation farming to make California the greatest food producer in the history of the world? Yes or no, whiners? Did Mexicans form the core of construction crews that built the roads and buildings of a booming West? Yes or no, whiners?

The Mexican haters used to be Irish haters and posted "Irish need not apply" signs. The Mexican haters used to be German haters and, like Benjamin Franklin used to say, the "Germans are dirty, filthy, corrupt people." The Mexican haters used to be Italian haters who forced the Italians to seek economic opportunities with Tommy guns. Welfare, as we know it, was designed for the English and Irish, certainly not for Blacks or Hispanics. It was designed for whites by whites.

The Mexican haters, who now hold Japanese Americans in high esteem, locked them up in concentration camps in 1942. The Mexican haters claim Mexicans choke the welfare rolls; that Mexican immigrants are importing poverty, but forget that most of the poor people in America are Black or Appalachian whites of Scotch/Irish or English backgrounds.

The Mexican haters tell us that 25% of our prison inmates are illegal aliens (from Mexico of course). That is a blatant lie. Fact: 12.5% of California prison inmates are illegal aliens; source-State of California, Dept. of Corrections.

The Mexican haters say Mexicans have not contributed to America. Mexican soldiers helped defeat the British at St. Louis, and in what is now Michigan. Mexicans (and Spanish, Puerto Ricans and Cubans) defeated the British at Baton Rouge, Mobile Bay, and Pensacola, and fought at Yorktown, in, of course, the American Revolution. Mexicans died for this country before there were many Irish, any Italian, Russian and Polish immigrants, or Japanese Americans, Swedish, Danish or Norwegian Americans, et al in America. Source: Department of Defense.

Another critic falsely states that, "Our grandparents knew how to respect the contributions made to our nation by immigration. They cut the numbers from time to time. We haven't followed their wise example for 40 years and are reaping the result of an increasingly Balkanized population, infrastructure meltdown and cultural dislocation." This is a flagrant lie.

Immigration has only been curtailed by "Yellow Peril" exclusion laws and in the 1920s. Those had nothing to do with cutting immigration; they were designed to keep out Asians, Italian Roman Catholics and Jews from Eastern Europe because these "swarthy" "thieving" immigrants were not Nordic Europeans.

A hundred years ago, Mr. Morris M. Estee uttered these words before the Agricultural Society of California: "I am satisfied that if in our orchards, vineyards, hopfields and grainfields our farmers, instead of hiring the thieving, irresponsible Chinaman (Mexican), who like the locusts of Eqypt, are eating out our substance, would give some encouragement to our boys (white boys), and by hiring them instead, that in a few years we would be rid in California of the curse to farmers and ranchmen, the irresponsible character of farm labor and have in its stead a far more valuable and intelligent class of farm laborers. If this is done, then the question, what shall we do with our boys would be answered."

Nothing has changed, like Mr. Estee, the Mexican haters have to lie, of course, because truth destroys their arguments, their societal impact and, them.

Contreras's book, *"The New American Majority, Hispanics, Republicans & George W. Bush,"* is available at **www.amazon.com**, **www. barnesandnoble.com**, and **www.iuniverse.com**
E-mail: **sdraoul@att.net**

ANTI-ILLEGALS FAIL, AGAIN

Raoul Lowery Contreras
January 1, 2002

There are readers of this newspaper who continue to blame Mexicans for the September 11th attacks on America. Moreover, they spread their hate by dissembling to an unwarranted and blatantly false degree.

Is it not true that agriculture is California's largest employer and dollar volume industry outside of the American military? And, is it not true that most, if not all, of California farmers hire Mexicans to work the fields and deliver the crops that feed us, or decorate our homes? Further, is it not true that despite what wages American farmers pay they can't hire Americans to do field work?

Why, then, do some people live in denial and claim that the hired Mexicans, here legally or illegally, are taking jobs away from unemployed Americans? In fact, there are very, very few unemployed Americans at all in my county or anywhere in California outside Los Angeles. The unemployment percentage rate, mostly made up of Blacks and Hispanics anyway, is not much higher than it was a year ago here in San Diego or in Orange County. In both areas, the unemployment rate continues to be at or less than 3%.

According to year-end reports now appearing in our newspapers, even the 2001 demise of the dot.com industry hasn't affected Southern California much. Housing prices are increasing, our population is increasing, service and construction industries are growing, so where is the damage, the damage claimed by those among us who can't find an American working in the fields?

They claim there exists an evil conspiracy in the Mexican Government to export its labor surplus to the USA to avoid a bloody revolution, despite the fact that Mexican labor has gravitated north into the U.S. since California entered the United States in 1850. They also are bereft in their knowledge of Mexican history for no revolution has ever occurred in Mexico because of unemployment. Moreover, Mexico's economy is ranked 9th in the world and is growing.

Furthermore, no terrorist incident, as we define them, has ever been perpetrated by illegally resident Mexicans in the United States-EVER. Yet, we read that September 11th is a reason to shut the Border with Mexico. Before the letters fly, the 1916 raid of Pancho Villa in New Mexico was a military raid designed to draw the United States into war with the government Villa was fighting. It worked. President Woodrow Wilson sent the U.S. Army under General "Blackjack" Pershing into Mexico to "punish" Pancho Villa. That effort failed.

In fact, General Pershing wrote a letter describing his troops as looking like spent dogs coming back into the United States with their "tails between their legs."

History refutes anti-Mexican critics, as does economic reality. They claim the evil Mexican government is conspiring to violate America's sovereignty with illegal workers yet never utter a peep when Canada, France, Spain and other European countries truly violate our sovereignty by refusing to extradite criminals who might face a death penalty for their crimes.

They also claim Mexico is corrupting America with drugs. Baloney! Americans corrupt America by using drugs, especially heroin, from Afghanistan, Pakistan, Southeast Asia and Turkey, and cocaine, not an ounce of which is manufactured in Mexico. Author Martin Gross, no friend of Mexico, writes that over 300 American politicians and government officials-A-DAY are imprisoned for corruption and/or drug dealing. Corruption is endemic wherever there are illegal drugs.

History, economics, free enterprise, common sense and labor supply/demand totally discredit rabid anti-Mexican critics. And, in case they didn't notice, not a single one of Osama Bin Laden's murderous martyrs on September 11th was a Mexican immigrant, legal or illegal. Nor, did any of the Paradise/Virgin seekers that crashed the planes into the Pentagon and the World Trade Center even come into the United States from or through Mexico.

Liars lie; racists lie; lying racists run amok among us and we see them in Letters to the Editor, on talk radio, on the Presidential campaign trail (Pat Buchanan) and in the editorial pages of some newspapers. We see pure unadulterated ignorance in print or hear it on the airwaves and it is hard to combat for there appears to be a great willingness to believe the baloney dished out by these ignorant and evil people.

ARE HISPANICS A CRIMINAL CLASS?

By Raoul Lowery Contreras
May 21, 2000

Crime rates are plunging while illegal immigration continues at the high pace of recent years. Crime rates are plunging, yet legal immigration continues at almost a million people a year. Crime rates are plunging, immigration is high, but there appears to be few links between the two.

According to Orange County, California, authorities gang member-
ship and activities are down, despite a growing Hispanic population, a
source of traditional gang crime and activities. Why? The normal knee
jerk reaction of anti-immigrants is that American and immigrant Hispanics are a criminal class. They are wrong.

Are Hispanic criminals criminal because they are Hispanic? No. Are
Hispanic immigrants a criminal class? No. Are blue-collar working
Hispanics prone to criminality? No. Are middle-class Hispanics prone
to criminality? No. Are most murderers in the United States Hispanic?
No. Are most people arrested in the USA Hispanic? No. Are most Hispanics arrested immigrants? No. Are most Hispanics arrested from the
lowest economic classes? Yes. Are most drug dealers and smugglers in
the USA Hispanic? No.

There is absolutely no evidence that any of these questions can be
answered yes on a national scale, except for the question about the lowest economic classes and arrests. That's a fact that cannot be disputed.
There might be some specific cities and towns where Hispanic crime
rates are higher, or even the highest in the area, but that is based on
population, not genetics. For example, there are towns in Texas and
California that are 100% Hispanic. Any crime in such cities will be
Hispanic, just as any crime in the state Maine will be mostly non-Hispanic white.

Oh, there is the occasional crackpot criminal like the "Railroad Murderer", Angel Maturino Resendiz, who was just convicted of murder in
Texas and will be tried for a number of other murders. But, people like
Resendiz are rare. This is true even in the drug business where so many
Hispanics are involved (from Colombia, Mexico, Central America and,
of course, Cubans in the government of Fidel Castro). Drug crimes are
limited to drug people, as a rule, thus the general population isn't too
affected. General crime sprees like that of Resendiz aren't the rule.

Occasionally, one sees that some Hispanics are involved in insurance fraud, what with staged car accidents on Los Angeles freeways, but the kingpins of such crime are usually not Hispanics, they are just the pawns on the street. One rarely sees a Hispanic rob a bank. One rarely sees a Hispanic running scams of any sort. One rarely sees Hispanics murder whites or blacks for racial reasons, though it happens. One rarely sees Hispanics commit multiple murders.

Studies in California conclude that most crimes committed by Hispanics are crimes of property, not violence. Even among illegal alien Hispanics, crimes of property outnumber other crimes. This fact requires even closer examination. In the federal prison system, for example, approximately one-fourth of the 135,000, or so, inmates are Mexican nationals, but they aren't in prison because they are "illegal aliens." They are there mostly because they are international smugglers, not violent criminals.

There are approximately 2.5-million illegal aliens in California, mostly of Mexican-origin, mostly male, yet there are less than 22,000 of them in prison and less than 3 or 4% of the county jail populations of the state. That is about 15-18% of the total California prison/jail population.

Every illegal alien is technically a law-breaker. That being the case, one has to be amazed at the low percentage of them in state prison. Also, considering the large number of illegals, say more than 2.5-million in California, less than 1% are in prison at any moment and no more than 3% of all incarcerated in all jails and prisons in California.

If, then, one looks at the numbers, there is the knee-jerk reaction of anti-immigrants combined with the shrill hysteria of the Los Angeles media, one sees that the public perception of Hispanic crime rates is nothing but another "urban myth."

Urban myths continue with little or no evidence if there is an organized effort to promulgate the myth. It is in the best interests of the
anti-immigrants, especially those with racial bias as their philosophical
foundation, to push the myth of Hispanic crime. It buttresses their
positions, despite the falsity of their views.

Question: Are the real criminals Hispanics who mostly commit crimes
of property, the rates of which are going down, or the anti-immigrants
who lie and propagandize their lies about millions of innocent, hard-
working, family-oriented, God-fearing patriots with Spanish-surnames?

21

THEY PAY THEIR WAY

LIES AND MENDACITY SINCE SEPTEMBER 11

Raoul Lowery Contreras
October 29, 2001

We are at war against thugs and murderers. Yet, despite, clearly demarcated enemies, complete with substantial proof, proof enough to convince their fellow religionists, there are Americans who can't shed their vile anti-Mexican bigotry and hatred.

One completely ignorant fool penned words to the effect that anyone can see that by crunching the numbers, one can see that for every dollar an illegal pays in taxes, he gets ten times that in public benefits. That is a blatant lie, an ignorant statement and one that simply cannot be proved by anyone.

Now, please tell me who gets more in public benefits. Is it the average welfare woman, who is a white, high school dropout, unmarried and the mother of two or more children? Or is it a young Mexican man who sleeps in the fields of Carlsbad to save on rent so he can send money home to his children who do not have a welfare system to suck off of?

Who contributes more to the economy, that welfare sucking white high school dropout with kids, or that Mexican man who puts food on our table?

253

Perhaps the answer comes in studies of the 2000 Census that indicate that there are far more illegals in the country than ever estimated. These uncounted illegals may be the secret to the economic success of the Clinton years. Yes, there are professional economists wondering out loud whether or not these illegals are truly the key to the longest economic expansion in history. Productivity increased by leaps and bounds during the 90s and productivity is, according to experts, the key to economic success.

What are the facts? Do Mexican men who come here illegally bring their wives and families with them? No. Border Patrol apprehension statistics are clear, most illegals caught are men without wives and children in tow. So, our schools are not being flooded with illegal alien Mexican children. Such is impossible. Children legally brought in by legal immigrants account for the growth of Spanish speaking children in our schools. There is no proof to counter that statement.

So, if illegal alien Mexican men and women, adults almost exclusively if the INS and Border Patrol are to be believed, don't enter our classrooms as students, they don't cost us much in school tax dollars, do they? They are, in fact, working and paying taxes in their payrolls or in their purchases, not collecting benefits.

Let's examine the pay-check phenomenon. The Immigration and Naturalization Service reports that it conducted a multi-thousand person study that revealed that 75% of the interviewees were paid with regular paychecks, complete with all regular withheld taxes, including Social security, Federal and state income taxes, Medicare and state disability taxes.

A ha, the cynics will say, how did these people get Social Security numbers? Well, some did and some didn't. Many used duplicate numbers, inauthentic documents and numbers that simply didn't exist, anything to get work. Needless to say, these people don't file tax returns so the taxes that are collected from their paychecks stay in the system and are used to pay others, like the welfare white unmarried female high school dropout who doesn't work to support her own two to three children.

Those men we see working in the fields throughout the country are not our enemies, those who attack them with lies are.

"THEY PAY TAXES...THEY PAY TAXES!"
Raoul Lowery Contreras
March 25, 2002

Blah! Blah! Blah! Fanatic Mexican haters scream: Illegals don't pay taxes! Illegals don't want to pay taxes! Illegals steal benefits from American citizens, citizens who pay taxes! Blah! Blah! Blah!

Then, we find these words in the Christian Science Monitor, "Immigrants...are flocking in record numbers to IRS offices and seminars such as this one (Houston) to learn how to become legal US taxpayers."

The first step was the 1996 creation of a taxpayer identification number by the Internal Revenue Service (IRS) for use by people who don't have a Social Security number. The IRS declares this is good business. Its job is to collect taxes, not decide who is legal or illegal. Critics say this is bad business because it makes illegals more secure in their presence, albeit illegal presence. I say this is good business because it totally knocks down the argument that illegals don't pay taxes.

That is like saying that because some Americans cheat on their income tax that all Americans cheat on their income taxes. Some illegals don't pay income taxes, but do pay any and all state and local property and sales taxes. It is impossible to truthfully say that illegals don't pay taxes. It is, in fact, a blatant lie.

Some IRS-sponsored tax paying seminars are attended by as many as 500 people in Houston—a night. "We had to do something," says

Leandro Leon, education and communication director in the Houston IRS office. "These undocumented aliens were working here, using bogus Social Security numbers, and not reporting their income." Notice, he said "not reporting their income," not that they weren't paying taxes. If they weren't filing, that didn't stop their employers from issuing W-2 forms and collecting federal income taxes and Social Security and Medicare taxes for the government.

As for the argument by the Mexican-haters that these people don't make enough money to pay taxes, baloney. It doesn't matter what they make, they pay Social security taxes and Medicare taxes to the federal government, plus whatever income tax withholding they might incur. They pay state and local taxes regardless of what they make—THEY PAY TAXES, JUST LIKE WE ALL DO. Now, what part of that don't the Mexican-haters understand?

500 seminar attendees a night—those high numbers can be seen at seminars all across the US. The IRS has signed up 5.3 million such people—newly acknowledged taxpayers, since the taxpayer ID program began in 1996.

Naturally, the Mexican-haters pooh-pooh the large movement by illegals to make their tax paying status normal and formal. "It does show how even talk of amnesty begins to affect behavior," says Steven Camarota, of the Center for Immigration Studies (CIS) in Washington. He believes anticipation of amnesty is motivating illegal immigrants to use tax paying so they can establish residency.

Camarota's CIS is a rabid anti-immigrant, anti-Mexican institution funded an directed by Dr. John Tanton who also founded the Federation of Americans for Immigration Reform (FAIR) with money from the Nazi-founded Pioneer Fund. Camarota claims his research shows that immigrants cost us more than they pay in taxes, but he conveniently ignores the fact that almost ALL people who receive government benefits receive more than they pay in taxes.

How typical of an anti-immigrant Mexican-hater to challenge the motives of people wanting to file their taxes properly and to get their refunds just like the rest of us. As usual, however, the illegals are one step ahead of the haters. By normalizing their tax paying status, they do squash one more lie that is spread by the CIS and fanatical Mexican-haters about the millions of illegals who work and live among us.

ENGLISH + SPANISH == THE USA

Raoul Lowery Contreras
May 15, 2001

Ola, como esta usted? Donde esta la biblioteca? Everyone who took high school Spanish knows that those phrases are probably all they recognize from their teenaged efforts to learn one of three most spoken languages in the world.

Nonetheless, almost everyone knows how to order tacos, fajitas and jalapenos; almost everyone can actually pronounce San Francisco or San Diego, or El Paso or San Antonio; almost everyone can pronounce Antonio Banderas' name, or Julio Iglesias' name.

Our politicians and their strategists are described as politicos and are crafty and "savvy." Savvy, of curse, comes from the Spanish verb—saber, to know.

Well, we now know (sabemos) that the campaign to make the United States of America an official English-speaking country is only an exercise for a fringe lobby group of nutcases existing out of the American mainstream. They carry the names of the usual suspects—Dr. John Tanton, founder of U.S. English and the Federation of Americans for Immigration Reform, (FAIR) and Roy Beck, a Tanton protégé. Glenn Spencer of the virulently anti-Mexican group in Los Angeles, The American Patrol, and Barbara Coe, the former civil service clerk, and founder of the California Coalition for Immigration Reform (CCIR) lead the English-only fight in California.

Another leader, a Chilean immigrant, hired by the fringe to make it look like Hispanics demand English-only, is sought out by the media to capture a heavily accented immigrant spouting words that he is paid to utter. He was hired after the famous Linda Chavez, yes the same Linda Chavez President-elect Bush named Labor Secretary, resigned the U.S. English post because comments made by the group's founder (Tanton) in a secret memorandum struck her as racist in tone and content. She was not alone. Famous newscaster Walter Cronkite also resigned from the organization's Board of Directors when the memo surfaced. So, Tanton searched out the Chilean immigrant and he has represented Tanton's anti-Hispanic view with a heavy Spanish accent-for money, of course.

According to public Internal Revenue filings of non-profit groups, Tanton has made a career of raising money for anti-immigrant and anti-Hispanic causes from the Pioneer Fund, a non-profit group founded by the same people who founded the American Nazi Party in the 1930s. Those founders were also the prime movers of the immigration restriction bills of 1922 and 1923 that passed an almost all white (one black) and Protestant Congress of the United States. These bills were designed to keep more Jewish and Italian immigrants out of America.

Despite the efforts of "English-Only," a campaign directed by extremists and full of irritated average English-only speaking Americans, the country appears to have adopted Spanish as an unofficial second language. This phenomenon is not limited to Spanish-speaking immigrants or their American born children. Many, many non-Hispanic Americans are diving into Spanish lessons in order to work with and supervise Spanish-speaking workers, or to work in businesses exporting billions of dollars worth of goods and services to Latin America, a trading area with almost 400-million Spanish-speaking potential customers.

Certainly, the huge influx of Spanish-speaking immigrants has influenced the spread of Spanish throughout the country, nonetheless, I believe it is the spread of Mexican food that has influenced most of Spanish usage in recent years. Almost every supermarket I have visited in urban areas outside of California have sections of "Hispanic" food, meaning, of course, mostly Mexican foodstuffs.

For the benefit of those fringe English-only people, let me lay on some mainstream American words like the "whole enchilada." It may be that I'm full of "beans" being a "beaner" or, as more sophisticated people say, a frijolero. It may be that I am so wrong I should be hauled off to the "hoosgow" or, in real Spanish, juzgado-bar of justice, or to the "calaboose" which originally was the Spanish, calabozo, jail.

There was a time in which only the American elite or the newest immigrants to America spoke anything other than English. The elite spoke French or German. The immigrants spoke their native languages until they learned English—if they ever did, and few did, or their children did. A few Yiddish words made it into mainstream American English, but only a few. So did some French and German words, but not many.

Will Spanish overtake English in our everyday America? No. Will Spanish enrich American English? Yes. Will the Spanish language become America's second language? Yes. If that is not in the cards, how did cowboy become such a driving cultural word and way of life? Cowboy is a direct translation of the Spanish/Mexican word for men who ride herd on cattle—vaquero, which comes from the Spanish word for cow, vaca.

You see, Spanish language usage by Americans isn't even a recent occurrence. It goes back to the very birth of the country, Los Estados Unidos de America.

22

AMNESTY

THE AMERICANIZATION OF ILLEGAL IMMIGRANTS

Raoul Lowery Contreras
July 23, 2001

As each moment passes in this year of our Lord, 2001, American opinion makers and politicians are focusing on "regularizing" the presence of, maybe, three, four or five million Mexicans illegally in the United States—regularizing, that is, in a positive sense.

Emanating from the George W. Bush White House are hints at "amnesty" for Mexicans, a "guest worker program," the "right" thing to do and the "compassionate" thing to do. Signing up in support of these ideas are House Minority Leader Richard Gephardt and Senate Leader Tom Daschle, both Democrats, with provisos for "fairness" to all, not just Mexicans.

A few conservative Republicans made it clear that they would never support general "amnesty" because it would reward lawlessness and encourage more illegal immigration. There were, however, no surprises in who came out against amnesty. The question is—are there enough of these critics to stop the White House and its goal to "regularize" millions of essential workers?

Lining up in journalistic support of the Bush ideas are the "usual suspects" led by the Wall Street Journal and business leaders. Joining

261

them are newspapers like the Los Angeles Times—normally anti-Bush, the ultra-conservative Washington Times, columnist and thwarted Bush Cabinet nominee, Linda Chavez, the San Francisco Chronicle and assorted columnists and newspapers that normally cry aloud about "loose" borders and "sovereignty."

Though outright amnesty ideas flamed out quickly, the amnesty trial balloon exposed who was on what side of the Guest Worker proposals that are sure to formally surface in the next few weeks. For example, the United Farm Workers Union is dead set against any guest worker program, as are their allies like the California Rural Legal Assistance and Quaker-religious related groups. Contrarily, the AFL-CIO has joined with business leaders to focus on some sort of legalization.

More importantly, rank and file Mexican Americans and legal resident Mexican nationals seem to be very appreciative of the Bush White House efforts and seem to justify the Presidential counselor Karl Rove's increasingly successful efforts to raise Bush's positives in the Mexican American community. Polls have been published that show that positive support among Hispanics for President Bush range from 49% to 58% before this week's news on Bush's push for "regularization."

Surprisingly, words from the anti-fanatical point group, Project USA (famous for anti-immigrant billboards around the country) indicate that a political consensus maybe forming in the country to "regularize" millions of Mexican workers; workers who work hard every day to feed us, build our houses and to work in slaughter houses, mines, mushroom caves, ad infinitum, etc., and, of course, to support their families so many miles away.

ProjectUSA: "The two immediately obvious solutions to the problem of millions of foreign nationals illegally residing in the United States—mass amnesty or mass deportation—are both politically unfeasible. For that reason they should both be rejected. However, a humane and sensible plan to document illegal immigrants and allow them to come out of the shadows as legal temporary guest workers might be a workable alternative."

ProjectUSA declares that for a guest worker program to be successful and effective it must contain these elements: "A new tamper proof identification card, including a thumb print..." "Local law enforcement must...assist (INS)" in the legalization process. It demands that legalization limit guest workers to "two year stints." Mandated government enforced savings programs of 15% of wages to be redeemed only in Mexico after work permits expire. Government mandated health insurance and or coverage would force employers to provide these services as apart of the work agreement with individual workers. They also advocate Congress deny American citizenship to babies born of illegal aliens.

If an anti-immigrant group can suggest a legalization program can work by including these elements, is there a guest worker program in our immediate future? Yes.

A national ID card is out of the question, but a legalization card combined with an actual Social Security card would not trample my rights as an American. And, as Congress can do nothing to change the 14th Amendment that defines citizenship, that demand is dead on arrival. The other suggestions, however, are feasible.

A guest worker program is in the offing and it appears it will come to pass with support of some, if not many, illegal immigration critics.

Reason: Mexican nationals working illegally in the country violated some law or another when they crossed the border, but are essential to our economic health. President Bush's plans to regularize the multi-million person workforce bring order to chaos. Regularization will benefit the President immensely politically, more importantly, it will benefit the country immeasurably even more.

AMNESTY, BASEBALL AND APPLE PIE

Raoul Lowery Contreras
July 29, 2002

The coming amnesty of illegal aliens will pass Congress and be signed by President George W. Bush. This despite protestations of a vocal minority who, themselves, offer no real solutions to solve the problem of filling millions of jobs that would go begging causing great harm to the country without illegally-present workers.

Is collapse of our economy acceptable? Are labor shortages acceptable in California, Iowa, Nebraska, Arkansas, North Carolina, Iowa, and Oklahoma? Is it acceptable for millions of working mothers to be forced from the work force because there isn't enough organized child-care available, at any price? Are food prices 10-20-30% higher acceptable to the average American family? Is it acceptable for new home prices to increase 10-20% when they are already over $350,000 in California?

These people would rather destroy the American nation than make simple accommodations in law that will stop the country's potential demise, like that presently occurring in Japan, Italy, Spain and Germany.

They scream like banshees about the Mexicans who solve the huge labor shortage we have in the country, but screaming "criminality" is all they do.

Criminalities, by the way, in America's executive suites are assaults on American sovereignty that dwarf little misdemeanors committed by men and women seeking work to support their families.

Thank God for the illegal workers in the country, for they, among other things, soften the blow of the assaults on our wallets and sovereignty by executive suite crooks. By accepting work and wages most

Americans won't touch, recent immigrants, legal and illegal, keep prices and inflation down. So declares Chairman Allan Greenspan of the Federal Reserve Board, a man with far more information about our economy than the screaming banshees.

As for jobs, of the more than 120-million workers in the country, 8-9-million might be here illegally. There are fewer than 3-million real unemployed Americans, thus, the math indicates that upwards of five or more million jobs would be unfilled if the illegals weren't here and each and every "unemployed" American filled jobs illegals presently hold.

Before Mexicans responded to recruitment by the beef, poultry processors and agriculture, many areas of the country were dying and food price hikes were in the offing.

What would we call food price increases caused by a lack of workers in the fields or processing plants? How about we call exorbitant food price increases a cruel and unforgiving tax on all people, especially those with families. Every American family would suffer and many would plunge into poverty, increasing welfare expenditures by billions of dollars. A reminder: Many military families are already using federal welfare and food stamps.

We have the least expensive food in the world. No country can match our food prices, farm productivity or food distribution. Question: Who makes this possible? Answer: Good farmers and many illegal immigrants willing to work for them at $6-10-an-hour. Those better-than-home wages result in greater productivity and lower prices that are a gift of billions of dollars to we Americans.

Illegals make hotel beds, wash restaurant dishes, dig ditches, pound nails, cut lumber, assemble electronics, pave streets, collect garbage, take care of pre-school children and clean the homes of working women. Illegals work throughout the American economy, gladly and productively.

The net effect of illegals in the country is a higher standard of living for all—even when factoring in the expense of their presence. Much of the expense is ameliorated irrefutably by the taxes they pay in their rents, purchases and withholding from their paychecks, taxes they pay just like the rest of us.

Now comes a congressional proposal to bestow amnesty and legalization on millions of these workers. What do the screaming banshees do—they scream: "AMNESTY REWARDS LAWBREAKING!"

Amnesties are as American as baseball and apple pie. Thousands of Anglo young men ran off to Canada and Sweden to avoid military service during the Vietnam War and they were amnestied. Thousands of Americans are given amnesty every day for not filing tax returns or paying taxes. Southern whites rebelled against America in 1861 and were amnestied at the Civil War's end. Confederate mass murderers like General Nathan Bedford Forest weren't even charged despite murdering hundreds of black Union soldiers for the crimes of being black and daring to fight white Confederate soldiers.

Amnesty is more American than the screaming banshees are willing to accept. So, I think, are the very illegal immigrants who, in reality, come here to work like Americans, to contribute to the highest standard of living and the most productive and free economy in the entire world or its history.

23

THE BORDER PATROL

CHECKPOINTS...PAPERS AND THE COURTS

By Raoul Lowery Contreras
April 15, 2000

Is it possible that the expensive charade played out every day throughout the American Southwest may be coming to an inglorious end? The charade is the ersatz imitation of roaming patrols and checkpoints made famous by the Nazi Gestapo of Germany. At this time and in this place, however, the patrols and checkers are United States officers of the Border Patrol.

The Southwest, in particular in San Diego County at the San Clemente, Temecula, Highway 94 and Interstate 8 Border Patrol checkpoints, is dotted with Gestapo-like checkpoints where anyone the Border Patrol wants to hassle and harass is subject to everything from warrantless searches to strip searches. The San Clemente checkpoint is just minutes from what used to be the Western White House of President Richard Nixon.

With a bumbling sworn officer staff of thousands, the Border Patrol normally resembles an Inspector Cloo-sow run operation. Given this bumbling institutional reputation, are the checkpoints running out of time? Not because they are keystone-cop-like and like a thin green-uniformed sieve, but because Solomon-like federal judges have now spoken, clearly and concisely. Can we apply the millions of dollars spent at these checkpoints to border enforcement—maybe? Why?

The 9th Circuit Court of Appeals is just one step shy of the United States Supreme Court. It has ruled in the U.S. vs German Espinoza Montero Camargo that the Border Patrol cannot "profile" (stop, frisk and arrest) Hispanic-looking people just because they look "Hispanic." Oops, is this a speed bump for those who defend cops/officers who use color and ethnicity instead of thorough police work to stop and/or arrest people? Is this an impenetrable legal wall that "profiling" believers won't be able to ignore as they have so many times before when judges have clamped down on these badge-wearing lawbreakers?

The decision covers all Border Patrol officers in the West and Southwest and puts them on notice that they can't pull people over just because they look Hispanic. Sure, they can pull people over if they do suspicious things like do a quick U-turn before a checkpoint, use dusty side roads off the Interstate, or throw out contraband during a chase. But, they can no longer pull someone over because they look Hispanic, which, by the way, along the Mexican border means looking Mexican. Looking Mexican normally means having skin color that more closely resembles mahogany than ash.

"Stops based on race or ethnic appearance send the underlying message to all our citizens that those who are not white are judged by the color of their skin alone," wrote Judge Stephen Reinhardt for the majority seven judges of the eleven-judge panel that heard the case. Is the "profiling" by federal officers a giant institutional hate crime against millions of people?

Further, "Such stops," wrote the court, "also send a clear message that those who are not white enjoy a lesser degree of constitutional protection—that they are in effect assumed to be potential criminals first and individuals second." With such words, is it any wonder that this writer has stated numerous times that this court would have buried the infamous and unconstitutional California Proposition 187 even deeper than a federal District judge did?

University of Toledo professor, David A. Harris, an expert on "racial profiling" says, "It is significant any time a court stands up and says that taking note of ethnicity as a mark of criminal activity is wrong."

More importantly, Harris says, "For too long, judges, not just police, have either implicitly or explicitly used race of ethnicity as a proxy for greater propensity to be a criminal." Judges, can you believe it? Believe it!

We have, therefore, a situation here that places legal obstacles in the way of Border Patrol officers who consistently use "driving while Hispanic" as an excuse to stop people, Hispanic looking people. That's what they do at checkpoints throughout the Southwest. They spend all that money and assign dozens of Border Patrol officers to the large checkpoint on Interstate 5 in San Clemente, then, brag they catch as many as 50 illegals a day. Whoopee, big deal. Actually, published reports have appeared that state that 50-a-day is not even true. In fact, the press reports that half of those arrestees are in fact picked up by local Orange County deputies and city cops and driven to the checkpoint for turning over to sedentary Border Patrol agents, not agents "patrolling" as the name of the force implies.

What a waste of money! Surely, if these officers and their back-up resources were assigned to the border they would stop more than 50 illegals from crossing the border, wouldn't they? Their ability to pull people over at a whim as they do at the checkpoints is based on ethnicity—I know from personal experience and observation. Unless they have a specific tip on a specific car and driver, they rarely pull anyone over that is not Hispanic looking. But, no more, no mas, says the 9th Circuit.

They'll have to stop every tenth or fiftieth car soon, for without the ability to stop criminal looking Hispanics, like me, on a whim, there is no reason for the checkpoints to continue. Moreover, the Court, looking at the huge Mexican-origin population of California, providently wrote, "Accordingly, Hispanic appearance is of little or no use in determining which particular individuals among the vast Hispanic populace should be stopped by law enforcement officials on the lookout for illegal aliens."

Good, maybe we can direct those resources and officers to the border, where they belong.

BORDER PATROL, BUSTED

Raoul Lowery Contreras
July 8, 2002

Federal law prohibits political activity and fund raising by government employees, your employees. The laws of slander and libel also protect many from being lied about and slandered, unless, the target is a "public figure." Federal law prohibits employees from lying about their official duties; it also prohibits employees from lying in court.

On the Internet at **www.borderpatrol613.org**, one finds rank-and-file Border Patrol agents lying about a Congressman.

There, there are reports about captures of illegal immigrants and alleged confiscations of illicit drugs at a Border Patrol checkpoint 60 miles north of the border. One also finds remarks that there are approximately 900 agents and family members in Republican Congressman Darrel Issa's district and that they should all work to unseat him. One also finds mention that Congressman Issa was stopped for "speeding" by a Border Patrol agent and that's a lie, according to a ranking Border Patrol manager furious at Patrol union members playing politics on government time.

The Border Patrol announced that in March they busted 494 illegals at the Temecula I-15 checkpoint. Big deal. That amounts to 2/3rds (.66) of an illegal an hour during the 744 hours in March. For this we paid millions of dollars in payroll and benefits to members of Local 1613.

The Patrol brags that it confiscated $56,411 worth of illegal drugs during the same 744 hours at the same checkpoint. Big, big deal ($75.00 worth of drugs per hour)! Big, big misrepresentation! As a former consultant to a local law enforcement agency, let me state that the dollar amount of illicit drugs is guessed high for income tax evasion purposes.

The Big Lie being bandied about by the Border Patrol about one of their agents stopping a "speeding" Congressman Issa comes apart on this web site because the agents can't get their stories straight. The agent who wrote the leaked written report stated that he stopped a Mercedes sedan speeding in excess of 90-miles per hour through a construction zone on I-5. Wrong! Congressman Issa drives a gold Lexus.

The Borderpatrol1613.org web site declares that the Congressman sped through a Border Patrol checkpoint at 80-miles per hour. These agents can't even get their lies straight.

Here is the capper quote from the site: "The (Border Patrol) union also strongly advises, based on past incidents, that all agents who encounter Mr. Issa request that the encounter be videotaped or recorded in some similarly approved agency method."

Consider this—Border Patrol agents have no power to stop alleged speeders on California highways. Congressman Issa thinks the Patrol is wasting million of dollars and not doing their job, thus the rank and file union Patrol agents hate him. They wage a hate campaign against him.

By way of contrast, a Deputy Sheriff recently stopped a "speeding" car at night in Imperial County, and shined a light on the passenger, Democratic Congressman Bob Filner. The deputy exclaimed, "Our new congressman," and let the car go with a warning. He didn't leak it to the press.

Did this web site suggest a videotape when a Border Patrol agent shot an unarmed Mexican in the back, dragged him into an Arizona arroyo, and left the scene allowing the man to bleed to death? The agent threatened his partner with death if he reported the killing. He was not fired, though his partner was because he didn't report the killing.

And, where was videotape when six agents chased some illegals into a river and threw rocks into the dark seriously injuring a man? The real story was that four of the agents stalked and harassed the two agents who did report the incident after the San Diego Police investigated the assault and recommended felon prosecutions.

And, where was videotape when a Border Patrol agent shot a Mexican twelve year old in the back and lied about it in federal court? The judge stated the agent lied and awarded $400,000 of our taxpayer money to the boy because the unarmed boy was guilty of nothing but running away—in Mexico—from throwing small rocks over a twelve foot high fence.

And, where was videotape when a burly 6-foot tall, armed Border Patrol agent was accidentally kicked in the face by a 100-pound 14 year-old who was climbing over a fence and didn't even see the agent trying to tackle him from behind. The big man Border Patrol agent actually convinced the U.S. Attorney to file a charge of assaulting a federal officer against the boy.

This column exposed that fraudulent filing and the agent was laughed out of court.

Unfortunately, we can't laugh the Border Patrol out of existence, for as this is read, another 2-3-4 or five thousand illegals have walked by the ineffective Border Patrol and more millions of taxpayer dollars have been wasted on the worst federal employees in history.

CHASING BORDER PATROL TAILS

Raoul Lowery Contreras
July 15, 2002

As this is read, three, four or five thousand illegals will cross the Mexican border into the United States, walking right by thousands of Border Patrol Agents who are more concerned about their "benefits" as union members and faulting "management" than in doing their law enforcement job.

It is no secret that millions of illegals are in country and more arrive every day. Almost all of them find work of some sort. Many wage rates are stabilized by their presence. Prices are stabilized as a result, not only in agricultural products, but many other products and services we buy every day. America's standard of living improves because of these very illegals. It is also no secret that the Border Patrol has added thousands of agents, given them six-guns and badges and turned them loose on the borders to "stop" this influx.

It is no secret, also, that they, like their predecessors, fail miserably in performing that job. There are illegals in every state, in every city and have been since the Border Patrol was created in 1922. The union agents complain that "management" is responsible for their deficient job performance.

The history of Border Patrol management is one of corruption. One Patrol district manager was forced to resign after helping two federal prisoners at the Terminal island prison partake in activities normally denied prisoners. Another Sector Chief was spared federal indictment for illegally receiving a Lincoln Town Car from the same federal prisoner as a retirement gift when he died of a heart attack. Later, the San

Diego Sector Chief was arrested for an accident while driving drunk. His arrest was covered up. When news of the arrest was published, he was not fired for the cover-up, just demoted to Marfa, Texas.

Even the Congressman in charge of the Border Patrol budget, New York Democrat John Murphy, went to prison for corruption.

The common thread through these incidents was corruption. Any senior Border Patrol management retiree (from the 70s, 80s and 90s) that retired without being forced to resign is plain lucky, or, they testified under immunity about the high-level corruption that was rife in the San Diego/Chula Vista Sector.

Nonetheless, even corrupt management can make a good decision. For example, after the recent tragic deaths of six people and injuries to 30 more in a wrong-way accident in the San Diego mountain stretch of I-8, one agent wrote a letter to Anti-Mexican talk show host Roger Hedgecock that he read on the air.

The letter stated that Border Patrol management prohibited agents from pursuing vehicles suspected of carrying illegals speeding the wrong way on highways. Fact: law enforcement agencies countrywide have restrained high-speed chases because so many innocent people have been killed in accidents during these chases. The National Traffic Safety Agency reports that 383 people were killed in or by high-speed chases in 1995. That's more Americans than lost by the American military in twenty years of Middle East strife.

Question: Should any law enforcement agency risk the lives of innocent bystanders in high-speed chases for misdemeanors, or violations of civil laws, which is what immigration violations mostly are?

The no-high-speed chase policy was implemented when a Border Patrol agent high-speed chase resulted in a number of deaths in the city of Temecula, California. The criminal smuggler did not hit high speeds until Border Patrol agents started the chase.

Thousands of illegals walk by complaining union members as if they weren't even there, everyday. Hundreds of them have died on that walk, and innocent Americans have died while Border Patrol cowboys recklessly thunder up and down the back roads and Interstates of the Southwest.

Why do we continue to waste millions of dollars on Border Patrol agents who chase their own tails and can't find them.

24

INS-THE IMMIGRATION AND NATURALIZATION SERVICE

THE INS TARGETS FARM WORKERS, NOT HIJACKERS

Raoul Lowery Contreras
September 28, 2001

Leave it to those among us who hate immigrants and Mexicans to rise from the ashes of the World Trade Center tragedy with calls for an American police state targeted at Mexicans.

A national identification card has always been a demand of theirs, as is a stop to almost all immigration into the U.S. as we know it. They demand the closing of the Mexican border, despite not one shred of evidence that these terrorists crossed into the USA from Mexico. They demand that President Bush abandon his call for legalization of Mexicans already in the United States. They see Mexicans as criminals and murderers who must be stopped at the border, by the Army, if necessary.

These people and their demands are wrongheaded. Some, me included, might say these people are the true enemies of freedom and liberty, not young men who, to support their families, want to work as busboys, pick lettuce or paint houses.

Facts: Not a single Mexican immigrant, legal or illegal, hijacked a plane on September 11th and crashed it into the World Trade Center or the Pentagon. Not a single Mexican immigrant, legal or illegal, has been associated with any of the identified hijackers, or their sponsors. Not a single identified or alleged hijacker has been tracked as having come through Mexico into the United States to commit their massive crimes.

Facts: According to studies at the University of San Diego, when Mexican immigrants, legal or illegal, do commit crimes, they are usually, crimes of property, not violence or armed robbery, murder or rape and pillage. The number of these people who are sent to prison or county jails is far less than one would expect, given the estimates of how many of these people there are in the country. If, for example, there are 4-million illegals in California as some declare, then why are there only about 20-25,000 in California prisons. The San Diego County Sheriff reports that only 500 such people are in his jail system that numbers 5,000 inmates on a daily average basis. For those who don't know, San Diego County shares a 70-mile border with Mexico and for generations has been the most popular entry point into the USA for illegals from Mexico.

Facts: Mexicans who apply for visas to come to the United States may wait months and years for permission to come to the United States to study or work while the alleged hijackers were granted visas with few problems and no wait.

Given these irrefutable facts, why, then, are American extremists turning their ire south instead of to the American officials in the Middle East who hand out student and visitor visas like pancakes at a pancake breakfast? Why do they insist on Americans giving up liberty for identification cards that are useless except when checked on a basis of skin color or ethnic appearance? Why, other than bigoted spite, do they call for closing the border with our second largest trading partner, our next door neighbor and treaty ally? What good will that do when the terrorists come in easily and legally though the JFK airport in New York City?

If American officials abroad simply sat on visa applications for six months while police and intelligence agents thoroughly checked out each applicant properly, the number of potential terrorists flying into the country will dwindle.

As for those already here, the Associated Press quotes California Congressman Darrel Issa as saying, if "the Border Patrol spent its time chasing terrorists instead of Mexican farm workers," there might not be a problem.

INS MUST GO!

Raoul Lowery Contreras
March 18, 2002

The Immigration and Naturalization Service (INS) must be disbanded, buried and tossed into the ashcan of history.

Next, the Congress of the United States must organize three new agencies, one to service permanent immigration, one to service temporary immigration and another to enforce immigration laws. The permanent immigration organization must be placed inside the State Department, the temporary immigration organization inside the Labor Department and the enforcement branch under the Justice Department. Presidential appointees, not civil servants, must run and direct these agencies.

Next, the Congress must craft a legitimate and workable immigration policy that truly meets the needs of the country.

The INS is a total failure as a government agency. 35,000 employees and over $5-billion to spend and the agency doesn't work.

Its employees go to jail more frequently than from any other agency. Some of its armed, uninformed agents—THE BORDER PATROL—smuggle drugs, murder immigrants, rape immigrants and then walk away free men with pensions.

Non-gun wearing employees sell work permits to immigrants for up to $5,000. The same employees approve visa applications for murderous, well-known terrorists (Mohammed Atta et al) six months after they die crashing jet liners into the World Trade Center.

I can't think of a single reason why the INS should continue to exist.

I would craft new agencies to take the place of the INS. I would not allow a single present INS employee to transfer to the new agencies. I would fire each and every Border Patrol agent. I would make sure that every management person in the agency, from local directors on up to the Commissioner, be a presidential appointment with the top people confirmed by the Senate.

The State Department Immigration Bureau would handle all immigration applications for residence or study; the Labor Department would handle all applications for work. The enforcers would enforce these laws at the border, in the workplace, or on the street, perhaps.

The first chore, however, is for Congress to craft a real immigration law that makes sense.

No nation that sends any terrorists to the US should be allowed to send anyone to the United States of America for any reason. Any student admitted must check in with his case officer every quarter or semester to re-qualify as a bona fide student. Any country that has any of its citizens commit a terrorist act in the United States will have all admissions to the United States curtailed for several years. This threat would probably cause their home nations do much more strenuous background checks of prospective visitors to the U.S.

Outside of student visa, temporary work permits would be the next area of importance. Agreements or treaties with countries like Mexico should be crafted that allows for a smooth legitimate flow of workers into the U.S. that meets the needs of the United States labor market. If we need 300,000 farm workers, then let them come, permits in one-hand and security clearances in the other. If nannies are needed in Los Angeles, let them come, work permits in one hand and security clearance in the other. If bilingual teachers are needed in El Paso, then let them come, college degree in one hand, security clearance and work permit in the other.

If we need 5-million workers, then let them come, certified by the Labor Department, the Justice Department and their home country's government. If hundreds of thousands of students wish to get bona fide educations in the best university systems of the world, then let them come, student visa in one hand and security clearances in the other.

One fact is certain: The INS must go. Their job is too important to leave to incompetents.

POLICE AS IMMIGRATION COPS?

Raoul Lowery Contreras
January 27, 2001

"I demand you arrest these wetbacks," the middle-aged nursery owner yelled at the 23-year-old police officer who had responded to the owner's call. As two other black and white patrol cars pulled up drawing the owner's attention, the policeman softly asked the six Mexicans, in Spanish, if the owner owed them any money. "Yes," they all answered, "He owes us two week's pay."

"Pay them," the young officer ordered the owner, "pay them now, before I arrest you for slavery!" That's how decent local police used to handle the illegal immigrant problem. They usually used common sense, caring more for cooperation from these working people in ferreting out and combating crime than their "green card" status.

There is a movement twitching among us, however, to take local law enforcement, cops and sheriffs, into federal territory and turn our friendly neighborhood cops into immigration cops, into "la Migra (meegrah)." One can only envision police checkpoints on every highway with burly pistol packing men demanding "papers."

Many Americans are unaware that immigration is a federal responsibility assigned by the Constitution's Article 1, Section 8; to wit: "The Congress shall have the power to establish a uniform Rule of Naturalization." Congress can, however, delegate some of its authority as in mandating that local welfare authorities can and must prove legality of potential welfare or job training clients. In its wisdom, Congress legislated in the 1996 immigration "reform" effort that local police could arrest illegal aliens within a strict set or rules.

The Courts say this is legal in general, and specifically, in the case of immigration. The courts say that local police, state authorities and the federal government must, however, adhere to rules. Number one, the State must sign a contract with the federal government to train the local police. When trained, they must be paired with immigration officers or Border Patrol agents to make arrests for immigration law violations. They may not deport people, nor deny them any of the rights of hearings before federal officers and judges, nor may they arrest people for immigration violations without the presence of federal immigration officers.

No city or state in the country has entered into such an arrangement, but one, California's Anaheim, has a police officer, H. Martin, who is also an elected school board member, who introduced the proposal to the Anaheim City Council. The subject was not officially discussed because no city council person brought the subject up during a council meeting. Nonetheless, the issue was emotionally fanned by outside agitators and Mexican haters.

Leading the charge is Huntington Beach's Barbara Coe, founder and leader of the anti-immigrant California Coalition for Immigration Reform (CCIR). From claiming co-authorship of the infamous and unconstitutional immigrant targeting Proposition 187 in 1994, to acknowledging her "racism" on ABC Television, to sponsoring anti-immigrant billboards alongside California highways, Ms Coe has agitated against illegal immigrants, against Mexicans and against any American who disagrees with her. She is a former entry-level civil service clerical worker.

The proposal hasn't yet made it past the conversation stage in Anaheim. It should never see the light of day anytime, anywhere. No greater danger than this proposal has threatened the American population since our Japanese origin neighbors were rounded up and sent to concentration camps under the signatures of California Attorney General Earl Warren and President Franklin Delano Roosevelt. That vicious and horrible violation of the Constitution was racist based and so is this proposal, though on ethnicity, not pure race.

Who would the police stop and question for citizenship and legal residency—people who look like Robert Redford, or me? There are lots of people who look like me in the country and police could spend all their time checking papers of millions of American citizens and legal residents instead of fighting crime or writing parking tickets. The question must be asked, also, what standards of identification and verification would be implemented by thousands of city police and sheriff's deputies? Would each jurisdiction require different documents? Would each individual officer determine who is and isn't a citizen?

My grandfather died at 82 with a copy of his 1906 California birth certificate and a sixth grade report card in his wallet to prove he was a U.S. citizen. I object to and refuse to do that, now or ever.

So did my younger brother when he arrested the nursery owner for stealing the wages of four hard-working Mexican men who were guilty of nothing more than not speaking with an immigration officer at the U.S./Mexican border.

AUTHOR'S BACKGROUND

Raoul Lowery Contreras, newspaper columnist, radio and television commentator, has been active in the media since the HISPANIC LINK of Washington D.C. purchased and distributed his first op-ed pieces in January of 1988.

He came to commentary after working for years in public relations in both the United States and Mexico. He worked for non-profit and for-profit organizations and companies, and did similar professional work in the United States Marines during the Vietnam-Era.

He honed his communications skills as a California political speech-writer and in preparing campaign literature for dozens of candidates for public office, including running once himself.

In 1998, Contreras was chosen to be the statewide spokesman against a Hollywood-sponsored initiative involving millions of dollars in crushing taxes from Californians least able to afford them. He coined a media favorite sound bite that has become part of the California language—GOVERNMENT BY HOLLYWOOD. The Rob Reiner-Barbara Streisand liberal Hollywood Axis was not amused.

Starting a long student career as a child speaking Spanish-only recently arrived from Mexico, Contreras attended both public and parochial schools and graduated from high school as an Honors History and English student. In college, he earned numerous Dean's List Honors at San Diego State College, now University, served in student government and represented the college in athletics and student activities like the Model United Nations.

San Diego State tapped him to represent moderate political views on local media, unofficially, of course, as balance to on-campus radical organizations and the speakers they brought on campus, such as the ever-popular Fair Play To Cuba Committee, Young Socialists League and the Communist Party USA. He majored in Political Science and minored in History and Economics.

He broke ground as San Diego's first Hispanic radio talk show host, substituted on the national Michael Reagan radio talk show as the first Hispanic national talk show host, albeit occasionally. His commentary is regularly sought out by NBC and Fox news programs.

His columns have been published weekly since February of 1988 making him the longest continuously published national Hispanic columnist in the country. The New York Times Syndicate New America News Service distributed his columns throughout the Western world. His column is published weekly at **www.calnews.com**, from where these published columns where drawn for publication in this book.

Contreras's first book, THE NEW AMERICAN MAJORITY, HISPANICS, REPUBLICANS & GEORGE W. BUSH was published by Writer's Showcase in August of 2002. He currently is organizing San Diego's first VHF television station granted a federal broadcast license in 52 years. His next book is an examination of American Hispanics who have fought for the United States since before there was a United States, A HISPANIC VIEW: HISPANIC AMERICANS, TROOPS OF THE LINE...

E-mail address: sdraoul@att.net

0-595-25691-0

www.ingramcontent.com/pod-product-compliance
Lightning Source LLC
Chambersburg PA
CBHW061337280526
45784CB00001B/41